Sports, Power, and Resistance

Sports, Power, and Resistance

An Introduction to Critical Sports Studies

Edited by

THOMAS P. OATES and **TRAVIS VOGAN**

UNIVERSITY OF ILLINOIS PRESS
Urbana, Chicago, and Springfield

1 2 3 4 5 C P 5 4 3 2 1
♾ This book is printed on acid-free paper.

Library of Congress Cataloging-in-Publication Data

Names: Oates, Thomas Patrick editor | Vogan, Travis editor
Title: Sports, power, and resistance : an introduction to critical sports studies / Edited by Thomas P. Oates and Travis Vogan.
Description: Urbana : University of Illinois Press, 2026. | Includes bibliographical references and index.
Identifiers: LCCN 2026008294 (print) | LCCN 2026008295 (ebook) | ISBN 9780252049941 cloth | ISBN 9780252089619 paperback | ISBN 9780252049118 ebook
Subjects: LCSH: Sports—Political aspects | Athletes—Political activity | Belonging (Social psychology) | Sports—Sociological aspects | Power (Social sciences)
Classification: LCC GV706.35 .S723 2026 (print) | LCC GV706.35 (ebook)
LC record available at https://lccn.loc.gov/2026008294
LC ebook record available at https://lccn.loc.gov/2026008295

The manufacturer's authorized representative in the EU for product safety is Mare Nostrum Group B.V., Mauritskade 21D, 1091 GC Amsterdam, The Netherlands. Email: gpsr@mare-nostrum.co.uk

Contents

Acknowledgments

This collection grew out of the 2023 Obermann Arts & Humanities Symposium, which was a cooperative effort with many contributors. Thanks to Jake Mayer, Sofia Restiffe Favoretto, Jennifer Sterling, Melissa Tully, and the School of Journalism and Mass Communication at the University of Iowa; Janet Weaver and the staff of the Iowa Women's Archives; the staff at FilmScene, especially Andrew Sherburne, Ben Delgado, Jane Kerenan, and Angie Mabeus; Beth Fischer and Jason Paulios at the Iowa City Public Library; Kimberly Datchuk at the Stanley Museum of Art; the University of Iowa Libraries Special Collections and Archives; and Heather Heddens, Jane Rubel, Connie Shafar, and Susan Birrell. The symposium was partially funded by grants from the Arts and Humanities Initiative program through the Office of the Vice President for Research at the University of Iowa, and the Ida Cordelia Beam Distinguished Visiting Professorships program through Iowa's Office of the Executive Vice President and Provost. We extend special thanks to Teresa Mangum, Erin Hackathon, Lauren Cox, Jenna Hammerich, and everyone at the Obermann Center for their assistance preparing and executing the symposium, and to the American Studies graduate students, especially Glenn Houlihan, Janeanne Levenstein, and Ashley Loup. Thanks also to Danny Nasset and Gary Smith at the University of Illinois Press.

Introduction

Sports through a Humanistic, Critical, and Interdisciplinary Lens

THOMAS P. OATES and TRAVIS VOGAN

On February 9, 2025, the Super Bowl LIX halftime show featured a performance by the celebrated rapper Kendrick Lamar. It marked the first time that a solo hip-hop artist had been chosen to headline the vaunted show. As has become customary, the Fox network's broadcast of Super Bowl LIX was dripping with patriotic imagery. During the pregame performance of the national anthem, Fox cut to President Donald Trump saluting alongside his daughter Ivanka. It was the first time a sitting president had attended the Super Bowl. Fox's shot of Trump saluting at attention also evoked the president's enmity toward athletes who, following the lead of blackballed former NFL quarterback Colin Kaepernick, refused to stand during the anthem, in protest of police murders of Black people. In a 2017 rally, Trump had famously disparaged these dissident and disproportionately Black athletes as "sons of bitches." Just before Super Bowl LIX, the NFL removed from its endzones the "End Racism" banners, which it installed after the murder of George Floyd in 2020 to showcase its apparent commitment to social justice. It replaced the "End Racism" banners with comparatively vapid messages that read "Choose Love" and "It Takes All of Us," statements of unity that identify no specific problem or action. The NFL field redesign seemed to acquiesce to Trump's outspoken battle against diversity, equity, and inclusion.

Kendrick Lamar's history of weaving biting social commentary into his Pulitzer Prize–winning work created considerable speculation about whether the rapper would use his hyper-visible platform to make a political statement at halftime. Lamar's performance was introduced by the actor Samuel L. Jackson, who played the patriotic icon Uncle Sam. "This is your Uncle Sam," Jackson hollered by way of introduction. "And this is the great American game!" Lamar proceeded to offer a medley of his recent songs that was characteristic of most halftime performances. But Uncle Sam interjected after the first song to remind Lamar of the expectations—and skepticism—he faced from mainstream America. "No! No! No! No! Too loud! Too reckless! Too ghetto! Mr. Lamar, do you really know how to play the game?" Jackson's Uncle Sam offers a winking meta-commentary on the pressures that Black entertainers like Lamar face in such high-profile circumstances. Lamar, Uncle Sam implied, was expected to walk a fine line that exudes authenticity without alienating audiences.

After Uncle Sam's warning, Lamar transitioned to the song "Humble," which he performed while surrounded by an all-Black troupe of dancers clad in red, white, and blue costumes. As part of their choreography, Lamar's dancers formed an American flag and raised their fists, a nod to the sporting dissent that so rankled Trump. The undulating flag—made up entirely of Black bodies—was both patriotic and rebellious. It showed Lamar playing "the game" from multiple sides by offering up a predictable symbol and then sprinkling it with notes of irony and critique. Amid the performance, one of Lamar's dancers unexpectedly unfurled a flag that combined the flags of Sudan and Palestine to demonstrate his solidarity with the political struggles in these nations. The rogue flag was barely visible to TV viewers, but images of the protest immediately circulated on social media. The dancer, who displayed the flag without Lamar's or the NFL's knowledge, was chased off the field, tackled by a group of all-white security guards, and arrested. The Fox network, which periodically interspersed the Super Bowl broadcast with promotions for its conservative news division, ignored the rebel dancer's protest and did not subsequently comment on it.

The halftime performance demonstrates sport's position as a visible, powerful, and multifaceted cultural formation. Sport unites and divides diverse groups; reinforces the status quo while providing a forum for dissent; sells goods as well as values and beliefs; and sometimes becomes the direct target of political action. But moments like Lamar's performance are not particularly exceptional or even surprising in the contemporary sports landscape. Sport is as complex, contradictory, subtle, and brazen as the cultures that produce it. It is fun and games and deadly serious. We cannot adequately understand and appreciate sport without putting it into dialogue with the dynamic cultural circumstances that shape and are shaped by it. This articulation unlocks sport's richness as a site where power is exercised, negotiated, and challenged. It illustrates why sport has such a pull and elicits such passion as both commercialized spectacle and cultural practice.

Power and resistance compose two key themes that animate and connect the study of sport across the humanities. Sport's capacity to showcase power relations constitutes perhaps its greatest significance as well as the most capacious avenue through which to explore its contours. Team owners, league executives, and elected politicians use leagues and franchises to promote political views, while players and fans use sport as a platform from which to oppose the status quo. Controversies over patriotic ceremonies, protests against police violence, and demonstrations for the rights of women, people of color, and LGBTQ+ people draw attention, sympathy, and backlash. As the sport sociologist John Bale wrote in 1986, "Sport is, after war, probably the principal means of collective identification in modern life."[1] Thirty-five years after Bale's comment, sports media scholar Victoria E. Johnson (a contributor to this anthology) added, "Sport remains the most prominent weekly and seasonal space for the idealization of homosocial bonds and the conservation of consensus, while also, increasingly, serving as the primary social institution at the forefront of civil discourse, calling for systemic transformation."[2] Sport is, in short, an exceptional part of popular culture. It provides some of the few moments that are still collectively experienced in an increasingly fragmented culture. The Super Bowl, for instance, is routinely the most watched annual TV program in the United States, and it is the second most commonly celebrated event after New Year's Eve. Super Bowl LIX, which the Fox network broadcast as part of its $2.2 billion annual contract with the NFL, drew 127.7 million viewers to become the most watched television program of all time. It broke the record held by the previous year's Super Bowl broadcast, which broke the record held by another Super Bowl. While exceptional in this sense, sport is also utterly banal in others. It constantly surrounds us in advertisements, clothing, bumper stickers, and so on. But these quotidian objects also illustrate how sport constantly sits in dialogue with power and resistance. Wearing a Caitlin Clark, Shohei Ohtani, or Patrick Mahomes jersey is—whether intentional or not—a statement about identity and politics.

This anthology focuses on the intersections across sport, power, and resistance in a North American context. Our approach is humanistic, critical, and interdisciplinary. It is *humanistic* because we situate sport as an institution that has no inherent meaning or value outside of the social, cultural, and historical circumstances that shape it. It is *critical* because we believe the practice of criticism is necessary to showcase sport's meanings, which are often implicit, fuzzy, and even contradictory. It is *interdisciplin-*

ary because we believe that critical analysis of sport is most useful when it does not confine itself to a single disciplinary paradigm. A multifaceted topic, sport demands a capacious theoretical and methodological approach that considers a variety of intersecting historical, social, and textual elements. We are primarily interested in understanding sport, not in contributing to any specific discipline or in suggesting that one approach provides a superior way to explore this topic. Scholarly disciplines are sometimes more preoccupied with advancing disciplinary conversations than in illuminating their objects of study and opening up new lines of inquiry. However, disciplines carry useful traditions, theories, and methods that, when combined with approaches from other disciplines, can shed exciting new light on their topics. This anthology is an attempt to foster and demonstrate a sensibility that will encourage this sort of humanistic, critical, and interdisciplinary inquiry.

It was not too long ago that scholars of sport could introduce their work by maintaining that sport had not received much academic attention. This was an admittedly convenient entry point. We could justify our approaches by contending that we were forging a place for critical discourse about sport in disciplines that had given it very little consideration, or ignored it completely. There are certainly plenty of scholars who continue to dismiss sport as an unserious topic.

Nevertheless, these easy justifications are no longer quite as tenable. Sport, although still marginalized in academe because of its relatively "low" cultural status, is now attracting steady attention from scholars across the humanities and social sciences. There are, of course, legacy communities like the North American Society for the Sociology of Sport, North American Society for Sport History, and the International Sociology of Sport Association that have been fostering this scholarship for decades. But a raft of new scholarly organizations, journals, and book series have launched in recent years. Sport is also getting attention from more traditional disciplines through the formation of new divisions, interest groups, and the publication of special issues. These new developments have helped to explain what can be gained from studying sport, and how we might most productively approach this project. One recent special issue, published in the American Studies Association's flagship journal *American Quarterly* and coedited by Joseph Darda and Amira Rose Davis, urges an interdisciplinary approach that "invites sports studies to undiscipline itself."[3] We read this statement not so much as a critique of sport studies, which is interdisciplinary and has been since its inception, but a reminder that truly interesting intellectual work requires scholars to stretch beyond their comfort zones.

But there is a trade-off with these new developments in the study of sport. It remains to be seen whether larger disciplines will demonstrate sustained engagement with this topic. Will the study of sport remain confined to the space of occasional special issues, forums, and designated book series rather than integrating into larger disciplinary conversations? If so, will these efforts further marginalize an already marginalized topic? Similarly, do the new sport-specific journals, special issues, and book series discourage scholars from publishing their work in non-sport-oriented venues that might reach a broader audience?

We do not intend to disparage these welcome scholarly developments. The editors, as well as the contributors to this volume, have benefitted significantly from the communities and opportunities that these new venues have provided. In fact, many of us have driven these developments. But how do we ensure that these communities create work that does not simply talk to itself? Building on Darda and Davis's invitation, how do we undiscipline our work to ensure a broad impact while resisting the urge to gatekeep for anything other than generative ideas?

Our work also corresponds with the rapid rise of sports management in American universities. Sports management is one of the fastest-growing undergraduate majors in the United States. Its proliferation coincides with decreased support for the humanities and social sciences, which is where sports studies classes were traditionally housed. These days, most university students encounter the study of sport through the primarily instrumental and profit-seeking prism sports management provides. This is not to say that sports management cannot teach students how to think critically about sports. It certainly can, and many of these programs incorporate critical elements into their curricula. But its principal goal is to support and sustain the sports industry, not to criticize or contextualize it. Our approach maintains an interest in business and institutions, but it is ultimately driven by a quest to understand sport's relationship to culture. To do this, it is necessary to criticize, and perhaps even dismantle, the status quo in sport.

We are, as is probably clear by now, deeply ambivalent about sport. We are not killjoys who were always picked last at recess and are now seeking revenge by attempting to eradicate this cultural practice that can bring so much happiness, excitement, and community. Many of us became sport scholars because of our formative experiences participating in and consuming sport. But we think that sport, because of its tremendous power, has a responsibility to live up to the high standards it so often claims to embody.

At minimum, we hope this collection encourages folks to look at sport critically and to recognize that sport is never divorced from the sociopolitical contexts surrounding it. Sport, like the larger culture of which it is a part, is dynamic. As such, sport does not have to be any one way. It can transform to become more just, more decent, and even more exciting. Nothing guarantees this, however, and sport can also transform to become more repressive, indecent, and boring. We have seen sport drift in both directions, sometimes simultaneously, and we are interested in exploring the complex mechanisms that drive these politicized migrations.

Sport is idealized across the political spectrum as a formation that teaches teamwork, leadership, humility, and other laudable virtues. If sport can instill these qualities, which we tend to agree are ingredients necessary to concoct a better world, then sport can help to improve the world. The chapters in this volume offer critiques that might help, in small ways, to usher these shifts—or to foster a sensibility that is open to such changes. It would be unrealistic for us to think that scholarship on sport might transform this massive, established, and corporatized industry. But it can foster useful critical awareness. And, who knows? Perhaps a more just sports ecosystem would also establish unforeseen commercial pathways for those who are principally interested in sport as an engine of consumer capitalism.

This collection grew directly out of a September 2023 symposium hosted at the University of Iowa. The symposium, which we titled *Sports, Power, and Resistance: Legacies and Futures,* was made possible by generous funding from the Obermann Center for Advanced Studies and the Office of the Vice President for Research. The three-day event mostly consisted of research presentations that evolved into the chapters that make up this volume. But it also included public-facing screenings, archival exhibits, and conversations about scholarship and pedagogy. At the risk of sounding overly sentimental, the symposium was a sort of dream project. It was a once-in-a-career opportunity that enabled us to build an event populated by a diverse collection of scholars whose work, personalities, and values we admire.

While our research focuses mainly on the intersections across sport and media, we wanted to cast a wide net with the symposium. We therefore invited dexterous scholars whose work jibed with our humanistic, critical, and interdisciplinary ethos but also challenged us to think about sport from different angles. We also sought scholars who would accept the very small honoraria we could provide.

We organized the symposium around the themes of power and resistance to give the event some shape while also providing flexibility. These themes complement a tradition of scholarship at the University of Iowa, which has been a hub for the humanistic, critical, and interdisciplinary study of sport since the 1970s. This status can largely be attributed to emeritus faculty members Susan Birrell and Catriona Parratt, as well as the many graduate students they mentored who went on to become leaders in the study of sport. One of their most notable legacies is the approach to "Reading Sport" that Birrell developed with Iowa alumnus Mary G. McDonald. This "critical analytic strategy" advocates using sport "as the site for exploring the complex, interrelated and fluid character of power relations" in order to "connect seemingly discrete incidents and events that are generated within the world of sport to the larger world."[4] Their approach now provides a largely taken-for-granted starting point from which much critical humanistic analysis of sport builds. We do not claim that the University of Iowa is the center of humanistic sports studies, but it is important to acknowledge the work that has been done at this institution and to build on it. Our goals differ from those that animated our predecessors, but they would not exist apart from their durable contributions.

As we organized the symposium and invited scholars whose work spoke to its themes in different ways, more specific lines of inquiry emerged that we used to give the symposium and edited collection additional structure. We organized the project into three sections. Part one, "Imagining Belonging," probes how sports build communities that foster belonging as well as exclusion. Part two, "Athletes and Resistance," explores multiple forms of resistance in sport through various performances and representations. The final part, "Political Activism," analyzes more explicit efforts to use sport as a platform for activism from various political viewpoints.

"Imagining Belonging" opens with Abraham I. Khan's "The Racial Contract, the Discourse of Ignorance, and Black Coaches in the National Football League," which theorizes a "discourse of ignorance" to critique the racial politics of the NFL's hiring practices. Michael L. Butterworth's "The Team that United a City: Sports Documentaries and the Rhetorical Construction of Unity" explores how a recent collection of sports documentaries build specific cities' communal identities while nevertheless obscuring those who are already marginalized in those locales. Theresa Runstedtler's "White Hopes in a Black Game: Race and the 1974 NBA Finals" complements Khan's and Butterworth's explorations of racial politics by exploring media coverage of the 1974 NBA Finals between the Milwaukee Bucks and the Boston Celtics. Runstedtler explains how the championship series became a microcosm for intensifying battles over segregation and was emblematic of ongoing racial struggles in professional basketball during the 1970s. The section closes with Victoria E. Johnson's "'I Was Raised on This Sport': Football and Female Expertise," which considers how a cluster of overlooked films depicting women in football align participation in the stereotypically masculine sport with the "possessive investments" of middle-class, white feminism.

We kick off the anthology's second part, "Athletes and Resistance," with Jaime Schultz's "Women's Distance Running, Disordered Eating, and Sport Autopathography," which analyzes a wave of memoirs published between 2013 and 2023 that focus on women distance runners' struggles with various eating pathologies. Shultz offers a close reading of eight autopathographies, or personal illness narratives, to explain how women distance runners critique issues of gender, embodiment, autonomy, and control in their sport. Next, Adrian Burgos's "In Clemente's Wake: Afro-Latino Players and the Quest for Respect" considers the racially caricatured way in which the Afro-Latino baseball legend Roberto Clemente was treated by the sports press. He then explains how the sports press posthumously exalted Clemente as a godlike standard against which his Afro-Latino successors have been unfairly judged. Noah Cohan's "Raising A Glass Helmet: How Black Athletes and Artists Resist Football's Headgear," highlights the football helmet's iconic significance in American sports. Cohan focuses on two media and art projects that have critiqued the helmet's dehumanizing and racist contours. We end this second section of the anthology with Samantha N. Sheppard's "'Bout that Action, Boss: Signifying and the Cultural Politics of Marshawn Lynch's Sporting Celebrity and Media Persona," which considers the famously enigmatic sports celebrity Marshawn Lynch. Sheppard analyzes Lynch's "mediagenic resistance" to his racial and commercialized exploitation through his recalcitrant press conference performances and other media appearances.

We begin the final part of the anthology, "Political Activism," with Travers's "Trans Participation in Sport: Female Eligibility in the Context of a Moral Panic," which critiques efforts to banish transgender people—especially transgender women and girls—from participation in competitive sport. Travers explains how these reactionary efforts reflect broader bigotries against transgender people and offers some pathways through which such intolerance might be resisted. With "Weaponizing Sport Ideology: OutKick's 'Anti-Woke' Brand and Women's Sports," Jason Kido Lopez explores how the sports media company OutKick brands itself through appeals to alt-right ideologies. Lopez focuses in particular on how OutKick unapologetically champions white heterosexual masculinity and marginalizes women as participants in and consumers of sport. We end the book with Douglas Hartmann and Ali Bouterse's "The WNBA and the 2020 Georgia Senate Race: A Multimethod Case Study of the Cultural Power of Sport." Hartmann and Bouterse offer a mixed-methods case study that explores the impact of the WNBA and its Atlanta Dream franchise on the

2020 Georgia Senate race, which elected Raphael Warnock and briefly gave the democratic party control over the United States Senate.

Hartmann and Bouterse conclude their chapter, which closes this collection, by suggesting the need for a critical approach to sport that "emphasizes sport's primary role and social significance as a dramaturgical platform, a theater wherein audiences and observers are exposed to and learn about social issues and problems." Sport, they continue, is best explained "as a site of contestation and struggle that, because of its cultural prominence, informs public audiences about social dynamics and power struggles outside of sport." In other words, sport's relationship to power and resistance most poignantly illustrates its unique significance as a cultural formation. We hope our humanistic, critical, and interdisciplinary inquiries can demonstrate this significance and open new avenues that reveal more questions and invite others into the growing conversation. Studies of culture have long been applied and adapted to explore sport. Perhaps it is time for studies of sport to fuel and inform studies of culture.

Notes

1. John Bale, "Sport and National Identity: A Geographical View," *The International Journal of the History of Sport* 3, no. 1 (1986), 18.
2. Victoria E. Johnson, *Sports TV* (London: Routledge, 2021), 18.
3. Joseph Darda and Amira Rose Davis, "The Body Athletic," *American Quarterly* 5, no. 3 (2023): 443–68, 447.
4. Mary G. McDonald and Susan Birrell, "Reading Sport Critically: A Methodology for Interrogating Power," *Journal of Sport & Social Issues* 16 (1999): 283–300, 284.

PART I

Imagining Belonging

1

The Racial Contract, the Discourse of Ignorance, and Black Coaches in the National Football League

ABRAHAM I. KHAN

"I am America," Muhammad Ali once declared. "I am the part you won't recognize. But get used to me—black, confident, cocky; my name, not yours; my religion, not yours; my goals, my own. Get used to me."[1] Though the precise historical context for this original quotation is not altogether clear, its frequent invocation reflects what Daniel Grano calls "Ali's ghostly presence," which "extracts his voice from any particular historical moment or bodily capacity," and "functions to express the anxieties and *ethos* of his era and our own."[2] Racial anxieties central to the American ethos found sharp expression in 2016 as Donald Trump's political ambitions activated dormant strains of white nationalism in reaction to the nation's first Black president. Upon Ali's death that summer, Barack and Michelle Obama's eulogistic remarks offered something akin to a ghostly rebuke to the racial cruelties of Trump's ascendant whiteness. Quoting Ali's assertion that he "is America" in their press release, the Obamas emphasized Ali's fighting spirit, not just as a boxing champion, but "as a man who fought for us," as, perhaps, a people's champion. "Ali stood his ground," they wrote, "and his victory helped us get used to the America we recognize today."[3] *The America* we *recognize today*.

With the benefit of hindsight, it is easy to doubt the optimism bundled within the tidiness of Obama's "we." Since the summer of 2016 we have sufficient warrant to believe that our common patterns of political recognition and national belonging are not as common as Barack Obama implored us to hope. Centering a political rhetoric, "Make America Great Again," as Matthew Houdek and Kendall Phillips have recently written, "calls forth a postracial nostalgia for a mythical great white past, and reproduces the futural orientation of whiteness and hegemonic masculinity." Noting that MAGA is "not an aberration," Houdek and Phillips argue that it "is a demand to go back to a time when white supremacy was mostly unquestioned in the mainstream and where Black people and people of color, especially women, had no recourse to make critical claims against the state."[4] In tracing the temporal dimensions of white supremacy's expression, they evoke Paul Gilroy's well-known formulation of racism as a "changing same,"[5] or, as Kirt Wilson has called it, in citing Frederick Douglass, "the snake of slavery,"[6] shedding its skin for new appearances as it cuts a venomous path through history. What is MAGA, after all, besides the enduring refusal to get used to the likes of Muhammad Ali?

In this chapter, I want to explain how the snake both feeds on and winds its way into American sport. Specifically, I argue that the recent case of Brian Flores (fired as head coach of the National Football League's Miami Dolphins in 2022, but as of this writing the defensive coordinator for the Minnesota Vikings) illuminates the path through which complex American institutions disavow the racialized political logics on which they are predicated and through which they operate. To arrive at what I mean, we might pause on the defiant thrill contained in Ali's declaration that he "is America," but we learn more if we emphasize the clause in Ali's quote that qualifies his defiance, the phrase that registers the eternal recurrence of white racial backlash: *I am the part* you *won't recognize*. Ali's blackness, his self-assurance, his name, his Islam, and his ambitions were each spun from the frayed threads of fabric made-in-the-USA, yet each remained a source of contemptuous befuddlement to the listener he addresses as "you." His use of the second person registers not just a fissure in the "we," but also a condemnation. For Ali, the "you," the white racial other, harbors a blind spot, a bottomless hole in American vision into which falls all the vibrant expressions of Black triumph, confidence, courage, joy, and, by implication or explication, Black humanity itself.

The blindness to which Ali referred is not synonymous with inattention. Blindness is not so much neglect as it is an active, predatory force. Agonizing over the violence, terror, and inheritance of trauma American whiteness bequeaths through generations, James Baldwin writes in *The Fire Next Time* about "the crime of which I accuse my country and countrymen and for which neither I nor time nor history will ever forgive them, that they have destroyed hundreds of thousands of lives and do not know it and do not want to know it."[7] American whiteness is an ostrich, Baldwin wants us to see, that plunges its head into the sand to hide from its shame.

Of course, if we add Baldwin's renowned suspicion of progress fables to the image, then perhaps "this country" is more like another of its iconic birds—Foghorn Leghorn—strutting around and flapping its wings in a flightless, blundering spectacle of idiotic self-congratulation. Ali's declaration and Baldwin's lamentation find scholarly expression in what Charles Mills calls the "epistemology of ignorance." In what follows, I first sketch out the epistemology of ignorance, show how it is derived from Mills's formulation of the "racial contract," and explain why it implies what I call the "discourse of ignorance." I then address three dimensions of the discourse of ignorance evident in the racial politics of coaching labor in the NFL: the construction of memory, the racialized mind/body dualism, and the rhetoric of intent.

The Racial Contract, the Discourse of Ignorance, and the National Football League

In *The Racial Contract*, Mills indicts classical political theory by demonstrating how the social contract is in fact an unacknowledged, but very much enforceable, racial contract. In an ambitious critique that runs through Hobbes, Locke, Rousseau, and Rawls, Mills argues that the European tradition of political philosophy relies on the social contract to explain "how society was created or crucially transformed, how the state was established, and how a particular moral code and a certain moral psychology were brought into existence."[8] As Grano explains in his elucidation of Mills's argument, the social contract "never literally existed,"[9] but instead operates as a fable that explains why citizens submit to the rule of law and enter into relationships of social and political interdependence. Both descriptive and normative, the social contract provides an account of humanity's ascent from the so-called state of nature and valorizes the Eurocentric rationality that purportedly clinched the grand accomplishment of civilization.

Mills argues that contract theory is predicated on a system of enduring assumptions regarding the invention of race as a consequential category of human identity. Influenced by Carole Pateman's work on the sexual contract,[10] which shows how the social contract establishes the conditions for patriarchal domination, Mills uses the term the "racial contract" to designate "a set of formal or informal agreements . . . between the members of one subset of humans . . . with the class of full persons . . . to categorize the remaining subset of humans as 'nonwhite,' and of a different and inferior moral status, subpersons." The resulting hierarchy entails that "the moral and juridical rules normally regulating the behavior of whites in their dealings with one another . . . do not apply at all in dealings with nonwhites or apply only in a qualified form." Moreover, as Mills specifies, "the general purpose of the contract is always . . . the exploitation of their [nonwhite] bodies, land, and resources, and the denial of socioeconomic opportunities therein."[11] Mills's narrative of the racial contract holds that the pursuit of imperialism, colonization, enslavement, and genocide is authorized through the positing of sub-persons and nonpersons—those to whom the social contract does not apply—those who, in the parlance of political theory, are consigned in perpetuity to the nasty and brutish state of nature.

In practice, however, the *racial* contract reveals the limits of the *social* contract. Mills grasps this problem through a distinction between the "ideal and nonideal society," the social contract naming the former as a "defensible moral code" and the racial contract naming the latter as "an unjust exploitative society, ruled by an oppressive government and regulated by an immoral code."[12] Noticing that Mills's account implies a contradiction between principle and practice—a tension between how a society imagines itself and how it actually behaves—Mark McPhail describes the difference between the ideal and non-ideal as a problem of incoherence. "The refusal to speak to the incoherence of the claim that a free nation can be built upon slavery and that a just and equitable society is fundamentally at odds with the near genocidal displacement and dispersal of the land's original inhabitants," writes McPhail, "that simultaneously conceals the material facts of history and reveals the shameful reality of that history."[13] In other words, the social contract is a kind of self-flattering myth that, when put into practice, produces results at odds with the social contract's promises of freedom, equity, and justice. The actual reality is a racial contract, an agreement on how the racial hierarchy works, and as the mythology is reinforced by historical repetition, a general silence about the difference between myth and reality protects the beneficiaries of the myth from the political obligations or social responsibilities that might arise from shame in acknowledging how non-white persons suffer in reality. In order for such silence to go unchallenged, says Mills, "one has to learn to see the world wrongly, but with the assurance that this set of mistaken perceptions will be validated by white epistemic authority. Thus, in effect, on matters related to race, the racial contract prescribes for its signatories an epistemology of ignorance, a particular pattern of localized and global cognitive dysfunctions (which are psychologically and socially functional), producing the ironic outcome that whites in general will be unable to understand the world they themselves have made."[14] The racial contract captures why Ali saw himself as the part of America that

America won't recognize, and why, as Baldwin reminds us, his country does not know who has been destroyed and does not want to know.

For McPhail, the epistemology of ignorance supports an "adaptive theory of racism," which holds that "even when the underlying assumptions that define white racial consciousness and unconsciousness are brought into awareness, they remain immune to alteration and transformation."[15] The adaptive theory of racism presents profound challenges for liberal political strategies grounded in civic pedagogy or public persuasion because it means that evidence of racism's material reality, instead of urging a reconsideration of practice, forces the racial contract to adapt, to generate novel ways of thinking that redirect white attention around obvious cases of inequality, domination, and exploitation. As Mills says, "Given the actual class, gender, and racial hierarchies of nominally inclusive and egalitarian liberal democracies, an epistemology of knowledge-seeking must simultaneously constitute itself as an epistemology of knowledge avoidance."[16] Put differently, the epistemology of ignorance names not the absence of knowledge, but the kind of knowledge that secures the racial contract's hierarchy. Linda Alcoff reads Mills as saying that "ignorance is not primarily understood as a lack—a lack of motivation or experience as a result of social location—but as a substantive epistemic practice that differentiates the dominant group."[17] Vincent Jungkunz and Julie White characterize this epistemic practice as "representations of reality that obscure the presence and meaning of racial practices and ideas," such as "official proclamations, political communications, and legal apparatuses" that amount to an "agreement to misinterpret the world."[18] Though it might seem akin to finding shapes in the negative space of an optical illusion, the epistemology of ignorance contains positive content identifiable in the forms of expression that emerge in response to claims of racial injustice.

McPhail's adaptive theory holds that "racism is characterized by a refusal to accept the empirical evidence of a racial contract, one that is grounded in a moral psychology that manifests itself in a sustained capacity to rationalize injustice, and which is characterized by the discursive dynamics of denial, projection, and positive self-representation."[19] Without modifying Mills's central insights, then, to the epistemology of ignorance, I want to add the *discourse of ignorance*, an elastic repertoire of delusions, rationalities, tropes, interpretive frames, and rhetorical strategies that work to disseminate cognitive dysfunction and thereby render it socially and psychologically functional. Though his work operates at what we might call the world-historical level, Mills says that "the racial contract continues to manifest itself in unofficial local agreements of various kinds,"[20] including employment discrimination. Put differently, if the epistemology of ignorance underwrites the racial contract, if it sustains racist forms of collective behavior in a world that denies the existence of racism, then ignorance must take local form as a discourse available for utterance, transmission, adoption, and reinvention, thus enabling its migration between historical contexts and various institutions. Put simply, the discourse of ignorance is how the snake of slavery molts and slithers along.

Though NFL history is replete with accomplished Black assistant coaches never hired to lead a franchise, one recent example offers an illustrative anecdote for how the epistemology of ignorance manifests as employment discrimination in professional football. In 2022, the Chicago Bears hired Matt Eberflus to replace Matt Nagy, fired only weeks before. Eberflus had served previously as defensive coordinator of the Indianapolis Colts, which at the time was a mediocre unit with limited success. At the time of both hirings by the Bears, neither coach, both of whom are white, had previous professional experience as head coach. Nagy had been hired after serving as offensive coordinator by the Kansas City Chiefs, and though Kansas City under Nagy had some success, the team was not of championship caliber. Eberflus replaced Nagy but was fired in November 2024 after starting the season with a 4-8 record. To put things bluntly, Chicago has been a bad football team under Eberflus and an undesirable destination for top athletes who have employment options as free agents.

Among the coaches the Bears interviewed and passed over to hire Eberflus is Eric Bieniemy, a Black coach who had been hired in Kansas City to replace Nagy. In the five years that Bieniemy coached the Kansas City offense, his team hosted the conference championship every year, winning three, along with two Super Bowls. Perhaps, according to the theory that he sought to emerge from the "shadow" of Andy Reid, the Kansas City head coach during their Super Bowl run, Bieniemy voluntarily left the Chiefs in a lateral move to coordinate the offense of the Washington Commanders. ESPN noted at the time that "Reid's shadow wasn't an obstacle for Doug Pederson or Nagy, his first two offensive coordinators after joining the Chiefs. Each moved on from there to a head-coaching job," but offered hope that "getting away from Reid and [quarterback Patrick] Mahomes and being successful with the Commanders will make him a more attractive head-coaching candidate."[21] Of course, both Nagy and Pederson are white, and the lateral move to Washington set Bieniemy up for failure. The Commanders were sorely lacking in talent, finishing the 2023 season with the second-worst record in the League. Head coach Ron Rivera (the League's only Latino head coach) was fired and replaced by Dan Quinn, another white coach, and Bieniemy was replaced by Kliff Kingsbury, a white coach plucked from college football whose most recent head coaching experience was with the NFL's Arizona Cardinals, where, from 2019 to 2022, his team achieved a record of twenty-eight wins, thirty-seven losses, and one tie. Kingsbury's Cardinals did not win a postseason game. Bieniemy stands as a living refutation to the enduring myth of sport's racial meritocracy.[22]

Some two decades earlier, civil rights attorneys Johnnie Cochran and Cyrus Mehri directed an extensive quantitative study of employment discrimination in the NFL with respect to hiring head coaches. In 2002, they released a seventy-eight-page report titled "Black Coaches in the NFL: Superior Performance, Inferior Opportunities." Supported by rigorous statistical analysis, Cochran and Mehri wrote that the "reality well-known in the world of football" is that "Black coaches are the last hired and the first fired." "In case after case," they said, "NFL [franchise] owners have shown more interest in—and patience with—white coaches who don't win than Black coaches who do."[23] For an explanation, they turned to sportswriting legend Frank Deford, who told them "there is almost surely some kind of submerged racism, which presumes that a heavy-duty football operation is really too complicated to trust to a minority."[24] Cochran and Mehri's report had an explosive effect, and to forestall the employment discrimination lawsuits that might have followed, the NFL quickly implemented a form of affirmative action called the "Rooney Rule." This policy requires every franchise to interview at least one non-white candidate for head coaching vacancies.[25] Since its adoption in 2003, the Rooney Rule has produced uneven results, and by 2020, the league extended its interview requirement to two non-white candidates for head coaching vacancies. Nonetheless, in 2023 the *Yale Law & Policy Review* published a lengthy analysis of the Rooney Rule prepared by DeMaurice Smith, who had spent the previous fourteen years as Executive Director of the NFLPA (the players' union), and Carl Lasker. Smith and Lasker's top-line finding states, "The lack of diversity in the NFL's coaching and executive ranks is not an accident but rather the result of a deliberate—or deliberately indifferent—policy of control exerted by the NFL owners. The Rooney Rule has failed."[26]

Smith and Lasker's gesture toward deliberate indifference resonates with the critical potential of the epistemology of ignorance. Though few would accuse NFL franchise owners of harboring generous hearts, the Rooney Rule's failure cannot be attributed to avarice alone. Avarice, as Mills shows, is structured by a racial hierarchy that prescribes who is entitled to accumulate wealth and who is subject to exclusion and exploitation. Against any official proclamation, the racial contract exposes the terms of exclusion and exploitation, and the epistemology of ignorance shields white consciousness from the shame entailed in the exposure. It is the talent for seeing the world wrongly, the agreement to misinterpret the world, that best helps make sense of the racial politics of coaching labor in the NFL. Addressing the dearth of Black head coaches throughout League history, Troy Vincent, NFL Vice President of Football Operations, recently said, "At the end of the day, we don't make the hires. We've exhausted ourselves with programs, initiatives, making sure that owners *know* who's out there, but we don't make the hire."[27] With all due respect to Troy Vincent, attempting to change the behavior of NFL owners with awareness campaigns sounds a bit like trying to thwart fascism with newsroom fact-checkers. Awareness isn't the problem. *They don't want to know.*

Ignorance and Memory

Mills writes that "white normativity manifests itself in a white refusal to recognize the long history of structural discrimination that has left whites with the differential resources they have today, and all to its consequent advantages in negotiating opportunity structures."[28] In an extensive *Washington Post* profile by David Maraniss and renowned sportswriter Sally Jenkins, Dallas Cowboys owner Jerry Jones demonstrates how ignorance structures white memory. Jones grew up in Little Rock, Arkansas, in the 1950s as the son of John Watson "Pat" Jones, a grocery store owner described as a "carnival barker trying to woo the masses under the big top."[29] Whether as a sincere commitment to public service or as part of a publicity scheme, Pat Jones ran for a seat on the Arkansas state legislature in the late 1950s. Despite the fact that Pat Jones ran one of the few racially integrated groceries in the state, Maraniss and Jenkins report that "selling food to Black people was one thing; attending school with them was another."[30] Pat Jones was a vocal supporter of "states' rights," Jim Crow–era code for racial segregation.[31] As Ian Haney López has put it,"'States' rights was a paper-thin abstraction from the days before the Civil War when it had meant the right of Southern states to continue slavery. Then as a rejoinder to the demand of integration, it meant the right of Southern States to continue laws mandating racial segregation." López calls "states' rights" a "fig leaf to allow persons queasy about black equality to oppose integration without having to admit it."[32] In other words, "states' rights" centered a political discourse of ignorance in the Civil Rights era.

When Maraniss and Jenkins asked Jerry Jones about his father's support for "states' rights," Jones turned the conversation back toward the ostensibly race-neutral terrain of professional football. "I'm a states' rights guy in the NFL," Jones replied. "I just believe the club should have the power." Even if it is possible to bracket Jones's reflexive deployment of a racial dog whistle in a discussion of racist employment practices, his blinkered pursuit of corporate decision-making power evokes the central prerogative of the racial contract. Mills writes that "the Racial Contract is calculatedly aimed at economic exploitation. The whole point of establishing a moral hierarchy and juridically partitioning the polity according to race is to secure and legitimate the privileging of those individuals designated as white/persons and the exploitation of those individuals designated as non-white/subpersons. The bottom line," writes Mills, "is material advantage."[33] The Cowboys have never had a Black head coach, and since 1995, when the Cowboys last won the Super Bowl, according to Maraniss and Jenkins, Jones "has elevated a succession of often-unremarkable white men, frequently based on personal relationships."[34] The Cowboys haven't won a meaningful game in over a quarter century, but in the same time they have become the most valuable sports franchise in the universe.[35]

As his states' rights gambit perhaps demonstrates, Maraniss and Jenkins write that Jones "is an enthralling storyteller but also a master of deflection, so absorbed in his own success story that he tends to filibuster and evade when questions get close to a racial reckoning."[36] Asked about a photograph in which he appears with a group of young white men blocking Black students from entering North Little Rock High School in 1957, Jones calls himself "mischievous," merely "curious," expressing adolescent anxiety about his football coach's prior warning to not "see any of you knot-heads near the front of that school."[37] Jones drapes a sepia-toned haze that falls like a veil over his memory, as if the camera's lens just missed Barney Fife ambling in from around the corner to scold the rowdy boys before they headed off to the soda fountain. Maraniss and Jenkins refuse to acquit Jones, however, at least not in print. Citing North Little Rock's contemporaneous history of hanging effigies, threatening mobs, cross-burnings, and an assault on a fifty-eight-year-old Black woman walking to work, they surmise, "Jones did not see what Black people in his community saw." But I wonder: *didn't he?*

The epistemology of ignorance helps to reframe the question from *whether* Jones saw white violence and intimidation to *how* Jones and powerful white men like him remember what they saw. "The editing of white memory," says Mills, "enables a self-representation in which differential white privilege, and the need to correct for it, does not exist. In other words, the mystification of the past underwrites a mystification of the present."[38] Jones is only one franchise owner, but his rhetorical dexterity around the question of Black coaches points to the forms of collective memory that sustain the discourse of ignorance in the NFL's institutional environment. "As individual memory is assisted through a larger social memory," Mills says, "so individual amnesia is then assisted by a larger collective phenomena."[39] Jones, in other words, is not alone in refusing to recognize the history of racial exclusions that accounts for the NFL's shameful record of not hiring Black coaches, but the self-editing of his memory works as a kind of synecdoche that reaches (a) toward other franchise owners resistant to affirmative action regimes and (b) further still toward a broader cultural discourse where the need to remedy racial discrimination does not exist. Ignorance, put simply, *endures*, and along with it the racial hierarchies that stack up like layers of rotten sediment. At its core, the racial contract secures a tacit consensus among powerful white men that Black and brown people exist to be exploited. To make the last two points, I turn my attention to Brian Flores.

The Racialized Mind/Body Dualism

The 2021 NFL season was Flores's third as head coach of the NFL's Miami Dolphins. Miami struggled early in the season, but aided by the development of second-year quarterback Tua Tagovailoa, Flores engineered an unprecedented turnaround and the Dolphins became the first team in league history to win seven consecutive games after losing seven consecutive games. For the second year in a row, the Dolphins finished with a winning record. Be that as it may, Flores was fired at the conclusion of the season in January 2022. As the national sports media lamented his firing and celebrated his efforts in Miami, his job prospects seemed bright. So, three weeks after being fired, Flores interviewed to be the head coach of the New York Giants, who instead hired Brian Daboll, the offensive coordinator for the Buffalo Bills. Four days later, on February 1, Flores filed a federal lawsuit alleging that his termination by the Dolphins and his interview with the Giants violated federal and state laws prohibiting racial discrimination in nongovernment employment.[40] Moreover, Flores's suit was brought as a class action and was thus later joined by Steve Wilks, former head coach of the Arizona Cardinals, and Ray Horton, a former NFL assistant coach who was once a candidate for the Tennessee Titans. Litigation is ongoing, and while the district court has ruled that Flores's claim against the Dolphins is bound by the NFL's internal arbitration procedures, claims against the League and the Giants may proceed.[41]

Flores's case illustrates how the racialized mind/body dualism rationalizes the discourse of ignorance. In the context of imperialism and colonialism, Mills writes that "for the racial contract, a basic inequality is asserted in the capacity of different human groups to know the world and detect natural law. Subpersons are deemed cognitively inferior, lacking in the essential rationality that would make them fully human."[42] Ben Carrington observes sport's role in positing subpersons when he describes "the Black athlete" as a "political entity . . . an attempt to reduce blackness itself and black people in general into a semi-humanized category of racial otherness." Western societies regard Black athletes in particular, he says, as "nearly human, and sometimes even super-human. Human-lite or human-plus. But very rarely, simply, ordinarily, human."[43] Critical sport scholars have been attuned to this formulation of "the Black athlete" since at least 1969, when Harry Edwards wrote that "the Black athlete in professional athletics is regarded by most of his white comrades and owners as a machine—a machine to be used as white men see fit and then discarded after youth or injury has reduced it to the point where cost has surpassed production."[44] Thousands of pages of existing scholarship on race and sport are devoted to unpacking the sources and consequences of the racialized mind/body dualism, and though space does not permit me to review it all here, it refers in essence to the belief, drawn from Cartesian rationality, racial folklore, and nineteenth-century junk science, that not only are mind and body distinct, but their variable capacities can be mapped onto prevailing conceptions of racial difference.[45]

Although the most comprehensive account of the racialized mind/body dualism's expression in sport is John Hoberman's *Darwin's Athletes,*[46] its dubious entailments are elucidated most succinctly by Mike Marqusee in *Redemption Song*, a brilliant biography of Muhammad Ali. "Black sports heroes long ago destroyed the myth of the white man's physical superiority," writes Marqusee, "but its place has been taken by the equally insidious myth of black physical superiority—with its unspoken concomitant, black intellectual ineptitude."[47] Marqusee's observation urges a reckoning with the scientific legacy of racial biology. Though eugenics purported to be advanced science in the nineteenth century, it relied on creationist just-so stories rampant in European intellectual circles. Among the most infamous of its scientists was Louis Agassiz, the well-known proponent of "polygenism," the belief that racial phenotypes designated distinctions between species.[48] Agassiz gained fame in Switzerland as a geologist but pursued work in biological taxonomy at Harvard in the late 1840s. With the institution of American slavery on the public agenda in 1850, Agassiz declared that "human affairs with reference to the colored races would be far more judiciously conducted if guided by a full consciousness of the real difference existing between us and them, and a desire to foster those dispositions that are eminently marked in them."[49] Or, as Stephen Jay Gould summarizes in his landmark scientific history *The Mismeasure of Man*: "train blacks in hand work, whites in mind work."[50] Pairing this historical record with Flores's lawsuit, we can grasp how the racialized mind/body dualism lives on in sport—like that old snake—as the epistemic heir of plantation slavery. Specifically, Flores's lawsuit points to how football's division of athletic labor is guided by assumptions of racial difference and a desire to foster those dispositions presumed since the nineteenth century to be marked in Blackness and whiteness: Black folks toil on the field, and white folks call the plays.

Flores pointed in his legal filing to the League's practice of so-called "race-norming" in concussion settlements.[51] As lawsuits against the NFL by retired players over the lasting effects of brain trauma began to multiply over the last decade, the League either denied compensation claims or offered discounted settlements to Black players according to the nakedly racist medical theory that Black players begin their football careers with inferior baseline cognition. Tracie Canada and Chelsey Carter explain that "race norming depends on the belief that race is a binary, biological concept, and therefore that differences in Black bodies and minds are not only existent, but quantifiable."[52] Carter and Canada link race-norming to the history of eugenics and plantation slavery, practices predicated on the racist assumption that there simply is no Black mind to quantify and thus deem worthy of concern. Borrowing terminology from Saidiya Hartman, they conclude that the NFL is "wrong on all accounts: race norming is an inherently anti-Black form of scientific racism that is evidence of slavery's afterlife."[53] The League agreed to end race-norming in 2021 after a dismissed lawsuit by former players ignited "public outrage" over the previously hidden practice.[54] As the abandonment of race-norming only called attention to its original application, Flores and his attorneys said in their filing with the US District Court, "the NFL insisted that white people simply have better cognitive function than Black people. This is the very definition of racism." They are surely right about that, but perhaps their position does not go far enough.

The adoption of race-norming and the process by which the NFL promised to abandon it also illuminates how the discourse of ignorance circulates. As the Associated Press reported, "The NFL noted that the norms were developed in medicine 'to stop bias in testing, not perpetrate it.' And both [NFL attorney Christopher] Seeger and the league said the practice was never mandatory, but left to the discretion of doctors taking part in the settlement program."[55] So the lawyers blame the neurologists, the neurologists blame the League, the League acts confused, and not only does the ability to identify racism's precise agency get lost in the rhetorical shuffle, but the persisting inequities generated by the legacy of biological racism never enter the discursive frame. Flores highlighted race-norming to place his firing into a historical pattern of racist mistreatment, and the NFL pled ignorance in deferring to its own medical experts.

Flores made an additional argument, though, that invokes a trope common to Black critiques of sport. In the lawsuit's fourth paragraph, Flores and his attorneys call the NFL a "plantation," noting that "its 32 owners—none of whom are Black—profit substantially from the labor of NFL players, 70% of whom are Black. The owners watch the games from atop the NFL stadium in their luxury boxes, while their majority Black workforce put their bodies on the line every Sunday, taking vicious hits and suffering debilitating injuries to their bodies and their brains while the NFL and its owners reap billions of dollars."[56] Much of the contemporary sport scholarship that uses the plantation analogy as a critical lens concerns intercollegiate sports, where universities' ongoing refusal to compensate athletes for their labor makes the exploitation of Black bodies most apparent.[57] Flores emphasizes not the lack of compensation, but the racial patterns evident in who gets assigned the leadership functions associated with mind work and whose body is designated for exhaustion or destruction.[58] Flores's reference to the owners watching games in their luxury boxes evokes theories of social power predicated on who is authorized to look and who is consigned to being looked at.[59] Flores portrays a power relationship defined by an ignorance of Black mental capacity, a "denial of equal intellectual and cognizing ability."[60] For Mills, this point is crucial, since it explains why the social contract is really a racial contract. Whereas the social contract ostensibly guarantees each member of society an equal opportunity to exercise and benefit from their cognitive gifts, Black folks are presumed to exist outside of society in the mythological state of nature. As Mills puts it, "the Black body in particular is seen as paradigmatically a *body*";[61] unfit, in other words, for cognitive work or decision-making power in the suites or on the sidelines where white men ruminate. White men can know the world, and Black men are simply in it.

The Rhetoric of Intent

The NFL, of course, denies that it treats anyone unfairly. Following Colin Kaepernick's demonstrations against racist police violence before NFL games in 2016, the Black athlete protests that followed from them in other sports, and the social movement pressure that began to build throughout sports as racial violence intensified in the summer of 2020, NFL commissioner Roger Goodell issued a statement "condemning racism and the systematic oppression of Black people." "We, the National Football League, admit we were wrong for not listening to NFL players earlier and encourage all to speak out and peacefully protest," Goodell stated, adding, "we are listening, I am listening, and I will be reaching out to players who have raised their voices, and others on how we can move forward together for a better and more united NFL family."[62] A handful of symbolic initiatives followed, including a policy allowing players to wear one of six league-approved social justice messages on their helmets, including the facile two-word slogan "End Racism." Noticing that the NFL's symbolic behavior in 2020 was no different than McDonalds's or Netflix's, Carl Rhodes notes that "in making statements about Black Lives Matter, the NFL was not doing anything that would make any material difference to the real lives of Black people in America."[63] As Akane Kanai and Rosalind Gill write, "the circulation of this corporate messaging relies on the increased visibility of populations that have been historically marginalized, *without dismantling the oppressions that such branding glibly references*."[64] Approved social justice messages and national anthem spectacles function to perpetually reassert an institution's principles of justice and equity in direct rejoinder to the institution's racist practices; that is, the NFL's promises and slogans underwrite the good intentions that serve to rebut criticisms of its conduct.

In response to Flores's lawsuit, NFL commissioner Roger Goodell similarly asserted the league's purported values. "We won't tolerate racism," Goodell told the press. "We won't tolerate discrimination. If there are policies that we need to modify, we're going to do that. If we've seen evidence of discrimination, we will deal with that in a very serious way that will reflect the fact that we won't tolerate that."[65] Statements like these illustrate the third dimension of the discourse of ignorance: the rhetoric of intent is strategic in that it renders cognitive dysfunction institutionally functional. Put another way, the ignorance that produces racially unjust employment outcomes demands little institutional remedy so long as the League communicates to its audiences (and itself) that it *intends* better outcomes. The second paragraph of Flores's filing points out that "rules have been implemented, promises made—but nothing has changed. In fact, the racial discrimination has only been made worse by the NFL's disingenuous commitment to social equity."[66] This is a reference to the Rooney Rule, which was adopted to pierce through the professional networks that keep Black coaches out of the right conference rooms. When implemented in 2003, three head coaches in the NFL were Black. Twenty years later, at the start of the 2023 season? Also three. Although the number of Black coaches has varied since 2003 (the high mark being seven in 2017–18), when Flores says that nothing has changed, snapshots taken two decades apart lend credence to his assertion. Three additional Black head coaches where added in the 2024 offseason, though Flores was not among them.

Regardless of where the number has been for the last century, however, the League and its franchise owners retreat with regularity into a rhetoric of intent, proclaiming with obtuse reassurance that they *mean well*.

Among Flores's most incendiary claims is that his interview with the Giants was a sham, a tokenistic performance meant to symbolically satisfy the Rooney Rule while shirking its requirement to give Black candidates a fair shake. His proof is a text message from New England Patriots coach Bill Belichick congratulating him for getting the job, *but Flores had yet to even interview*. "Coach, are you talking to Brian Flores or Brian Daboll," Flores inquired. "Sorry, I fucked this up," Belichick replied.[67] The Giants would announce Daboll as their hire days later. Owing to its "malice" standard, proof of intent in racial discrimination cases is almost always an insuperable burden for plaintiffs. Arguing that "intent and colorblindness are profoundly connected,"[68] López notes that "the requirement that malice be proved is so exacting that, since this test was announced in 1979, it has never been met."[69] Discrimination cases thus tend to move predictably: "The result is that, under intent doctrine, the Court defaults to the most lenient level of review and then rejects the discrimination claim in all cases involving allegations of discrimination against non-Whites."[70] In the form of rare access to the white whisper network, however, Flores seemed to deliver the goods on the question of intent.

The Giants' public response to Flores's proof was an attempt to demonstrate their good faith, a statement laughable in the flatness of its denial. "Our hiring process and, most certainly, our consideration of Mr. Flores was sincere and genuine. We are disappointed to learn that Mr. Flores was under the mistaken impression that the job had already been awarded."[71] Similarly, the League office asserted its "deep commitment to ensuring equitable employment practices and continue[s] to make progress in providing equitable opportunities throughout our organization. Diversity is at the core of everything we do, and there are few issues on which our clubs and our internal leadership team spend more time."[72] And despite the fact that the League statement was issued *before the end of the same business day* on which the lawsuit was filed, the NFL was at ease insisting that the claim was "without merit." Obviously, the appeal to progress is false on its face, but the function of the statement is not to disclose dispositive facts. It was meant to mobilize public defenses of their good intentions. The plain translation of these statements amounts to an insistence that Brian Flores's cognition has gone awry, that he is mistaken to believe that which is in his direct perception, that his interpretation of his own experience cannot be trusted. "The governing epistemic principle," writes Mills, "could be stated as the requirement that—at least on controversial issues—nonwhite cognition has to be verified by white cognition to be accepted as valid."[73] The blanket refusal to verify Flores's cognition was obvious to at least Tony Dungy, the first Black head coach to win a Super Bowl, who noticed that "you can tell by the reaction most people are in total denial."[74]

As real as the denial may be, as deeply felt as it may be, and even if we take the Giants' or the NFL's good faith in good faith, the rhetoric of intent is corrupted by an epistemology of ignorance that categorically blocks knowledge claims drawn from the specificity of Black experience. The *epistemology* of ignorance simply cannot process the radical disjunction between intent and effect, between ideal and non-ideal states of affairs, nor can it generate the moral architecture required to comprehend the damage it causes. According to Mills, "in whatever discipline that is affected by race, the 'testimony' of the black experience and its distinctive conceptual and theoretical insights will tend to be whited out. Whites will cite other whites in a closed circuit of epistemic authority that reproduces white delusions."[75] Thus, the *discourse* of ignorance is a delusion generator, like a chatbot in eternal beta that keeps cranking out the same vapid press releases about "diversity and inclusion," as if painting "End Racism" onto the football field delivers a sufficient alibi for the perpetuation of racial injustice. As Jenkins puts it, "the owners are always so perplexed, so baffled, so thinly rueful that there are so few minority coaches in a league in which 70 percent of the labor is Black. This has been their tone for decades, without an iota of shame."[76] Shamelessness is possible, I contend, even encouraged, as long as NFL franchise owners and their peers each accept by default the benevolence of their collective intent. Sham interviews are not violations of good faith, they are the *rational* outcome of a collective hallucination about good faith.

Conclusion

Toward the end of *The Racial Contract*, Mills urges a "frank appreciation of how the Racial Contract creates a racialized moral psychology. Whites will act in racist ways while thinking of themselves as acting morally. In other words," he says, "they will experience genuine cognitive difficulties in recognizing certain behavior patterns as racist, so that quite apart from questions of motivation and bad faith they will be morally handicapped simply from the conceptual point of view in seeing and doing the right thing."[77] By layering the *discourse* of ignorance over the *epistemology* of ignorance, we notice that grandiose claims to progress and sober promises of moral accountability are not exactly lies, but evidence of a failure, if not refusal, to comprehend the world the League itself has made. League officials and franchise owners may be handicapped in seeing and doing the right thing, but they have mastered the art of *saying* the right thing. Their evasions, retreats, and self-serving mythologies about their commitment to diversity will always be validated by white epistemic authority convinced of its own innocence. "It is not permissible that the authors of devastation should be so innocent," wrote James Baldwin, but "it is the innocence that constitutes the crime."[78]

Jerry Brewer, the brilliant sports columnist for the *Washington Post*, remarked in the days after Flores filed his lawsuit, that "Flores is dangerous to the league because he no longer operates from a place of need. He isn't working humbly within the system to realize a dream of job stability. He's gripping a sledgehammer."[79] This is a cathartic characterization, one worth an optimistic emotional investment as we consider the way sport intersects with questions of social justice. At the same time, it is impossible to escape the cynicism arising from the suspicion that Flores and other Black coaches are simply snakebitten. The law, after all, has far more experience with the racial contract than even the National Football League, which is perhaps why Mills was careful to include juridical structures in his critique. Football may take up more cultural space, and so may sometimes seem more important, but the Courts? The Courts *are* "the system." Should Flores avail himself of binding arbitration in his complaint against the Dolphins, the sole arbitrator, appointed by league owners, is NFL Commissioner Roger Goodell. In October 2023, about a year and a half after Flores first filed suit, Goodell agreed to a three-year contract extension with the owners reportedly worth around $65 million per year.[80] Arbitration was stipulated in Flores's employment contract, which, of course, was a racial contract all along.

Among the NFL's most ubiquitous and nauseating promotional slogans is one that says the NFL "inspires change." Perhaps if Flores's sledgehammer strikes a blow or two, the slogan might manifest at least an ironic truth. Alas, I am reminded of Baldwin one final time: "It is clear that white Americans are simply unwilling to effect these changes; they are, in the main—so slothful have they become—unable to even envision them."[81] Perhaps like Muhammad Ali, Brian Flores also is America—another part of America that America won't recognize.

Notes

1. Muhammad Ali, "In His Own Words," Muhammad Ali Center, 2024, https://alicenter.org/meet-ali/in-his-own-words/.

2. Daniel A. Grano, "Muhammad Ali Versus the 'Modern Athlete': On Voice

in Mediated Sports Culture," *Critical Studies in Media Communication* 26, no. 3 (2009): 195.

3. Barack and Michelle Obama, "Statement from President Barack Obama and First Lady Michelle Obama on the Passing of Muhammad Ali," White House Press Office, June 4, 2016, https://obamawhitehouse.archives.gov/the-press-office/2016/06/04/statement-president-barack-obama-and-first-lady-michelle-obama-passing.

4. Matthew Houdek and Kendall R. Phillips, "Rhetoric and the Temporal Turn: Race, Gender, Temporalities," *Women's Studies in Communication* 43, no. 4 (2020): 373.

5. For an elaboration of Gilroy's account, first formulated in *The Black Atlantic: Modernity and Double-Consciousness* (London: Verso, 1993), see George Lipsitz, "The Changing Same," *Social Identities* 24, no. 1 (2018): 16–20. Gilroy locates the concept of the changing same within the history of jazz music, but other scholars trace its origins to Amiri Baraka on the same subject in 1966. (Compare Brandon Erby, "The Changing Same of American Racism: African American Rhetoric and the Rejection of Normalcy," *Spark: A 4C4Equality Journal*, July 2022, https://sparkactivism.com/volume-2-call/vol-2-intro/same-american-racism/). Erby argues that one possible formulation of the changing same "represents how forms of structural and systemic racism shift and reconfigure in the United States."

6. Kirt H. Wilson, "Dreams of Union: Days of Conflict: Communication Social Justice and Civil Rights Memory in the Age of Barack Obama," Carroll C. Arnold Distinguished Lecture 2016, National Communication Association, https://www.natcom.org/sites/default/files/annual-convention/NCA_Convention_Video_Archive_2016_Arnold_Lecture.pdf, p. 6–7.

7. James Baldwin, *The Fire Next Time* (New York: Vintage, 1993), 5.

8. Charles W. Mills, *The Racial Contract* (Ithaca: Cornell University Press, 1997), 10.

9. Daniel A. Grano, "Ritual Disorder and the Contractual Morality of Sport: A Case Study in Race, Class, and Agreement," *Rhetoric & Public Affairs* 10, no. 3 (2007): 451.

10. Carole Pateman, *The Sexual Contract* (Cambridge: Polity, 1988).

11. Mills, *The Racial Contract*, 11.

12. Mills, *The Racial Contract*, 5.

13. Mark Lawrence McPhail, "(Re)-Signing Reconciliation: Reading Obama's Charleston Eulogy through a Rhetorical Theory of Adaptive Racism," *Rhetoric & Public Affairs* 23, no. 3 (2020): 542.

14. Mills, *The Racial Contract*, 18.

15. McPhail, "(Re)-Signing Reconciliation," 541.

16. Charles W. Mills, "Epistemological Ignorance," in *50 Concepts for a Critical Phenomenology*, ed. Gail Weiss, Ann V. Murphy, and Gayle Salamon (Evanston, IL: Northwestern University Press, 2019), 110.

17. Linda Martín Alcoff, "Epistemologies of Ignorance," in *Race and Episte-*

mologies of Ignorance, ed. Shannon Sullivan and Nancy Tuana (Albany: SUNY Press, 2007), 47.

18. Vincent Jungkunz and Julie White, "Ignorance, Innocence, and Democratic Responsibility: Seeing Race, Hearing Racism," *The Journal of Politics* 75, no. 2 (2013): 439.

19. McPhail, "(Re)-Signing Reconciliation," 541.

20. Mills, *The Racial Contract*, 73.

21. John Kiem and Adam Teicher, "What Eric Bieniemy's Move Means for the Chiefs, Commanders and His Career," ESPN, February 17, 2023, https://www.espn.com/nfl/story/_/id/35675202/why-offensive-coordinator-eric-bieniemy-left-chiefs-commanders.

22. It is worth noting here that the NFL and its franchises are corporations whose primary objective is to pursue profit. Winning football games may correlate to greater revenues, but not necessarily (as the point below about the Dallas Cowboys proves). From this perspective, the NFL is less a pure sporting endeavor than it is a lucrative television show. Nonetheless, football maintains its cultural presence through its meritocratic mythos, and even if it did not, decisions about whom to hire as coach still amount to casting decisions in unscripted programming, which follows the same racial logics this essay identifies. I credit Nick Marx for posing the question that generated this point.

23. Johnnie L. Cochran, Jr., and Cyrus Mehri, "Black Coaches in the National Football League: Superior Performance, Inferior Opportunities," Mehri & Skalet, PLLC, i. Though this report no longer appears to be publicly available from its original source, www.findjustice.com, the author is in possession of the document accessed and downloaded in spring 2003.

24. Cochran and Mehri, "Black Coaches in the National Football League," 3.

25. "The Rooney Rule," National Football League, accessed February 1, 2024, https://operations.nfl.com/inside-football-ops/inclusion/the-rooney-rule/.

26. DeMaurice Smith and Carl Lasker, "The Rooney Suggestion: How the 'Rule' Has Failed to Defeat Institutional Barriers to Equitable Hiring Practices in the NFL and Recommendations for Meaningful Reform," *Yale Law and Policy Review* 42, no. 1 (2023): 243.

27. Quoted in Dave Sheinin, Michael Lee, Emily Giambalvo, Artur Galocha, and Clara Ence Morse, "How the NFL Blocks Black Coaches," *Washington Post*, September 21, 2022, https://www.washingtonpost.com/sports/interactive/2022/nfl-black-head-coaches/.

28. Charles H. Mills, "White Ignorance," in *Race and Epistemologies of Ignorance*, ed. Shannon Sullivan and Nancy Tuana (Albany: SUNY Press, 2007), 28.

29. Tom Stephenson, "Jerry Jones: The Grocer's Son," *D Magazine*, September 16, 2013, https://www.dmagazine.com/publications/d-ceo/2013/october/jerry-jones-the-grocers-son/.

30. Dave Maraniss and Sally Jenkins, "Jerry Jones Helped Transform the NFL, Except When It Comes to Race," *Washington Post*, November 23, 2022, https://www.washingtonpost.com/sports/interactive/2022/jerry-jones-black-coaches-nfl/.

31. Maraniss and Jenkins, "Jerry Jones Helped Transform the NFL."

32. Ian Haney López, *Dog Whistle Politics: How Coded Racial Appeals Have Reinvented Racism & Wrecked the Middle Class* (New York: Oxford University Press, 2014), 16.

33. Mills, *The Racial Contract*, 32–3.

34. Maraniss and Jenkins, "Jerry Jones Helped Transform the NFL."

35. In 2023, *Forbes* valued the Dallas Cowboys at $9 billion, nearly $2 billion more valuable than the Major League Baseball's New York Yankees, who rank second. See Mike Ozanian and Justin Teitelbaum, "The World's 50 Most Valuable Sports Teams 2023," *Forbes*, September 8, 2023, https://www.forbes.com/sites/mikeozanian/2023/09/08/the-worlds-50-most-valuable-sports-teams-2023/?sh=5d5dddb72b44.

36. Maraniss and Jenkins, "Jerry Jones Helped Transform the NFL."

37. Maraniss and Jenkins, "Jerry Jones Helped Transform the NFL."

38. Mills, "White Ignorance," 31.

39. Mills, "White Ignorance," 31.

40. *Flores v. The National Football League*, 1:22-cv-00871, US District Court for the Southern District of New York: 1–58, https://www.wigdorlaw.com/wp-content/uploads/2022/02/Complaint-against-National-Football-League-et-al-Filed.pdf.

41. Ken Belson and Jenny Vrentas, "Brian Flores's Discrimination Case Against the N.F.L. Can Move to Court," *New York Times*, March 1, 2023, https://www.nytimes.com/2023/03/01/sports/football/brian-flores-discrimination-nfl.html.

42. Mills, *The Racial Contract*, 59.

43. Ben Carrington, *Race, Sport and Politics: The Sporting Black Diaspora* (Thousand Oaks, CA, 2010), 2–3.

44. Harry Edwards, *The Revolt of the Black Athlete* (New York: Free Press, 1969), 25.

45. I offer a fulsome review of this literature in Abraham I. Khan, "Sport and Race: A Disciplinary History and Exhortation," in *Defining Sport Communication*, ed. Andrew C. Billings (New York: Routledge, 2016), 107–20.

46. John Hoberman, *Darwin's Athletes: How Sport Has Damaged Black America and Preserved the Myth of Race* (Boston: Houghton Mifflin, 1997).

47. Mike Marqusee, *Redemption Song: Muhammad Ali and the Spirit of the Sixties* (London: Verso, 1999).

48. Louis Menand, "Morton, Agassiz, and the Origins of Scientific Racism in the United States," *The Journal of Blacks in Higher Education* 34 (2001), 110–13.

49. Quoted in Steven Jay Gould, *The Mismeasure of Man* (New York: Norton, 1996), 145.

50. Gould, *The Mismeasure of Man*, 145.

51. *Flores v. The National Football League*, 4.

52. Tracie Canada and Chelsey R. Carter, "The NFL's Racist 'Race Norming' Is an Afterlife of Slavery," *Scientific American*, July 8, 2021, https://www.scientificamerican.com/article/the-nfls-racist-race-norming-is-an-afterlife-of-slavery/.

53. Canada and Carter, "The NFL's Racist 'Race Norming.'" Hartman's notion of the "afterlife" of slavery is elaborated in *Lose Your Mother: A Journey Along the Atlantic Slave Route* (New York: Farrar, Strauss, and Giroux, 2007). Hartman's work has been enormously influential in interdisciplinary Black studies, particularly on scholarship in the emerging tradition of Afro-pessimism.

54. Associated Press, "NFL Agrees to End Race-Based Brain Testing in $1B Settlement on Concussions," October 20, 2021, https://www.npr.org/2021/10/20/1047793751/nfl-concussion-settlement-race-norming-cte.

55. Maryclaire Dale, "NFL Pledges to Halt 'Race-Norming,' Review Black Claims," Associated Press, June 2, 2021, https://apnews.com/article/pa-state-wire-race-and-ethnicity-health-nfl-sports-205b304c0c3724532d74fc54e58b4d1d.

56. *Flores v. The National Football League*, 2.

57. See, for example, Billy Hawkins, *The New Plantation: Black Athletes, College Sports, and Predominantly White NCAA Institutions* (New York: Palgrave Macmillan, 2010), and Taylor Branch, "The Shame of College Sports," *The Atlantic*, October 2011. Branch writes, "to survey the scene—corporations and universities enriching themselves on the backs of uncompensated young men, whose status as 'student-athletes' deprives them of the right to due process guaranteed by the Constitution—is to catch an unmistakable whiff of the plantation."

58. Though Mills's racial contract serves as my primary theoretical resource here, compare Achille Mbembé and Libby Meintjes, "Necropolitics," *Public Culture* 15, no. 1 (2003): 11–40.

59. Along similar lines, see Thomas P. Oates, "The Erotic Gaze in the NFL Draft," *Communication and Critical/Cultural Studies* 4, no. 1 (2007): 74–90. Oates writes that "in an age when blacks are perceived as athletically dominant, especially in macho team sports like football and basketball, the draft, and the looking it enables, serves to reassert the white male power structure by positioning increasingly non-white athletic bodies as commodities, and encouraging fans to imagine themselves as potential possessors of these bodies," 88.

60. Mills, *The Racial Contract*, 60.

61. Mills, *The Racial Contract*, 51.

62. Roger Goodell quoted in Carl Rhodes, *Woke Capitalism: How Corporate Morality is Sabotaging Democracy* (Bristol, UK: Bristol University Press, 2022), 125–26.

63. Rhodes, *Woke Capitalism*, 130.

64. Akane Kanai and Rosalind Gill, "Woke? Affect, Neoliberalism, Marginalised Identities, and Consumer Culture," *new formations: a journal of culture/theory/politics* 102 (2021): 26. Emphasis in original.

65. Quoted in Madeline Coleman, "Roger Goodell Addresses NFL's Diversity Issues, Allegations in Flores Lawsuit," *Sports Illustrated*, February 9, 2022, https://www.si.com/nfl/2022/02/10/brian-flores-lawsuit-roger-goodell-addresses-nfl-diversity-issues-allegations.

66. *Flores v. The National Football League*, 2.

67. Ricky O'Donnell, "Brian Flores' Text Exchange with Bill Belichick Is Damning Evidence of NFL Hiring Discrimination," SBNation, February 1, 2002, https://www.sbnation.com/nfl/2022/2/1/22913143/brian-flores-bill-belichick-texts-nfl-discrimination-lawsuit.

68. Ian Haney López, "Intentional Blindness," *New York University Law Review* 87 (2012): 1,784.

69. López, "Intentional Blindness," 1783.

70. López, "Intentional Blindness," 1783.

71. WCBV.com, "New York Giants Respond to Lawsuit from Former Patriots Assistant Coach Brian Flores," https://www.wcvb.com/article/new-york-giants-repond-to-lawsuit-from-former-patriots-assistant-coach-brian-flores/38976854#.

72. The NFL's response was first posted in a tweet by ESPN reporter Adam Schefter (@AdamSchefter), "NFL Statement on Brian Flores' lawsuit," https://twitter.com/AdamSchefter/status/1488643379542077442.

73. Mills, *The Racial Contract*, 60.

74. Quoted in William C. Rhoden, "Will the Brian Flores Lawsuit Force a Racial Reckoning for the NFL?" *Andscape*, February 2, 2022, https://andscape.com/features/force-is-the-only-thing-that-nfl-owners-understand-in-the-fight-for-racial-justice/.

75. Mills, "White Ignorance," 34.

76. Sally Jenkins, "NFL Owners Are Committed to Diversity—Until It's Their Turn to Make a Hire," *Washington Post*, February 3, 2022, https://www.washingtonpost.com/sports/2022/02/03/brian-flores-new-york-giants-interview/.

77. Mills, *The Racial Contract*, 93.

78. Baldwin, *The Fire Next Time*, 6.

79. Jerry Brewer, "Brian Flores Is Done Pretending, and the NFL Is Losing Control," *Washington Post*, February 2, 2022, https://www.washingtonpost.com/sports/2022/02/02/brian-flores-black-coaches-nfl/.

80. ESPN News Services, "NFL Commissioner Roger Goodell Receives 3-year Extension," ESPN, https://www.espn.com/nfl/story/_/id/38687143/nfl-commissioner-roger-goodell-receives-3-year-extension.

81. Baldwin, *The Fire Next Time*, 85.

2

The Team That United a City

Sports Documentaries and the Rhetorical Construction of Unity

MICHAEL L. BUTTERWORTH

In September of 2021, ESPN debuted *Once Upon a Time in Queens*, a four-part documentary about the New York Mets team that won the 1986 World Series. Across the episodes, the narrative metaphorically links the fortunes of the team with that of the city itself. As the ESPN press release for the series stated, "as the grime and hopelessness that defined the city gave way to the high-flying, 'greed is good' rise of the 1980s, the Mets emerged, too. And the transformations—of the city, and the ballclub—ran in parallel paths in every which way imaginable."[1] The synergy between the team and the city peaked with a championship parade attended by more than two million people, which is featured late in the series' final installment. As the film presents slow-motion footage of the parade, *Slaves of New York* author Tama Janowitz declares, "New York City's a galaxy. We had the garbage collectors, we had struggling artists, we had seamstresses, we had rich people, poor people. And in that moment, the Mets brought that whole constellation together."[2] The Mets, therefore, were not merely a great baseball team; they were the very glue that held together the nation's largest and most dynamic city.

I open with *Once Upon a Time in Queens* for two reasons. First, its 2021 premiere situates it within a moment that journalist Jacob Feldman has named the "golden age of sports docs."[3] As Samantha Sheppard and Travis Vogan confirm, "Sports documentaries have never been more popular, prestigious, or visible."[4] This is especially true on television, where networks such as HBO and ESPN have used the genre to bolster their brands and "to examine sport's meaning and history."[5] Second, the narrative of

Once Upon a Time in Queens metaphorically equates sports to the identity of a community. The idea expressed by Janowitz, that a team brings a city "together," is one of the most common virtues attributed to sports.[6] Such declarations are often about more than binding communities together simply on their own terms; rather, the idea that sports facilitate "unity" is frequently paired with a lament or critique about the things that prevent such unity in the first place. From crises such as 9/11, Hurricane Katrina, and the COVID-19 pandemic to everyday struggles to build community against cultural, economic, and political challenges, sports are offered as the antidote to communal division or distress. There is certainly value in this concept, as there are moments when sports *can* facilitate communal bonds, even when they are fleeting or not universal. Too often, however, celebrating sports for bringing people together "relies on the abstract notion of unity for its own sake without taking account of the causes of political division or their variable forms of legitimacy."[7]

In this chapter, I argue that one of the most prominent themes in televised sports documentaries is the assertion that teams are uniquely able to constitute and define local communities. As a rhetorical critic, I am primarily interested in the use of sports in ways that simplify the complex reasons conflict and division exist in the first place, while reinforcing the idea that sports are the primary means by which a community can develop a collective identity. To make this argument, I begin with a brief discussion of the sports documentary genre and my orientation to rhetoric. I then turn to a substantive engagement with six films produced over roughly the past two decades. Following that analysis, I examine the limits of sports documentaries as a form of epideictic rhetoric, concluding that unity through sports is, at best, partial and temporary.

Sports Documentaries as Epideictic Rhetoric

Documentaries are premised on the presentation of "real" people and "true" events on screen. Yet any presentation of reality is shaped by the biases and interpretations of filmmakers. As Bill Nichols argues, "Documentary films stand for a particular view of the world, one we may never have encountered before even if the factual aspects of this world are familiar to us."[8] More pointedly, Jane Chapman asserts that "a documentary seeks to persuade, which means that representational issues are central to its inherent ideology."[9] Nichols and Chapman share the view that audiences should not view documentaries as "objective" presentations of reality; rather, they are subjective representations of one view of reality. In other words, documentary film is *rhetorical*.

If the affirmation of community is one of sports' most essential functions, then rhetoric is the means by which communal values are communicated. In classical rhetorical vocabulary, there are three forms rhetoric may take: *forensic*, *epideictic*, or *deliberative*.[10] Epideictic rhetoric, often defined as a discourse of "praise or blame," is focused on the affirmation or rejection of the present values that shape a community. I have argued elsewhere that much of the rhetorical scholarship about sports is at least indirectly grounded in the epideictic, especially "for scholars interested in the ways sport shapes identities at local, national, and global levels. Such an emphasis is also consistent with the way sport is typically upheld as a mechanism to promote peace and unity."[11]

The use of sports to shape identity and promote unity is commonly tied to public memory, a scholarly disposition that argues shared reflections of the *past* tell us more about the anxieties and crises of the *present*.[12] Such uses of sports are consistent with the aims of epideictic rhetoric. More specifically, Bradford Vivian defines "neoliberal epideictic," through which ostensibly nonpolitical expressions of memory are used not only to generate unity but also to deny the legitimacy of conflict. In his words, such texts can induce "a quietly pernicious mode of public forgetting and political judgment: a disavowal of institutional politics and difficult sociopolitical differences in favor of transcendent political symbolism and supposedly universal civic sentiment."[13] It is with these ideas in mind that I turn to a critical reading of sports documentaries.

Constituting Unity in Sports Documentaries

In this chapter, I analyze six films based on a few guiding principles. First, to evaluate projects similar in scope, I use only single-episode documentaries, which rules out *Once Upon a Time in Queens* among many others. Second, I have included films that feature each of the four major North American sports, primarily because those sports are more likely to capture large, diverse audiences. Third, I have incorporated films that recall each decade dating back to the 1960s. I do not mean to suggest that any single film can stand in for an entire decade; rather, I aim to trace rhetorical patterns located in public memory over time. I proceed thematically, featuring six documentaries: 1) HBO's *A City on Fire* (2002), which focuses on the 1968 World Series champion Detroit Tigers; 2) HBO's *Broad Street Bullies* (2010), which details the mid-1970s Philadelphia Flyers, known for their physical style of play in the NHL; 3) ESPN's *The U* (2009), which recounts the rise of college football at the University of Miami in the 1980s;[14] 4) ESPN's *Four Falls of Buffalo* (2015), which recalls the four consecutive losses in the Super Bowl by the Buffalo Bills; 5) NFL Films' *Rebirth in New Orleans* (2016), which locates the city's recovery from Hurricane Katrina in the Saints and the Louisiana Superdome; and 6) ESPN's *Believeland* (2016), a reflection on each of the three major teams in Cleveland that pivots around LeBron James leading the Cavaliers to their first NBA championship.[15] Through a close reading of each documentary, I emphasize that these films argue professional sports: 1) represent civic identity; 2) valorize the working class; and 3) promise an antidote to division, especially with respect to race.

Representing Civic Identity

In *Believeland*, after the Cleveland Cavaliers triumphed in the 2016 NBA Finals, at last delivering a championship to the city's long-suffering fan base, local radio host Tony Rizzo declared, "This is maybe one of the greatest weeks in the history of the city. Nothing has brought Northeast Ohio together like this Cavaliers championship."[16] This sentiment is representative of one of the most pervasive themes in these documentaries, which is that professional sports are a vital component of a city's civic identity. This theme is evident across the films but most strongly present in *Four Falls of Buffalo*, *Rebirth in New Orleans*, and *Believeland*.

Nearly everything in ESPN's *Four Falls of Buffalo* is shaped by the elements. The film's title and opening sequence reference the majesty of Niagara Falls while metaphorically hailing the fall of the NFL's Buffalo Bills over four consecutive seasons in the early 1990s. Meanwhile, Sam Cooke's "One More River to Cross" provides the soundtrack, giving the narrative the feel of a spiritual journey. The narrative anchor for that journey is former Bills quarterback Jim Kelly, as the story traces his initial reluctance to be in Buffalo, his ascent as one of the game's best quarterbacks, the four Super Bowl losses, the tragic death of his eight-year-old son, and his cancer diagnosis in 2015. In spite of all this, Kelly insists he is "a very blessed man." His journey also stands in for Bills fans, who, though not all touched by the same kinds of tragedy, have suffered alongside the team through its unprecedented run of near misses.

Beyond the spiritual heft of water, *Four Falls of Buffalo* makes frequent references to the city's notoriously lousy weather. As ESPN announcer Chris Berman laments, "No one, nationally, had much nice to say about western New York or Buffalo," the film cuts to images of snow covering the football stadium. Robert Thompson of Syracuse University follows this by stating, "This is a city, we should also remember, that nine months of the year, there is either snow or rumors of snow." And one of Buffalo's most well-known natives, the former newsman Tim Russert, observes, "Being a Buffalo Bills fan really isn't being a fan, it's a way of life." He adds, "It represents people who honestly believe that, against all the odds, against some of the worst weather imaginable, they have a magnificent life that they're proud of." In short, the brutal weather often experienced in Buffalo makes for something of a spiritual test, one that requires the city's residents to endure and thrive, together.

Four Falls of Buffalo recalls the development of the team in the 1980s and its rise to elite status by the early 1990s. To reach four consecutive Super Bowls is a remarkable achievement, even as fans and media outside of Buffalo grew weary of seeing them lose. Although sports are often celebrated for teaching lessons about perseverance and finding virtue in the challenges of competition, it is rare to see affirmations of teams and athletes who do not *win*; the very notion of being a "loser" is anathema in American culture. *Four Falls of Buffalo* finds its virtue in the journey, acknowledging that a team in defeat may still stand in for its city. Following their loss in Super Bowl XXV (their first), Bills head coach Marv Levy shared an anonymous poem with his team: "Fight on my men, Sir Andrew said / A little I'm hurt, but not yet slain / I'll just lie me down and bleed a while / And then I'll rise and fight again." An embodiment of such resilience is found in Scott Norwood, best known to NFL fans as the kicker who missed a field goal as time expired in Super Bowl XXV that would have given the Bills the victory over the New York Giants. That play, known as "Wide Right" because of the kick's trajectory outside the right goal post, provides the opening image of *Four Falls of Buffalo*, confirming for viewers that it remains the defining memory of the team in that era.[17] Nevertheless, the film is clearly sympathetic to Norwood, who appears several times and remains visibly shaken by his missed kick. After that loss, the Bills gathered in front of 30,000 fans in Buffalo's Niagara Square. Norwood addressed the supportive fans. "You know, we're struggling with this right now, and you know I am," he said, "but I know I've never felt more loved than right now." The extended sequence is rather eloquent, as the fans' commitment to the team is unshaken before Norwood's despair and humility. Sports audiences are rarely invited to linger over disappointment as a virtue *in and of itself*, making this an especially important moment. It reminds audiences that civic identity is less about a triumphant outcome and more about the spiritual bonds that are forged in the shared journey.

Rebirth in New Orleans takes the notion of civic identity even further, asserting that the Saints and the city's residents are part of the same *family*. That family has been built and shaped by New Orleans's rich cultural heritage, including its celebrated food, music, and party scenes. In the film,

New Orleans Times-Picayune writer Jeff Duncan claims the "Saints became a part of the cultural fabric of the city over the years. Even though they didn't win a lot, people loved them anyway." Former Saints wide receiver Rich Mauti likens the team to Mardi Gras, saying, "it's embedded in the city." And Louisiana Superdome engineer Nolan Ledoux confirms, "It's a family affair. Everybody loves the Saints because it's part of their family." The strength of a family might best be measured by its members' ability to support one another in times of tragedy or crisis, something that came to define New Orleans after Hurricane Katrina devastated the city in 2005.

At just under forty-three minutes, *Rebirth in New Orleans* provides only the minimum detail necessary to understand Katrina's effects. Nevertheless, the images remain shocking and unsettling, especially when trying to process the experience of 35,000 refugees inside the Superdome. In the wake of the storm, the documentary tells us, "The battered Superdome was the new symbol of New Orleans, not gone but uninhabitable." Meanwhile, the film makes connections to suggest that the people seeking shelter in the stadium were representative of the city as a whole. "It became an island of 35,000 stranded people," we hear, "so many of whom experienced the worst moments of their lives in the same place they had once felt the best." It is unlikely that the residents who found themselves huddled in the Superdome were frequent attendees at Saints games; but the narrative arc of the documentary ultimately depends on an assumption that they are.

Most of the film is dedicated to the efforts to rebuild the Superdome in time for the Saints to return for the start of the 2006 season. *Rebirth in New Orleans* asserts that a recovery in New Orleans had to begin with the stadium and, thirteen months after the storm, on September 25, 2006, the Saints hosted the Atlanta Falcons on ESPN's *Monday Night Football.* The "Domecoming," as it is known, was a spiritual revival, complete with an invocation, a chorus singing "Amazing Grace," and a performance of "When the Saints Go Marching In." What followed seemed to confirm that something miraculous was indeed taking place. The Saints defeated the favored Falcons, 23–3, in a game best remembered for the iconic moment in which Saints safety Steve Gleason blocked a punt that was recovered in the end zone for a touchdown. The play electrified the crowd and has become synonymous with the Domecoming itself. ESPN commentator Tony Kornheiser, who was in the booth for the broadcast, recalls, "You are hearing this noise, you are watching these people, you're watching what so many in that place thought was an absolute rebirth." Others, including Gleason's teammate Scott Fujita, echo the theme of "rebirth," which was eventually immortalized in a statue outside of the Superdome depicting

FIGURE 2.1: "Rebirth" sculpture of Steve Gleason outside of Caesar's Superdome in New Orleans (Brian Hanlon, 2012). Photograph by Yair Haklai, 2016. Wikimedia Commons.

the blocked punt. Its title, simply "Rebirth," anoints Gleason as the patron "Saint" of New Orleans and consecrates the Saints as the savior of the city.

Believeland similarly emphasizes the spiritual and familial ties that bind a city together. Before the Cavaliers won an NBA championship in 2016, no city in the United States had suffered more sports-related disappointment than Cleveland. It was not merely that its professional teams had failed to win titles, it was that they had failed by coming so close and losing in heartbreaking fashion. The NFL's Browns nearly reached the Super Bowl in 1987 and 1988, narrowly losing in both years to the Denver Broncos in iconic moments known as "The Drive" and "The Fumble." The NBA's Cavaliers had a dominant team in the late 1980s, but they are best known for losing in the 1989 playoffs to the ascendent Chicago Bulls on "The Shot," an iconic, series-clinching jumper from Michael Jordan. And MLB's Indians (now Guardians) lost the World Series twice in the 1990s, losing in 1997 to a Game 7, extra-inning rally by the Florida Marlins.[18] Beyond these failures, Clevelanders also felt abandoned in two dramatic moments: first, when Browns owner Art Modell moved the franchise to Baltimore in 1995; and second, when Cavaliers superstar LeBron James left in free agency for Miami in the infamous "Decision" of 2010.

The narrative of *Believeland* reaches its crescendo with the departure of James in 2010 and his return in 2014. As Denise Bostdorff and Daniel

O'Rourke have detailed, James's homecoming can be analogized to the parable of the prodigal son, with James achieving forgiveness by leading the Cavaliers to a title in 2016.[19] In the documentary, the sense of exaltation is obvious, best symbolized by sportswriter Scott Raab tearfully celebrating the championship. They are tears of joy, but also of release, as the film presents a permanently altered and unified city. As the film closes with images of the Cavaliers' championship parade, Raab turns to his son, "No father on earth could ask for anything better than to enjoy this with you." Much like the Saints in New Orleans, then, a sports triumph in Cleveland is anchored by family and its symbolic connection to the community.

The spiritual significance of needing to "believe" in the Cavaliers also echoes the themes present in *Four Falls of Buffalo* and *Rebirth in New Orleans*. Before James was the "prodigal son," he was the "chosen one" and "King James," a generational player and community savior. When he left Cleveland for Miami in 2010, the community's sense of betrayal was powerful, characterized at least in part by resentments rooted in racism. Many fans were angered and some went so far as to burn their jerseys bearing James's likeness, an act that might be understood as a symbolic lynching.[20] Cavaliers owner Dan Gilbert infamously scolded James in a public letter, his words formed by the paternalistic privilege of a white owner offended by the self-determination of a Black superstar. The point here is not to evaluate in full the racial dynamics underlying public reactions to "The Decision," which I will explore in detail through a discussion of other films; rather, it is to acknowledge how powerfully those dynamics were felt at the time yet were left unexamined in *Believeland*.

Watching *Believeland* makes it easy to root for Clevelanders. Indeed, the celebration is euphoric and, to a degree, indicative of sports' capacity to bring people together. Much like other films in this chapter, however, this one becomes overly dependent on the "sports will save us" narrative. One interview subject in *Believeland* is reporter Toni Grossi, who declares, "The purpose of a professional sports franchise is to lift the spirits of its community and also lead its economic recovery, revitalize our economy when we're going bad. And that's the importance, I think of professional sports and it is to Cleveland." This is a common perception but a gross distortion of the role of professional sports, especially with regard to their economic impact.[21] It also overestimates how much professional sports can sustain civic identity over time. The Cavaliers' victory in 2016 was worthy of celebration, but fleeting. After all, LeBron James left again, this time heading to Los Angeles in 2018, and the three major league teams have all had only sporadic moments of subsequent success. *Believeland* celebrates the city in 2016, but it cannot explain what might characterize Cleveland in the years before or since.

Valorizing the Working Class

The post-industrial transformation of the United States is well documented through the narrative of decline in the midwestern and eastern cities known as the "Rust Belt," and this theme is most prevalent in *Broad Street Bullies, Four Falls of Buffalo,* and *Believeland. Broad Street Bullies* grounds its narrative in the economic decline of Philadelphia in the 1970s. Early in the documentary, the narration describes the city as "a hard-scrabble, beer and a hoagie kind of town, heavily defined by close-knit ethnic neighborhoods and a working-class population set in its ways." Midway through the film, a photo montage of blue-collar workers—a line cook, a forklift driver, a barber—culminates with one commenter observing, "It was all about this, tough, let's grind it out every day. Men worked two and three jobs, they hustled. . . . They loved guys who'd sweat and bleed, who'd fight literally and figuratively." *Broad Street Bullies* makes clear that, in spite of Philadelphia's economic and cultural diversity, it is a working-class ethos that provides the impetus for the city's eventual embrace of the NHL's Flyers.

From the opening moments of the documentary, when a disembodied voice insists, "This team unified a city," it is clear that Philadelphia should be understood as uniquely suited to a combative ethos. The city had established teams in the other major sports, so hockey seemed an unlikely source of salvation. But the NHL's expansion in the late 1960s brought the Flyers to Philadelphia for the 1967–68 season and, just six years later, they won the Stanley Cup. The transformation from a struggling expansion team to NHL champion was most clearly signified by a shift in their style of play. *Broad Street Bullies* earns its title as an homage to sportswriter Jack Chevalier, who first penned that reference in 1972. The nickname, which hailed one of the main thoroughfares through the city (Broad Street), followed from players such as Bobby Clarke and Dave Schultz, whose physical style intimidated opponents, pushed the boundaries of fair play, and changed the league. Their behavior, largely coded as "toughness," provides the narrative anchor for the film, justified not only because it yielded success but because it presumably reflected the character of the city. Lou Scheinfeld, who was in charge of Philadelphia's arena the Spectrum, claims "the Flyers gave them hope." Local radio host Anthony Gargano suggests the city "had a complex—'I get no respect, I'm from Philadelphia'—until this band of crazy nuts from Canada come in." Not unlike Cleveland's reputation, this perceived lack of respect can be attributed to the city's economic challenges. More specifically to Philadelphia, its residents are also often overshadowed by their close neighbors, with the nation's political epicenter in Washington, DC, to the south and its economic epicenter in New York to the north. The film's narration confirms this sense of neglect, declaring, "Not much had come easy to the city of late, and the Flyers' gritty brand of hockey struck a chord. They were the perfect antidote for a city longing for a lift." Accompanying these words is a series of images showing the signs of urban decay.

The closing moments of *Broad Street Bullies* provide another photo montage of everyday Philadelphians bonding over their beloved hockey team. Against these images, Flyers players of the era recall their days fondly, insisting they have nothing for which they should apologize. The narration agrees, concluding, "The bullies may have bent a rule or two on their climb to the top, but the one that the team and its city have abided by is the chalky edict Fred Shero declared en route to their first cup. 'Win today, and we walk together forever.'"[22] Or, as one reviewer of the film puts it, "HBO has transformed the Flyers' story into an attractive, more narrowly focused feel-good story about a bunch of guys who went out and played for themselves and their fans, and what the rest of the world thought was and remains inconsequential."[23] That the Broad Street Bullies were polarizing, of course, only adds to the fondness felt for them by their fans. Although the documentary goes to great lengths to show the sense of unity felt by those in Philadelphia, it never examines what happens for those fans uncomfortable with the price of victory or the larger consequences of treating the Flyers as a romantic memory. Moreover, in its depiction of the city as a model of working-class America, it minimizes the substantial cultural and economic diversity that characterizes one of the nation's largest, most vibrant cities.

Returning to *Four Falls of Buffalo,* the city's civic identity is tied as equally to its working-class ethos as it is to its weather. It is less explicit than in *Broad Street Bullies,* but commentator Tim Russert's observations are telling. "Dallas doesn't need this. They have big oil. And big, blonde hairdos. . . . Washington doesn't need this. They've got the White House and the Pentagon and Congress," he insists. "Buffalo. We've got the Bills. That's who we are." Implied in this juxtaposition is that cities such as Dallas and Washington are enclaves of wealth and power, places that have other means through which to secure a collective identity. There may be some truth to the idea that Buffalo is more of a "working-class" town than the rivals named by Russert, but similar sentiments might just as well be expressed by residents of, say, Green Bay or Baltimore. Yet the argument finds its power in the long-standing romanticization of those with less economic power, one that suggests financial hardship produces or reveals superior character. Those with money and power might be seen as "elite," whereas "regular" people who struggle are "real." This is clearly a rhetorical construction, yet it finds traction equally in political and popular culture. In the words of Bills linebacker Darryl Talley, Buffalo citizens are "salt of the earth people," hard-working, normal folks whose sports teams should provide the status to them that their labor cannot.

In many ways, Cleveland can be seen as the most representative city of the nation's industrial decline. Once the fourth-largest city in the United States, and home to the stately mansions of its fabled "Millionaire's Row" (Euclid Avenue), Cleveland was an economic powerhouse in the early decades of the twentieth century. By the end of the century, it was much more common to hear the city referred to by the aforementioned moniker, the "Mistake on the Lake." That image is confirmed through archival footage of Cleveland's infamous moments, such as the Cuyahoga River catching fire in 1969 and the city falling into default in 1978. For many of *Believeland*'s participants, the negative perceptions of Cleveland are at odds with their more affirmative impressions. Former mayor Dennis Kucinich calls the city the "jewel on the lake," and radio host Aaron Goldhammer praises the residents' work ethic. "Everyone here works for what they have," he asserts. "They've gotten to where they are because of what they've done with their bare hands and their own intellect." Much like in Philadelphia and Buffalo, then, Cleveland is depicted as a city where everything is earned and nothing is given.

Goldhammer's reference to intellect is a bit of an outlier, as the portrayal of hard work in these films is overwhelmingly focused on *physical* labor. Images and descriptions of workers in factories, docks, yards, and restaurants are commonplace, simultaneously erasing depictions of similar people in "successful" or "glamorous" cities such as New York and Los Angeles and depictions of wealth and status within the cities celebrated as working-class strongholds. Nevertheless, it is clear that embodied labor has rhetorical resonance. As Janet Zandy explains in her study of labor, culture, and class, "The laboring body speaks the language of fatigue and frivolity, of sacrifice and shared experience. It is a vocabulary of gestures, an idiom of collective experience."[24] Through sports documentaries, such shared, collective experiences often define the narratives of these cities.

Promising an Antidote to Division

The documentaries I have reviewed also commonly dramatize sports as a mechanism to triumph over division, especially those characterized by racial identity. In particular, *A City on Fire*, *The U*, and *Rebirth in New Orleans* feature this storyline. Beginning with Detroit, the "Motor City" was among the most vibrant cities in the United States in the first half of the twentieth century. By the 1960s, it became perhaps the most dramatic example of the nation's post-industrial transformation. Beginning in that decade, Detroit became "one of the most embattled cityscapes in the United States, emblazoned in the national memory with the 1967 uprising and the Devil's Night arsons in the 1980s and 1990s. It has become a national symbol of urban decay, post-industrial neglect, and criminality."[25] *A City on Fire* alludes to the general economic status of Detroit, but the film is primarily focused on the city's racial transformation and the role of baseball's Tigers in potential reconciliation. It opens with images of the 1967 uprising that was prompted by police harassment of Black residents. The narrative is bolstered by numerous images from that summer's violence, and it is juxtaposed with the fortunes of the Tigers that season. In one illustrative moment, outfielder Willie Horton, a Detroit native and one of the few Black players on the team, traveled into the heart of the unrest while still wearing his uniform. Elsewhere, Horton has reflected on this moment, saying, "I was just trying to bring some peace to the people that were in the riots." In the film, Horton stands in for the city's hopes to bridge racial divisions. As one commentator in the film notes, "When he joined the Tigers it was like a connection had finally been made between the Black population of Detroit and this ballclub." That sense of optimism, however, was dimmed by declining attendance and a late-season playoff push that came up one game short.

The simmering racial tensions in the city provided a narrative anchor for the Tigers' ambitions for the 1968 season. The bulk of the documentary details Detroit's pursuit of a championship, culminating in a memorable Game 7 victory in the World Series. Throughout, numerous voices overtly connect the fortunes of the team to the prospects for racial healing in the city. The narration declares, "The team was singular in more than purpose. Their clubhouse was colorblind, free of the bigotry of former owner Walter Briggs," adding, "as the city's obsession with the Tigers shifted into overdrive, crowds Black and white packed the ballpark at a record-setting pace." Of the World Series victory parade, Tigers outfielder Gates Brown observes, "What really struck me is how the Blacks and whites were both celebrating." And legendary radio broadcaster Ernie Harwell summarizes:

> I think, for that one year, people could tune in on the radio or the TV and have a common interest to root for. They watched Willie Horton hit a home run and Jim Northrup hit one, whether he was Black or white didn't make any difference. They were Tigers, and the people could rally behind that one cause.

Undoubtedly, the Tigers' success generated considerable enthusiasm and may well have ameliorated some of the ongoing tensions. Yet, in one curious moment from the middle of the sequence cited above, a commentator suggests the resulting community was "like this big brotherhood, a true brotherhood that forgot about the problems of society." As these words are spoken, a dramatic black-and-white visual of the riots in 1967 appears on the screen. If the intent is to provide a contrast between that moment and the celebration inspired by the Tigers, the visual effect is quite the opposite. Instead, it seems to undermine the claim that the city had formed a brotherhood of any kind. In light of Detroit's troubled narrative that would be shaped in the decades ahead, the film's conclusion is all the more jarring. Emphasizing the Tigers as a means to unify a divided city, the narrator boasts, "25 Tigers, united, colorful and colorblind, may not have saved the Motor City, but there's little doubt they helped it to heal."

The film's central premise is certainly appealing. As baseball writer Craig Calcaterra suggests, "It's a great concept: Americans at odds over race and class coming together over the national pastime. . . . No matter how hard the filmmakers try, they never quite manage to show that the Tigers' World Series run had any healing effect on the city."[26] Despite the many images depicting the violence of 1967, there is little to no explanation of how Detroit's racial divisions emerged in the first place. Perhaps more importantly, the film cannot offer the Tigers' 1968 World Series championship as a salve against future divisions, which, history now tells us, only intensified in subsequent years and decades. As Thomas Sugrue details, Detroit's racial strife was neither random nor sudden. Rather, a long history of white flight and residential redlining hardened the divisions between Black and white Detroiters, which was then exacerbated by deindustrialization. Thus, "the bleak landscapes and unremitting poverty of Detroit in the 1970s and 1980s are the legacies of the transformation of the city's economy in the wake of World War II, and of the politics and culture of race that have their origins in the persistent housing and workplace discrimination of the postwar decades."[27] Given that history, the celebratory narrative of 1968 itself is questionable at best.

The U, meanwhile, is the seventh installment in the debut season of ESPN's now-celebrated documentary series, *30 for 30*. Directed by filmmaker and South Florida native Billy Corben, the film documents the rise of football at the University of Miami during the 1980s. It begins by recalling the futility of the program in the preceding decade. That opening sequence is followed by archival news clips detailing the crime and violence of the city. Former Hurricanes player Brett Perriman recalls, "You talk about the early '80s, there was a lot of turmoil in the city. It was so intense at that point, as far as the Black/white relationships." Throughout the remainder of the film, *The U* leans into the football team as a metaphor for confronting and, potentially, transcending racial divisions.

Part of what makes *The U* compelling is that head coach Howard Schnellenberger's transformation of the program is, frankly, astonishing. Taking over a bad team with minimal fan support in 1979, Schnellenberger led the Hurricanes to a national championship in the 1983 season, just his fourth (and last) with the team. Archival news reports of the celebratory parade confirm the team's civic role, with one declaring, "Miami's been waiting a long time to cheer together and, yesterday, 75,000 south Floridians hooted, hollered, and tossed confetti on the young men who united this city." Another boasts, "They made the city forget a drumbeat of bad headlines and news pictures, racial strife, riots, drug wars, and crime," and one more concludes, "For now, it doesn't matter what kind of accent you speak with or where you come from, around Miami college football has brought everybody together." To this point, *The U* functions quite similarly to *A City on Fire*, emphasizing the team's ability to bring about social harmony.

To *The U*'s credit, it provides a much richer discussion of racial politics than *A City on Fire*. As journalist Dan Le Batard states directly, "Miami scared the hell out of white America." This assertion is supported in various ways, including the acknowledgement that Schnellenberger's success could be attributed to his willingness to recruit in South Florida's Black neighborhoods and give young players the freedom to express themselves. *The U* argues that the attitude and swagger the predominantly Black players brought to Miami changed college football throughout the nation. As former player Melvin Bratton says of the sometimes brash behavior, "That's what the fans paid to see." The film further connects a cultural shift in college football with the rise of hip-hop, an association confirmed by the presence of 2 Live Crew's Luther Campbell, a significant booster of Miami football. Campbell is featured prominently in *The U*, arguing that Hurricanes football "eased all the tensions of Miami" and that the team "created what football is in college." This theme is echoed by several former players, all of whom are eager to defend their impact on the game.

While *The U* makes room for more visible and authentic expressions of Black identity, it also seems to suggest that all acts of transgression are inherently progressive. However, as one of Miami's best-known players of the era, Michael Irvin, admits, "We were bad boys, and we were enjoying being bad boys." Rather than contend with this tension, the film mostly reduces cultural change to "swagger," even comparing the players on a couple of occasions to boxing icon Muhammad Ali. This loose affiliation with Ali is representative of contemporary uses of his memory that too often celebrate his showmanship and gift of language at the expense of his political commitments.[28] Thus, equating Miami players with Ali may define them as brash and bold, but it does little to examine their racial consciousness or efforts to address racial divisions.

For a documentary that credibly attends to racial identity, *The U* is limited in at least two other ways. First, as Simon Darnell suggests, the praise of Schnellenberger for pioneering recruitment strategies in the inner city ignores larger structural questions about how college football exploits the labor of young, Black men and the challenges to Miami's academic mission prompted by its increased investment in the sport.[29] The film does take some time to position the football program against the university's president, Edward Foote, but only to depict him as a nearly villainous, stodgy snob. Second, viewers of *The U* might conclude that Miami's racial dynamics existed entirely in Black and white. Surprisingly, there is no substantive discussion of the sizable Latin American community in South Florida and, while it is plausible that only a few Latino players were contributors to the team, it is a significant oversight to suggest the Hurricanes could "unite" the city without ever acknowledging a vital population within the community.

The latter stages of *Rebirth in New Orleans* commit a similar oversight, as Gleason's blocked punt becomes the defining metaphor for the film and the storyline implies that *everyone* in the city felt its impact. At one point, the narration insists, "Even those watching in a FEMA trailer that night, like [Saints fan] Shelton Alexander and his family, felt the power of the rebirth." Another fan suggests the moment inspired others, including himself. "Everybody felt like, if the Saints can rebound like that, maybe I need to try to rebound," says Shack Brown. "Maybe I need to block a punt in my own life." In the abstract, this is a fairly absurd use of the metaphor, but Brown is absolutely earnest. And New Orleans Police Sergeant Mike Foster adds, "Just that blocked punt made such a big difference. We all needed that, that new beginning. And it inspired people tremendously to move forward." Toward its conclusion, the documentary channels this inspiration as it details the Saints' completion of the journey with a Super Bowl XLIV victory over the Indianapolis Colts in February, 2010. As the narration concludes, "It was a storybook run, which began the night of the rebirth."

Rebirth in New Orleans clearly argues that the reopening of the Superdome and the eventual Super Bowl championship saved the city of New

Orleans. However, the documentary offers little to no evidence of the city's overall salvation. Daniel Grano and Kenneth Zagacki summarize the problem well:

> The Superdome's rebuilding represented a frustratingly anomalous case of coordination and funding between the Governor's office, the National Football League (NFL, which donated 15 million dollars), FEMA (which contributed 116 million dollars), and 850 workers. How could this be justified when so many of New Orleans' citizens could not even get FEMA to wire their trailers? The answer, given throughout ESPN's broadcast, was that the symbolic rebirth of the Superdome was a necessary prelude to the city's material recovery.[30]

I do not mean to suggest that the "Domecoming" was without meaning, as it is clear that seeing the Saints' triumphant return was important to many in the city and, more importantly, those for whom the team represented a family. Yet *Rebirth in New Orleans* makes no effort to question the decisions that prioritized the Superdome's rehabilitation over the many needs across the city. When stadium architect Paul Griesmer boasts of the reopening, "We did it. We did what everyone said we couldn't do," it is fair to ask what the city did not do in exchange. As others have documented, there are many Black and poor residents of New Orleans who were left waiting months or years for a rebirth of their own.[31]

The Limits of Unity in Sports Documentaries

Can sports, especially at a moment of triumph, unite a city? Yes, or at least, *sort of.* No one can deny that sports are uniquely popular and play a role in any city's civic identity. At the same time, the recurring emphasis on "unity" in sports documentaries represents an overly romanticized form of public memory. The films included in this chapter consistently suggest that professional sports are a crucial component of a city's civic identity, often at the expense of other cultural and social influences. For each of these cities, however, the dependence on sports for community comes with risks. Based on these narratives, one might wonder if a city without a professional sports franchise could ever hope to have a civic identity, or whether its residents might rally around other sources of identification if and when their teams cannot be there for them. Meanwhile, characterizations of the "Rust Belt" correspond well with conventional sports narratives that celebrate the ethos of hard work and determination, attributes that suggest a kind of authenticity that is central to the myth of the American Dream. An added benefit of constituting a civic identity grounded in the mythic portrayal of "regular" people is that sports offer the promise of transcending conflicts and differences. This is especially true of narratives that depict sports as an antidote to racial tensions, even if the evidence for this claim is fleeting or incomplete. In doing so, the documentaries reinforce commonly held perceptions that sports are the ultimate meritocracy, a level playing field where race is transcended and talent and hard work rewarded.

Aside from these overarching themes, the documentaries have implications for our understanding of public memory and epideictic rhetoric. In particular, these films display a tendency to freeze history in a given moment and neglect significant precedents and antecedents. *A City on Fire* and *Rebirth in New Orleans* are especially guilty of this, which contributes to highly romanticized and exaggerated narratives about sports transcending conflict. Public memory draws upon moments from the past to provide assurances and guidance for the present and future. In doing so, it also requires omissions, what Vivian terms "public forgetting." As he explains, public forgetting has the potential to "play a positive, formative role in works of public memory."[32] Yet, in the case of these documentaries, by erasing or overly simplifying substantive conflicts, sports are presented as if they are unproblematically and universally the means for bringing people together. Given the "evidentiary value" of documentary film, this romantic vision can be highly persuasive.[33] In particular, viewers are invited to relive unifying moments from the past at times when relevant community conflicts are taking place in the present.

As Stephen Wieting and Judy Polumbaum argue, "Sporting events and sports personages, while far from unique in feeding the collective imagination, yield particularly vivid, compelling, accessible material to be memorialized and ascribed contemporary meaning in the retelling."[34] It would be fair to say that sports documentaries are also consistent with this observation, especially given the epideictic nature of sports discourse. Such narratives celebrate communal values, yes, but they are also relentlessly affirmative, often implying that sports either reveal or make possible social harmony. Moreover, sports are the means by which we can transcend otherwise irreconcilable differences. From this point of view, the 1980 US Olympic men's hockey team didn't just defeat the Soviet Union's heavily favored Red Army squad, it provided a symbolic triumph of democracy over communism. George W. Bush didn't merely throw a ceremonial first pitch at the 2001 World Series, he demonstrated the nation's resolve and his presidential mettle. And the Houston Astros didn't simply win their World Series in the wake of the devastation caused by Hurricane Harvey in 2017, they inspired the community to rebuild. It is easy to understand why such narratives are persuasive, but each one overly simplifies complex political problems and processes. In this way, the consonance between sports and neoliberal epideictic rhetoric yields an outsized emphasis on ritual affirmations of community that are stripped of cultural and political substance. The recurring portrayal of unity as a necessary outcome of a team's identification with a city reinforces the idea that unity, in and of itself, should be our goal. There is no consideration for what purpose people should be united, let alone any discussion of the legitimate reasons why some conflicts and divisions persist. Sports media tend toward romantic and heroic language as it is, but the exaggerated claims of these documentaries should compel us to exercise more caution and humility.

There are clearly important reasons to celebrate the shared values of a community, and epideictic rhetoric has long facilitated such celebrations; however, they should be accompanied by a more robust engagement with meaningful differences. One of those differences might be to account for audiences who do not follow or identify with sports or who seek community through other shared institutions. As Vivian reminds us, *neoliberal* epideictic rhetoric relies on assertions of universality that downplay or ignore the structural politics that make a truly unified community a virtual impossibility. Sports, far from detached from those structural politics, often exacerbate the very economic and social conditions that ensure divisions persist. The insistence, then, that fan affiliations are the means by which cities "come together" bolsters a mythic construction of unity through sports and diminishes other forms of civic engagement. Ultimately, although each film provides a compelling snapshot of a particular time and place, they all omit key details and are constrained by their narrative scope. Thus, sports may unite a city, but they do so only temporarily and in limited ways.

Notes

1. Isabelle Lopez, "ESPN Films Latest 30 for 30 Documentary 'Once Upon a Time in Queens' to Premiere September 14 & 15," *ESPN.com*, August 24, 2021, https://espnpressroom.com/us/press-releases/2021/08/espn-films-latest-30-for-30-documentary-once-upon-a-time-in-queens-to-premiere-september-14-15/.

2. *Once Upon a Time in Queens*, part 4, directed by Nick Davis, aired September 15, 2021, https://www.espn.com/watch/player/_/id/1e9006af-520a-43bc-bbc7-d18f17e4a952?om-navmethod=espn%3Aglobalsearch%3Aresults.

3. Jacob Feldman, "ESPN's 'Last Dance' Emmy Affirms a Golden Age of Sports Docs," *Sportico*, September 21, 2020, https://www.sportico.com/business/media/2020/espn-sports-documentaries-last-dance-emmy-1234613456/.

4. Samantha N. Sheppard and Travis Vogan, "Introduction," in *Sporting Realities: Critical Readings of the Sports Documentary,* ed. Samantha N. Sheppard and Travis Vogan (Lincoln, NE: University of Nebraska Press, 2020), 1.

5. Travis Vogan, "Chronicling Sport, Branding Institutions: The Television Sports Documentary from Broadcast to Cable," in the *Routledge Handbook of Sport Communication,* ed. Paul M. Pedersen (London: Routledge, 2013), 135.

6. Michael L. Butterworth, "Public Memorializing in the Stadium: Sport, the 10th Anniversary of 9/11, and the Illusion of Democracy," *Communication & Sport* 2 (2014): 203–24.

7. Michael L. Butterworth, "Sport and the Quest for Unity: How the Logic of Consensus Undermines Democratic Culture," *Communication & Sport* 8 (2020): 456.

8. Bill Nichols, *Introduction to Documentary*, 2nd ed. (Bloomington, IN: Indiana University Press, 2010), 13.

9. Jane Chapman, *Issues in Contemporary Documentary* (Cambridge, UK: Polity Press, 2009), 29.

10. For more on the uses and limits of these terms, see Michelle Kennerly, "Introduction: Term Limits," in *A New Handbook of Rhetoric: Inverting the Classical Vocabulary*, ed. Michelle Kennerly (University Park, PA: Pennsylvania State University Press, 2021), 1–22.

11. Michael L. Butterworth, "The Rhetoric of Sport," *Oxford Research Encyclopedia of Communication,* December 2023, https://oxfordre.com/communication/display/10.1093/acrefore/9780190228613.001.0001/acrefore-9780190228613-e-1393.

12. For a summary of this idea and others related to public memory, see Matthew Houdek and Kendall R. Phillips, "Public Memory," *Oxford Research Encyclopedia of Communication*, January 2017, https://oxfordre.com/communication/display/10.1093/acrefore/9780190228613.001.0001/acrefore-9780190228613-e-181?d=%2F10.1093%2Facrefore%2F9780190228613.001.0001%2Facrefore-9780190228613-e-181&p=emailA0e.XtejqPS.2.

13. Bradford S. Vivian, *Public Forgetting: The Rhetoric and Politics of Beginning Again* (University Park, PA: Pennsylvania State University Press, 2010), 64.

14. In 2014, ESPN released *The U: Part 2.* Because the first film was originally a stand-alone film, I do not define the pair as a documentary series, keeping *The U* within my selection criteria.

15. All subsequent quotations from the films come from my transcriptions. *A City on Fire*, executive produced by Rick Bernstein and Ross Greenburg, aired July 22, 2002, https://watch.plex.tv/movie/a-city-on-fire-the-story-of-the-68-detroit-tigers; *Broad Street Bullies*, directed by George Roy, aired May 4, 2010, https://www.youtube.com/watch?v=Ms68m8ZP528&t=1201s; *The U*, directed by Billy Corben, aired December 12, 2009, https://www.espn.com/watch/film/c11da66e-1b8a-4d09-a3e6-8fbcf124a863/the-u?om-navmethod=espn%3Aglobalsearch%3Aresults; *Four Falls of Buffalo*, directed by Ken Rodgers,

aired December 12, 2015, https://www.espn.com/watch/film/f844e1d2-b60a-4205-9b5e-e583a6a08bf7/four-falls-of-buffalo?om-navmethod=espn%3Aglobalsearch%3Aresults; *Rebirth in New Orleans*, directed by Rob Gehring, aired May 15, 2016, https://www.youtube.com/watch?v=FM2sAJpyO3I; *Believeland*, directed by Andrew Billman, aired December 12, 2015, https://www.espn.com/watch/film/8a4b7b8d-eca9-488a-87d9-5739391739aa/believeland?om-navmethod=espn%3Aglobalsearch%3Aresults.

16. *Believeland*.

17. "Super Bowl XXV—'Wide Right'," *NFL.com*, https://www.nfl.com/100/originals/100-greatest/games-10.

18. For a thorough account of these moments, see Edward T. Uszynski, "Implicit Religion and the Highly-Identified Sports Fan: An Ethnography of Cleveland Sports Fandom" (PhD diss., Bowling Green State University, 2013).

19. Denise M. Bostdorff and Daniel J. O'Rourke, "Religion, Sport, and the Return of the Prodigal Son: The Postsecular Rhetoric of LeBron James's 2014 'I'm Coming Home' Open Letter," *Rhetoric & Public Affairs* 21 (2018): 1–38.

20. Matthew Allen, "Burning Jerseys: The Distant Cousin of Lynching," *The Root*, October 1, 2017, https://www.theroot.com/burning-jerseys-the-distant-cousin-of-lynching-1819019964.

21. Sports fans, politicians, and community leaders commonly believe that sports drive economic recovery and/or growth. The evidence suggests otherwise. For a comprehensive review of relevant scholarship, see John Charles Bradbury, Dennis Coates, and Brad R. Humphreys, "The Impact of Professional Sports Franchises and Venues on Local Economies: A Comprehensive Survey," *Journal of Economic Surveys* 37 (2023): 1389–1431.

22. This mantra, written on a locker room chalkboard, is referenced earlier in the film.

23. Stu Hackel, "The Morning Skate: HBO Makes 'Broad Street Bullies' a Love Story," *New York Times*, May 3, 2010, https://archive.nytimes.com/slapshot.blogs.nytimes.com/2010/05/03/the-morning-skate-hbo-makes-broad-street-bullies-a-love-story/.

24. Janet Zandy, *Hands: Physical Labor, Class, and Cultural Work* (Piscataway, NJ: Rutgers University Press, 2004), 4.

25. Joshua Atkinson and Clayton Rosati, "DetroitYES! and the Fabulous Ruins Virtual Tour: The Role of Diffused Intertextual Production in the Construction of Alternative Cityscapes," *Critical Studies in Media Communication* 29 (March 2012): 49.

26. Craig Calcaterra, "Lukewarm: HBO's Unconvincing *A City on Fire*," *Shysterball*, August 12, 2002, http://shysterball.blogspot.com/2002/08/lukewarm-hbos-unconvincing-city-on-fire.html.

27. Thomas J. Sugrue, *The Origins of the Urban Crisis: Race and Inequality in Postwar Detroit* (Princeton, NJ: Princeton University Press, 1996/2005), 271.

28. For more on this idea, see Daniel A. Grano, "Muhammad Ali Versus the

'Modern Athlete': On Voice in Mediated Sports Culture," *Critical Studies in Media Communication* 26 (August 2009): 208.

29. Simon C. Darnell, "The U," *Journal of Sport History* 38 (2011): 130.

30. Daniel A. Grano and Kenneth S. Zagacki, "Cleansing the Superdome: The Paradox of Purity and Post-Katrina Guilt," *Quarterly Journal of Speech* 97 (2011): 209.

31. Wright Thompson, "Hurricane Katrina: Beyond the Breach," *ESPN.com*, August 24, 2015, https://www.espn.com/espn/story/_/id/13500835/breach.

32. Bradford Vivian, *Public Forgetting: The Rhetoric and Politics of Beginning Again* (University Park, PA: Pennsylvania State University Press, 2010), 6.

33. Roberto Arnau Roselló, "Images for the Interpretation of the Past: Uses and Abuses of Memory in Documentary Film," *Quarterly Review of Film and Video* 39 (2022): 465.

34. Stephen G. Wieting and Judy Polumbaum, "Prologue," in *Sport and Memory in North America*, ed. Stephen G. Wieting (London: Frank Cass, 2001), 4.

3

White Hopes in a Black Game

Race and the 1974 NBA Finals

THERESA RUNSTEDTLER

"Basketball is merely the most natural channel of a black tide that has been flooding professional sports," observed *Milwaukee Journal* sports columnist Terry Bledsoe in June 1973.[1] Once ruled by white stars, the National Basketball Association (NBA) was in the midst of a racial transformation. By the 1972–1973 season, African Americans held three of the five places on the NBA's first all-league team, and seven of the ten spots on the first two teams. This rising wave of Black talent had the potential to reshape American culture, Bledsoe contended: "Professional athletes are the dream stuff of a nation, and black dominance of sports is reshaping the hero symbols of a society." Despite Bledsoe's optimism, white team owners and fans were slow to embrace Black preeminence in pro basketball, or what African American sportswriter Sam Lacy once termed, "Jim Crow in Reverse."[2]

Although the NBA drafted its first Black players in 1950, it maintained a policy of "controlled integration," upholding an informal racial quota that restricted the number of African Americans on any one team.[3] However, this quota system fell away with the establishment of a rival league in 1967, the American Basketball Association (ABA), which challenged the NBA's monopoly on professional ball. The competition for top-flight talent between the NBA and the ABA from 1967 to 1976 (when the two leagues merged) not only opened the door to increasing numbers of African American players in the professional ranks, but also contributed to the exponential increase in player salaries over the course of the decade. By the mid-1970s, the NBA's labor force was about 75 percent Black, and throughout the decade the National Basketball Players Association (NBPA), the union representing the players, had outspoken Black presidents: Oscar Robertson (1965–1974) and Paul Silas (1974–1980). However, in this same period, professional basketball's fanbase remained majority white.[4]

Many sportswriters and league officials wondered if the NBA would survive what appeared to be a widening racial gap between the athletes and the fans. Black ballplayers seemed to be making all the money and having all the fun at the very same moment that white working-class men were facing diminishing salaries, employment prospects, and job security. By 1973, sixteen out of the twenty-three NBA players with million-dollar, multiyear contracts were Black, while the median income for white families was $12,600 (for Black families it was just $7,270).[5] The oil shocks and inflation of the early 1970s, alongside deindustrialization, globalization, and the decline of union power, had brought a sharp end to white working-class experiences of postwar prosperity. This economic downturn occurred just as African Americans, empowered by civil rights gains and emboldened by the Black Power movement, stepped up their demands for more access to schools, jobs, trades, and professions formerly reserved for white Americans.[6]

In the midst of this broader struggle over racial integration, African American men were reshaping the pro game, imbuing it with the unapologetically Black style of playground ball. Narratives of decline permeated public discourse about the NBA, reinforcing longstanding racial stereotypes and their attendant moral judgments: Black men's flashy, selfish, and above-the-rim play was replacing a once honorable white game of disciplined teamwork. Perhaps even more disturbing, rather than showing gratitude for their rising success in a heretofore white space, Black players dared to demand more, using legal strategies and union organizing to push for better contracts and more control over their careers. Meanwhile, off the court, their conspicuous consumption, masculine bravado, and flouting of respectability politics made them popular emblems of Black Power. As one of the few lucrative professional spaces where Black men dominated, the NBA seemed to defy the tenets of US racial politics, and the league became not only a repository for white working-class resentments, but also a lightning rod for wider debates about the place of African Americans in post-civil rights America.[7]

All of these racial, gendered, and class tensions came to a head in the 1974 NBA Finals, when the Boston Celtics and their two white stars, John Havlicek and Dave Cowens, took on the Milwaukee Bucks, with their two Black legends, Kareem Abdul-Jabbar and Oscar Robertson. Framed as a David and Goliath contest featuring "the small Celtics against the big Bucks," the championship series became a microcosm of the intensifying battles over desegregation in Boston and other urban areas across the United States.[8] It was also imagined as a contest between white and Black basketball—one that would determine the future trajectory of the sport at a moment of profound transition in US society.

The Backdrop

As the start of the NBA Finals approached, white working-class Bostonians found themselves on the frontlines of the economic crisis and growing conflicts over racial integration. Awash in grievances, some looked to the Celtics for a victory to call their own. As historian Ronald Formisano notes, the financial stresses caused by stagflation—a combination of rising prices and unemployment—had exacerbated racial tensions on a number of fronts in the city. Affirmative action lawsuits in the early seventies, which helped Black and Latinx workers gain a tiny foothold in public sector employment, had already challenged white (predominantly Irish American) control of the city's police, fire, and public works departments in a moment of austerity. At the same time, white Bostonians in the construction industry also saw their power eroding. Hit particularly hard by the economic downturn, the industry was wracked with high unemployment, and now white workers faced additional competition from African Americans for a diminishing number of jobs. In 1974, the city, construction companies, and unions had agreed to a plan to aid minority workers by requiring 30 percent minority employees on construction jobs in inner-city, minority neighborhoods.[9] Public debates about affirmative action policies in Boston and other US metropolitan areas gave rise to false narratives about Black advantage and "reverse discrimination" in an already tight job market.[10]

Meanwhile, Beantown's old order of racially segregated schooling was also under threat. It had faced challenges since the early 1960s, when Black parents and civil rights advocates began to confront the Boston School Committee (BSC) about its resistance to desegregation in the city's public schools. In 1964, thousands of students boycotted Boston schools in support of the National Association for the Advancement of Colored People's (NAACP) "Stay Out for Freedom Day," alongside similar protests in New York City and Chicago. A year later, Massachusetts legislators passed the Racial Imbalance Act, mandating that local school boards ensure that no school's nonwhite enrollment exceeded 50 percent. Yet the BSC remained recalcitrant to change, choosing to forgo state funding to maintain segregation. In March 1972, the NAACP filed a class action lawsuit on behalf of fifteen Black parents and their forty-three children, with mother of three Tallulah Morgan as the lead plaintiff. The suit accused the BSC's president

James Hennigan and other members with failing to comply with the 1965 Racial Imbalance Act.[11] By the start of the Celtics–Bucks series in May 1974, the battle over school desegregation was heating up. Federal district court judge W. Arthur Garrity, Jr., was on the cusp of rendering his decision in *Morgan v. Hennigan*—a decision that would bring crosstown busing to Boston—while other US cities, from New York City to Detroit to Chicago, were caught up in desegregation conflicts of their own.[12]

The Irish American enclave of South Boston was ground zero for these ongoing economic and racial transformations. In 1974, its unemployment rate was 9.9 percent, in comparison to the Boston-wide rate of 8.5 percent, while its median income ($8,704) was 5 percent below that of the city as a whole.[13] White ethnic pride combined with economic resentments to fuel racist opposition to the integration of their schools. As Alan Lupo of the *Boston Globe* noted, "Besieged by many problems, Southie draws strength from its traditions and its people to battle once more against a threat from outside. This time it's forced busing."[14] Yet, even though South Boston struggled, the conditions in nearby Roxbury and other Black neighborhoods were far more dire. Black Bostonians were simply seeking justice; however, their efforts to access better jobs and schools were cast as an unfair assault on white city dwellers "who felt their children, neighborhoods, and status to be threatened."[15]

The Celtics' fortunes seemed to follow a similar downward trajectory in the early seventies. After capturing eleven titles from 1957 to 1969, Boston failed to make the NBA playoffs in 1970 for the first time in twenty years. Although African American center Bill Russell had been pivotal to Boston's dynastic success in the sixties, as a player and then player-coach, sports journalists characterized him as exemplifying all of the best virtues of "white" basketball style, thereby enabling the Celtics to maintain their reputation as a "white team."[16] Despite this media framing, Russell, known for being outspoken about civil rights and unafraid to call out white prejudice in Boston, faced intense racism even at the height of his career. Local fans also remained somewhat ambivalent about supporting the team at the box office.[17] "During the years the Celtics were cluttering Boston Garden's rafters with championship banners," the *Los Angeles Times* observed, "Bostonians were selling out the Garden—to see the struggling Boston Bruins of the National Hockey League."[18] The Russell-era Celtics drew most of their fans from the surrounding suburbs, beyond Route 128, while Bruins supporters tended to be white working people who lived within the city limits.[19]

After Russell's retirement in 1969, General Manager Red Auerbach worked to restore the now languishing Celtics to their former glory, this time led by white stars. He hired former Celtics great Tom Heinsohn to replace Russell as head coach. He also built and marketed the team around the veteran Havlicek and the newcomer Cowens, with a supporting cast of highly talented Black players including JoJo White, Don Chaney, and Paul Silas. Auerbach's plan helped to bring the Celtics back into contention. They had already made it to the Eastern Conference finals in 1972 and 1973. While the New York Knicks had eliminated them both times, they were back within striking distance of the NBA championship.

Auerbach's revamped "white" Celtics also thrived financially, as Boston's hockey-crazed fans started to attend ballgames in larger numbers.[20] As a longtime resident of Roxbury later recalled, "Russell leaves and the fair-haired boy, Dave Cowens, comes in . . . and you can't get a seat."[21] When Cowens came on the scene in 1970, a new generation of white ethnic Bostonians could immediately identify with him. "He's not Irish, but people think he is," said one Celtics official of the redheaded center.[22] During Cowens's first few years in the league, he helped the Celtics to attain the greatest game attendance in their history. By the time of the 1974 NBA Finals, the slogan "Celtic Pride" appeared on bumper stickers all over the city.[23] By centering whiteness, Auerbach took a profitable page out of the marketing playbook of Boston's more popular sports franchises, the Bruins and the Red Sox of Major League Baseball.[24]

The Players

Havlicek and Cowens held a special appeal for the city's white working-class fans, as the heirs apparent in a line of "Great White Hopes" in the 1970s NBA, from Pete Maravich to Ernie DiGregorio to Bill Walton. They epitomized the stereotypical hardworking and unselfish white athlete, who was successful despite his supposed physical limitations.[25] They appeared to be throwbacks to an earlier era of basketball, before the influx of Black players into the NBA, when "grit" and "fundamentals," rather than "natural athleticism" and high-flying acrobatics, were key to winning games. Unlike the Bucks' Jabbar, who towered over everyone at seven-foot-two, there was nothing particularly distinctive about them physically. And there was nothing particularly fancy about their style of play. Their fast-breaking, team game evoked the Celtics of old, as they relied on relentless hustle to outrun, out-rebound, and out-pass opponents. With Havlicek and Cowens at the helm, the Celtics—a team whose name and branding paid homage to Boston's Irish history and resonated with contemporary calls for white ethnic pride—embodied a sense of white nostalgia for simpler times, when racial segregation held sway on and off the court. They offered a redemption story for white blue-collar fans who saw themselves on the losing end of the social changes wrought by the civil rights and Black Power movements of the 1960s and 1970s.[26]

Havlicek's own journey to stardom was a classic tale of bootstrap success. Born in Martins Ferry, Ohio, on April 8, 1940, he was the second son of Frank Havlicek, an immigrant from Czechoslovakia who came to the United States at age twelve, and Mandy (Turkalj) Havlicek, a Croatian-American who came from a long line of Midwestern mine workers. He had spent his formative years living above the general store that his parents ran in Lansing, Ohio, a small town of a few hundred residents near Wheeling, West Virginia.[27]

Because of his strong, silent personality, Havlicek's childhood friend nicknamed him "Hondo," after John Wayne's character in the eponymous 1953 Western film. Hondo was a three-sport star, excelling in football, baseball, and basketball at Bridgeport High School in the nearby Ohio River village of the same name. He decided to play college basketball at Ohio State University, even though OSU football coach Woody Hayes had tried to recruit him. As a Buckeye, Havlicek roomed with Jerry Lucas, another future NBA star, and together they won an NCAA championship in 1960.[28]

In 1962, the multitalented senior was drafted into two professional sports leagues. The Celtics chose Havlicek as the seventh pick in the first round of the NBA's college draft, while the National Football League's Cleveland Browns drafted him to play wide receiver. Havlicek initially decided to try his luck with the Browns, playing a few exhibition games during the preseason. However, when the Browns released him, he joined the Celtics. Hondo came to fill an important role as Boston's versatile sixth man, able to play both small forward and shooting guard.

With a broad-shouldered and sinewy six-foot-five frame, Havlicek had the appearance of a steelworker. He also had an uncanny ability as a clutch performer, having played an important role in six NBA championships with the Celtics. With the retirement of Russell in 1969, Havlicek finally moved from sixth man to starter and became the hub of the team's offense. In 1970, he became even more popular with Boston fans when he turned down an opportunity to jump to the ABA for more money, choosing, instead, to remain loyal to the Celtics.[29]

In spite of the fact that Havlicek was incredibly athletic, mainstream sports journalists tended to characterize him as an underdog: a hardworking and humble white everyman in an increasingly flashy Black sport. He "doesn't shoot as well as the best, isn't strong enough to smother a backboard, doesn't have breathtaking speed, can't dribble behind his back and isn't 7 feet tall," John Underwood of *Sports Illustrated* maintained. Instead, his indefatigable effort was key to the Celtics' system of team play: "Havlicek runs and runs (scoring, rebounding, defending tenaciously, making key passes, setting up plays), and when his opponent begins to go under, he runs some more."[30] Hondo was also a "vital link between the old and new" Celtics, leading his younger teammates by example on the floor. "Some superstars are moody and pout. But not John," Cowens told Larry Whiteside of the *Boston Globe*. "He goes about his job, accepts criticism and doesn't complain."[31]

In many respects, Cowens modeled himself after his mentor. Born on October 25, 1948, in Newport, Kentucky, Cowens had a similar underdog story of drive and determination. At just six-foot-eight, he was much smaller than most centers. Drafted by the Celtics in 1970 out of Florida State University, Cowens was, at the time, largely unsung in the national media.

Regardless of his relative lack of renown and experience, Cowens seemed tailormade for Boston. He had been trained in the same style of fast-break, pressing-defense game that the Celtics deployed. Auerbach had personally scouted Cowens, taking what others thought was a huge risk in picking him fourth overall and signing him to a three-year contract. Auerbach's original plan was to use Cowens as a forward or as a temporary center until he found a permanent replacement for Russell. However, Cowens's strength, jumping ability, and sheer perseverance had convinced both Auerbach and Heinsohn to keep him at center. Averaging seventeen points and fifteen rebounds per game in the 1970–1971 season, Cowens shared Rookie of the Year honors with Geoff Petrie of the Portland Trail Blazers. In his sophomore season, he won the Most Valuable Player award, and in 1973, he finished second behind Jabbar in the MVP vote.[32]

Cowens was "hustle personified," according to Jeff Greenfield of *Sport* magazine.[33] Sportswriters praised the young center for his untiring effort, as he held his own against the NBA's best Black athletes. "When you watch a ballplayer, over a period of a few weeks, outrun Calvin Murphy, outmuscle Willis Reed, steal the ball from Walt Frazier, out-hook Kareem Jabbar, and out-rebound Wilt Chamberlain, you are not talking about sheer hustle," Greenfield argued. "You are talking about achievement."[34] The implication was that Cowens's achievement came through hard work and tenacity, rather than innate talent. He was a White Hope for a league in flux—one reminiscent of the NBA before the Bill Russell–Wilt Chamberlain rivalry transformed the position of center. "He's super-quick," Heinsohn told Greenfield. "He's almost a throwback to the days when there was no big man in the pivot." And Cowens did all this in a quiet, unflamboyant manner.

Sports journalists lauded Cowens for being a private and unpretentious person off the court, at a time when African American stars such as Walt "Clyde" Frazier and Spencer Haywood flaunted their urban style and conspicuous consumption.[35] When talking to the press, Cowens avoided discussions of politics and money, instead keeping his public comments focused on basketball. Profiles of the white Celtic emphasized that he lived simply in a converted bathhouse in Weston, Massachusetts, largely eschewing visible symbols of wealth, such as fancy clothing and luxury cars. He preferred the peace and quiet of the country over the hustle and bustle of the city. If Havlicek had the appearance of a steelworker, Cowens fashioned himself a Kentucky farmer, who raised cattle, Christmas trees, and other crops in his spare time.[36]

Meanwhile, the Bucks' Jabbar and Robertson represented all of the frightening racial changes afoot in post–civil rights America. Seen by many as "basketball's big black villain," Jabbar became the target of white angst in the early seventies. "To many sports fans, he was a black giant who ruled his sport, looked serious and bored, punched white players who inflamed his temper, acted rude to reporters and fans, and cashed fat paychecks," historian Aram Goudsouzian argues.[37]

It did not help that he came into the league already branded as a troublemaker. As a star center for the University of California, Los Angeles, Jabbar (then known as Lew Alcindor) had been a vocal part of the revolt of the Black athlete—a wave of African American athletic protest against white authorities at colleges across the nation in the late 1960s. When the Black-led Olympic Project for Human Rights (OPHR) contemplated a collective boycott of the 1968 games in Mexico City, Jabbar had tried to rally his fellow athletes to the cause: "We catch hell because we are black. Somewhere each of us has got to make a stand against this kind of thing."[38] Although the OPHR's boycott never came to fruition, the young superstar stayed home to denounce racism in America.[39]

When he joined the Milwaukee Bucks in 1969, Jabbar continued to embody Black Power politics. His favorite book was the *Autobiography of Malcolm X*. He listened to the jazz music of Miles Davis, converted to Sunni Islam and changed his name, and studied African languages.[40] While he worked hard on the court, he felt in no way compelled to go out of his way to please white sportswriters and fans. "People have a feeling that I'm a nasty nigger, you know," he told WNET's *Black Journal* in 1972. "See, now I don't mind that. . . . That, to me, is a compliment."[41]

Even in Milwaukee, Jabbar did not have a great relationship with the local sports media. He was known for showing up late to interviews and being curt with reporters. In press conferences, he often refused to answer questions or responded with terse, one-word answers.[42] Instead of following the traditional rules of etiquette expected of Black athletes—be accessible, be humble, be cheerful, and be grateful—he spoke openly about the discomfort of being a minority in a white midwestern city: "The atmosphere is not what I'm used to—big city. Milwaukee is middle America, and things that are for me and what I am have nothing to do with middle America."[43] Jabbar was an unabashedly Black athlete, who seemed to care little about white approval.

Adding to the racial stakes of the impending Bucks–Celtics matchup, Robertson embodied the growing power of Black labor in the league. Also known as the "the Big O," Robertson became president of the NBPA in 1965 and made it his mission to revamp the union from the ground up. Previously the preserve of white stars who maintained a conciliatory stance with management, the NBPA under Robertson's leadership became more democratic, more racially integrated, and more demanding.[44] Borrowing from the spirit and tactics of the broader Black Freedom Movement, the NBPA contested league bylaws and customs that kept players underpaid and under the thumb of the team owners. In April 1970, the Big O became the face of *Oscar Robertson* et al. *v. NBA*, a class-action antitrust lawsuit that challenged the NBA–ABA merger and eventually brought down the reserve clause in 1976 (a clause in professional contracts that effectively bound a player to one team until that team decided to trade or release him). *Robertson et al. v. NBA* also coincided with two other successful Black-led antitrust actions against the NBA—*Hawkins v. NBA* (1969) and *Haywood v. NBA* (1971)—which exposed the league's illegal practice of blacklisting and took down its unjust four-year-rule, respectively.[45] With each incremental victory, Black players could not help but see their struggles against the all-white team owners as part of the wider push for African American economic equality in the post–civil rights era.

Nevertheless, in the midst of ongoing fights over racial integration in Boston and other US metropolitan areas, white fans saw the demeanor and demands of this new generation of Black players as an affront to not only the game, but to the nation's longstanding racial order. Havlicek and Cowens were the gritty white underdogs, up against ostensibly indolent Black players who, despite their physical advantages, would rather sit back and complain than work hard for their money. This racial narrative of the 1974 NBA Finals dovetailed with prevailing white working-class grievances off the court, as they saw themselves as victimized by unworthy African Americans, who received a host of "special advantages" and "government handouts," from affirmative action to busing and welfare.[46]

The Showdown

The drama of the Celtics–Bucks showdown was not just about the race of the star players involved, but also about the teams' clashing approaches to the game. Peter Carry of *Sports Illustrated* characterized the upcoming duel as "a sweet juxtaposition of styles and stature."[47] With their focus on team play, featuring a fast-break offense and full-court press, Auerbach's revived Celtics hearkened back to their predecessors of the 1950s and 1960s. "We've got to be constantly on the run," said Havlicek. "We can't afford to let them set up a defense. We've got to make them play our game."[48] Even though the teams were more or less evenly matched, having split two wins apiece against each other during the regular season, sportswriters still cast the Celtics as longshots. Only clever strategy and tireless effort would enable them to overcome the Bucks' "natural" advantages.

For some journalists the Bucks' half-court play, designed to capitalize on Jabbar's physical dominance, foreshadowed the NBA's descent into a dark age of professional basketball. "I hope somebody—anybody—beats Milwaukee, because a victory by them in the playoffs would be the best ammunition anti-basketball critics could ever hope to have," Bob Ryan of the *Boston Globe* argued. "You know and I know that there is just one major reason why they are contenders, and that reason stands about 7–3." If one player on an otherwise mediocre team could make that much of a difference, Ryan reasoned, "there must be something inherently wrong with the sport."[49] Unlike the supposedly more industrious white Celtics, the Black-led Milwaukee team had a reputation for being lazy on the floor. "There are not many Bucks who are willing to dive headlong after a ball," observed Dave Begel of *Basketball News*. The only exception, in Begel's eyes, was Mikey Davis, the Bucks' white reserve forward: "He doesn't have the talent a lot of players have, but he's going to stick around the Bucks and the league for a lot of years because he's not afraid."[50]

Milwaukee coach Larry Costello challenged the idea that the Bucks were just going to sit back idly and rely on Jabbar's height advantage. "This is the playoffs," Costello said. "We need balanced team play to win."[51] Costello knew this firsthand, having played with legendary center Wilt Chamberlain in Philadelphia. Having one great player did not necessarily mean an automatic win. The Bucks were more than just Jabbar. They also had the illustrious Robertson, veteran All-Star Bob Dandridge, and recent acquisitions Cornell Warner and Rob "Fritz" Williams.

Heinsohn felt he had no strategic choice but to focus on shutting down the Bucks' other players. "There's no real way to defense [*sic*] Jabbar," he said. "All you can do is get position on him and make his hooks a little longer and double team him. You can't overplay him too much because he's such a great passer." It certainly did not help that Cowens was almost half a foot shorter than Jabbar. "I'll try to take him outside," Cowens said. "That's the only thing you can do with a man that size." Recognizing that the Celtics played a running game, using their stamina to tire out their opponents, Costello countered with a plan to dictate the tempo. "What we've got to do is force them to play half-court basketball with us," he said. "They're not a great shooting team but if they can get the break they can kill you."[52] Ironically, despite their billing as a "Black" team, the Bucks knew that speed was not on their side. They had already lost their quickest guard, Lucius Allen, to a knee injury in March. Without Allen in the backcourt, the Bucks knew they would have to work extra hard to combat the Celtics' running style.[53] Still, the Bucks seemed up for the challenge. Because Milwaukee had the best regular season record of 59–23 (though the Celtics were close behind at 56–26), they had won homecourt advantage for the finals.[54]

Even though characterized as a racial battle between two sets of stars, in actuality the series defied that definition, as both teams dug deep into their rosters to stay in the game. Nevertheless, this racial rivalry helped make the finals a great success at the box office, at a time when the NBA was still a distant third in popularity behind Major League Baseball and the National Football League. Game 1 took place in front of a capacity crowd of 10,938 at Milwaukee Arena and a national television audience tuned in to CBS.[55] In spite of the Bucks' homecourt advantage, the Celtics pulled ahead in the first quarter and held on to win 98–83.[56] For Game 2, the Bucks played in front of another full house in Milwaukee. They knew they could not afford to lose again. Otherwise, they would be down by two when they traveled to Boston for Game 3. Buoyed by their fans, the Bucks sealed a 105–96 overtime victory.[57]

Milwaukee then faced a raucous sold-out arena of 15,320 Celtics fans at the Garden for Game 3. It was Boston's first NBA championship series game in the Garden since they won it all in 1969. A win over the unapologetically Black Jabbar and the uppity NBPA leader Robertson would be especially sweet against the backdrop of broader struggles over racial integration in Beantown. In the first thirty-five seconds, Cowens hit a twenty-foot jumper that set the tone for the rest of Game 3. Together, Cowens and Havlicek scored seventeen points, as Boston pulled ahead by nineteen points (32–13) in the first quarter. It was as if the Celtics of old had returned. They ran and executed on offense and worked the full-court press on defense. In contrast, Milwaukee was in disarray, shooting just 32 percent from the field, with eleven turnovers.[58] At the final buzzer, the score was 95–83 for Boston.[59]

The Bucks had two days to retool for Game 4 at the Garden. Costello made some changes to the starting lineup that helped the Bucks regain control of the tempo. The Milwaukee offense became a series of back-ins and baseline turnarounds, as they took advantage of their size to post up on shorter defenders.[60] The Bucks won 97–89, tying up the series at two games apiece. Jabbar scored thirty-four points but the real heroes were in the backcourt (Davis racked up fifteen points, while Robertson had nine assists), proving yet again, that Milwaukee was more than just a one-man team.[61]

With the series tied, it was as if the Bucks were getting a do-over. Home-court advantage was now back on their side as they were set to play two out of the next three games in Milwaukee.[62] Yet, despite the capacity crowd at Milwaukee Arena for Game 5, the Bucks struggled. Jabbar scored a series high of thirty-seven points, but it was not enough to overcome the Celtics' defense. The final score was 96–87 for Boston.[63]

This away victory gave the Celtics a 3–2 lead in the series. They only needed one more win in Boston to take the championship. On game night, the Celtics had two cases of champagne waiting in their locker room, but the Bucks caught them by surprise. Even with the Garden's sellout crowd on its feet, screaming for the home team, at the end of regulation the score was tied 86–86.[64] Although it took two tumultuous overtime periods, in the final possession of the game, Jabbar's signature skyhook gave the Bucks a 102–101 victory and another chance at winning the title.[65]

As the Bucks made their way off the court, Celtics fans peppered them with obscenities.[66] In the face of this abuse, Jabbar remained smug. Since his rookie year in the league, the Black superstar center had understood that he was a target for the NBA's largely white fanbase, especially on the road. "Out there you're a vector for all the hostility in the stands," he told *Sport* magazine in 1970. "It all comes and they're shouting that I'm not hustling and that I stink and I'm a bum."[67] Nonetheless, with his clutch basket and thirty-four points overall, Jabbar had saved the Bucks for another game. "They're not drinking champagne tonight," he laughed, referring to the Celtics. "We're going back to Milwaukee."[68] This epic struggle between white and Black basketball proved popular with sports fans across the nation. The broadcast of Game 6 garnered the highest ratings of any televised basketball game in history, with thirty-eight million sets tuned in. As CBS announcer Pat Summerall later remarked, "The double-overtime game drew more mail response than any other game—*in any sport*—I have ever broadcast. More than 1,800 letters were sent to me alone in the days immediately following the game."[69]

Meanwhile, anticipation for Game 7 ran high in Milwaukee. Not too long after the Bucks' win in Boston, a crowd had already started to gather outside the ticket office at the downtown Milwaukee Arena. By dawn, the throng had swelled to an estimated 5,000 fans. When the ticket office opened at 9:00 a.m., the crowd went wild, as people rushed from all directions toward the entrance. By this time, several police units and an ambulance had been dispatched to the scene. The crowd continued pushing toward the ticket office.[70] With the crush of fans creating a dangerous situation, the office decided to close just after 10:00 a.m., temporarily halting ticket sales. The police then escorted the ticket sellers and the 1,200 remaining tickets to the Milwaukee County Stadium, three miles away, where they were put on sale just before noon. The tickets were gone in an hour, with several hundred frustrated fans still waiting in line.[71]

Even with the rabid support of Milwaukee fans, the Bucks fell behind for most of Game 7, eventually collapsing in the fourth quarter. The final score was 102–87 for the Celtics, making them the first team in NBA history to win three games on the road in the finals. It was also Boston's twelfth league title in eighteen years. In the locker room, the Celtics finally cracked open their cases of champagne.[72]

The Celtics' triumph proved a reassuring salve for their white fans at a moment of profound racial change. After all, their two white marquee players had led the way, grinding down Jabbar, Robertson, and the rest of the Bucks with their hustle and perseverance. Cowens was not only the game's top scorer, with twenty-eight points, but he also made history. Not since 1958 had a team won an NBA championship with a white center. As for Havlicek, *Sport* magazine named him the series MVP.[73] "After five years, Boston again has a winner," Peter Carry of *Sports Illustrated* declared. "The ingredients that beat Milwaukee in seven games are the same: a lot of tradition plus gutty men like John Havlicek."[74] The Celtics offered hope that white men could still come out on top, both on and off the court.

Black sportswriters had a different take on the racial dynamics of the Celtics' win. Writing for the Memphis *Tri-State Defender*, Ulish Carter bemoaned the lack of attention paid to Boston's "unheralded" Black heroes, including Chaney, White, and Silas. "Chaney [and White] made the Celtics pressure defense work," Carter noted. "Silas' job [was] to stop the other team's top offensive player and to help Cowens off the boards and he did this and more."[75] Rather than viewing the series as a win for white basketball, A. S. "Doc" Young characterized the Celtics' victory as an encouraging sign of interracial cooperation: "Yes, Dave Cowens and John Havlicek are white. They are also marvelous basketball players. Boston didn't win, though, merely because those two stars are white. The Celtics won because black and white together, they are the best team."[76] Yet these interpretations of the series remained largely buried in a sports media landscape focused on lauding the Celtics' white stars and white basketball tradition as welcome antidotes to the increasing Blackness of the league.

The Aftermath

Back in Beantown, fans came out in full force to celebrate the Celtics' victory. A cheerful crowd of nearly 10,000 waited in City Hall Plaza for about an hour to catch a glimpse of their beloved team. A plane, meanwhile, circled overhead, pulling a sign that said "BOSTON SALUTES THE BOSTON CELTICS—YOU'RE ON TOP OF THE WORLD." The team arrived at City Hall, transported by motorcade from Boston Garden. According to police estimates, the crowd along the street likely numbered around 30,000. The players, especially those new to Boston, were flabbergasted by the enthusiastic turnout. After a short delay caused by Mayor Kevin White's late appearance, the players, wives, children, owner, general manager, and coaches took their place on the platform set up in front of City Hall. As Johnny Most, the radio voice of the Celtics, introduced the players one by one, the crowd reserved its biggest cheers for Havlicek and Cowens. When the Celtics held up the championship trophy, fans erupted in a chant of "We're Number One."[77]

If Havlicek was popular before, the championship made him an admired emblem of white American success. "If John Havlicek of the Boston Celtics were not real, he would have to be invented," said reporters of his folk hero status. A photo of Havlicek with his blonde wife Beth, holding their two blonde children, accompanied a post-championship feature in the *Boston Globe*.[78] The article painted a picture of domestic tranquility. They lived in the suburban community of Melrose, in a modest eight-room, split-level ranch house on a quiet, tree-lined street. Hondo met Beth in college at Ohio State and they later married in 1967 at the First Congregational Church in Plainesville, Ohio. These days, they split their time between Boston and Columbus, Ohio. A former elementary schoolteacher, Beth filled her time with her children, lunches with friends, and charity work. During the offseason, Hondo enjoyed hunting and fishing. He was also an avid fan of Westerns. At a moment when white hoops stars were in short supply, Hondo offered a clean-living, suburban counterexample to the stereotypically hedonistic pro Black athlete of the inner city.

Because of their connections and networks, white players like Havlicek could easily transition into businesses after their basketball careers ended. At thirty-four, Hondo was an aging man by pro ball standards. He planned to play out the two remaining years of his contract and then shift to running his Ohio-based manufacturing and marketing business full-time. He had also taken advantage of his marketability during his career, endorsing basketballs and sneakers. The Ohio media portrayed John and Beth as a "local version of Captain and Mrs. America," and together they did television commercials for shaving cream and a meat-packing company. Even though Havlicek enjoyed his time in Boston, he planned on moving back to Ohio when he retired. "It is less hectic in the Midwest," he explained. "The nature of the people there is not as fast-paced as that of Easterners. And there's a lot more room. More space to breathe there." Despite all of the media attention, the championships, and the financial success, the Havliceks seemed like a regular white suburban family with the traditional values of America's heartland. "The Havliceks," said neighbor Mrs. Rudy DiSciullo, "are very nice people. And what's so nice about them," she added, "is that they're so ordinary."[79]

In contrast, extraordinarily talented Black players such as Robertson garnered few accolades beyond the sports pages and relatively few financial opportunities outside their basketball contracts. In the early 1970s, white players routinely made more money for personal appearances and received more endorsement offers, regardless of their talent on the court. "What they [Black players] are paid TODAY in SALARY represents what they can expect," Sam Lacy of the *Baltimore Afro-American* explained. "The fringe benefits don't go to the black stars, and don't you forget it."[80] It had taken Robertson eleven years to get his first endorsement deal from a razor-blade company. After his retirement in August 1974, he managed to snag a multiyear contract to be a color commentator on CBS. However, the network had tried to censor him from making any negative comments about the officials, and when Robertson refused to comply, CBS fired him after just one season. He also sensed that the NBA was not keen on having a Black commentator on its broadcasts, particularly one who was the face of the lawsuit still tying up the NBA–ABA merger.[81]

Meanwhile, in the weeks after the NBA Finals, as Boston's battle over school desegregation heated up, Havlicek and his team became an important symbol of white triumph. In June 1974, Judge W. Arthur Garrity, Jr., finally rendered his decision in the case of *Morgan v. Hennigan*. Garrity ruled that the Boston School Committee had, in fact, contributed to the establishment of a racially segregated school system. His desegregation plan, which involved redistricting and the crosstown busing of Black and white students, proved explosive. According to Formisano, "Its most provocative feature was its pairing of Roxbury High School, in the heart of the black ghetto, with South Boston High, the pride of the Irish-dominated white enclave most associated with hardcore antibusing passion."[82] Residents of Southie criticized the desegregation orders as unjust, noting that the judges and politicians who crafted them tended to live in all-white suburbs, safely outside the areas considered for busing. White locals came to see themselves as the real victims in this social transformation, contending that African Americans, aided by government elites, would soon threaten Southie's already underfunded schools and impoverished neighborhood.

With the start of the new school year in the fall, the court-ordered plan went into effect, unleashing a fiery backlash. In the national media, South Boston became a symbol of white racism, dubbed the "Little Rock of the North." Mobs of white men and women confronted the police, while youths hurled rocks, bottles, and racial epithets at the buses transporting Black children to traditionally white school districts. Fights, riots, and protests against integration continued throughout the year.[83] Although the Celtics had won the NBA championship against the Bucks' Black superstars, they ultimately could not hold back rising Black demands for equality. White schools were not only under attack, but Black players were taking over professional basketball, whether white fans liked it or not.

The Legacy

By 1975, the league had reached a racial tipping point, as the NBA Finals, for the first time ever, featured two Black head coaches, Al Attles and K.C. Jones, leading two majority-Black teams, the Golden State Warriors and Washington Bullets, respectively. Even though the Warriors routed the Bullets in four games, the series seemed to prove that Black ball could be saleable to a white American audience by drawing a Nielsen TV rating of 10.1 (nearly a full point better than the ratings of the 2014 NBA Finals and better than any NBA Finals from 2005 to 2009).[84] However, media-driven moral panics about Black violence and drug use in the league, coupled with greed and mismanagement on behalf of a revolving door of team owners, continued to compromise the NBA's popularity into the late 1970s.[85]

When Havlicek retired in 1978 as the Celtics' all-time leading scorer (26,395 points) and an important factor in eight of Boston's NBA titles, it seemed like the end of an era. Sportswriters lamented his departure in emotional tributes to the decorated veteran. Hondo was, according to Mark Engel of *Basketball Weekly*, "perfect for the Celtics" and "perfect for all of basketball."[86] When the Celtics' fortunes took a nosedive in the same period, white journalists and fans alike tended to blame the team's Black players, from Sidney Wicks to Bob McAdoo. For Bob Ryan of the *Boston Globe*, Wicks was "practically useless and stupendously overpaid," while Beantown fans booed him at every turn.[87] Disgruntled by his poor treatment at the Garden, the talented center McAdoo described Boston as "a place that destroyed black careers."[88]

In 1979, rookie forward Larry Bird took up where Havlicek left off. Bird appeared to be the White Hope that the Celtics and the NBA needed. As John Papanek of *Sports Illustrated* noted, Bird embodied the "Celtic ideal of humility, teamwork and excellence," once again tapping into white fans' nostalgia about the good old days. In a few short years, he reversed the Celtics' fortunes, leading them to another NBA championship in 1981. Bird did all this, as Papanek argued, without the "natural" physical advantages that Black players reportedly possessed.[89]

Building on the racial lessons of the 1970s, the NBA had figured out how to market its majority-Black league by foregrounding Bird's blue-collar whiteness in opposition to the stylish yet safe Blackness of Earvin "Magic" Johnson of the Los Angeles Lakers. This cross-racial, cross-coastal rivalry not only spoke to the culture wars of the 1980s, but also helped the league to restore its reputation and grow its profitability and reach.[90] Since then, the NBA, far from being beyond race, has continued to monetize US racial tensions and curate aspects of African American urban culture in ever more sophisticated ways to suit the evolving ideas and preferences of its fans.

Notes

1. Terry Bledsoe, "White Man's Games a Path to the Black Man's Salvation," *Los Angeles Times*, June 10, 1973.

2. Sam Lacy, "Jim Crow in Reverse," *Baltimore Afro-American*, April 1, 1972.

3. Curtis Matthew Harris, "Hardwood Revolution: The NBA's Growth and Player Revolt, 1950–1976" (PhD diss., American University, 2021), 63–64.

4. For more on the role of the ABA in challenging the NBA's informal racial quota and monopolistic business practices, see Theresa Runstedtler, *Black Ball: Kareem Abdul-Jabbar, Spencer Haywood, and the Generation That Saved the Soul of the NBA* (New York: Bold Type, 2023).

5. Lacy J. Banks, "The Black Majority," *Philadelphia Inquirer*, February 7, 1973. For income figures, see "Money Income in 1973 of Families and Persons in the United States," *Current Population Reports: Consumer Income*, series P-60, no. 7, January 1975, 1, accessed June 7, 2024, https://www2.census.gov/prod2/popscan/p60-093.pdf.

6. Runstedtler, *Black Ball*, 135–35; Jefferson Cowie, *Stayin' Alive: The 1970s and the Last Days of the Working Class* (New York: New Press, 2010), 7, 12.

7. Runstedtler, *Black Ball*, 2, 13–14.

8. Peter Carry, "They're Centers of Attention," *Sports Illustrated*, May 13, 1974.

9. Ronald P. Formisano, *Boston against Busing: Race, Class, and Ethnicity in the 1960s and 1970s* (Chapel Hill, NC: University of North Carolina, 1991), 15.

10. Runstedtler, *Black Ball*, 170. For more on the embattled history of affirmative action, see Terry H. Anderson, *The Pursuit of Fairness: A History of Affirmative Action* (New York: Oxford University Press, 2004).

11. Formisano, *Boston against Busing*, 8, 29, 35–36, 54. For more on the Black activism surrounding *Morgan v. Hennigan*, see Zebulon Vance Miletsky, *Before Busing: A History of Boston's Long Black Freedom Struggle* (Chapel Hill, NC: University of North Carolina Press, 2022).

12. For a national study of the "busing crisis," see Matthew F. Delmont, *Why Busing Failed: Race, Media, and the National Resistance to School Desegregation* (Berkeley, CA: University of California Press, 2016).

13. Alan Lupo, "South Boston: Symbol of Urban Resistance," *Boston Globe*, June 2, 1974.

14. Lupo, "South Boston."

15. Formisano, *Boston against Busing*, 3. For more on the white ethnic and class dimensions of the antibusing movement in Boston, see Britney L. Brooks, "'Celtic Pride': White Nostalgia and Working-Class Masculinity in 1970s Professional Basketball" (master's thesis, University of Nevada, Reno, 2018), 15–74.

16. Brooks, "'Celtic Pride'," 1, 86–87; Santiago Colás, *Ball Don't Lie: Myth, Genealogy, and Invention in the Cultures of Basketball* (Philadelphia: Temple University Press, 2016), 67.

17. Jeffrey Lane, *Under the Boards: The Cultural Revolution in Basketball* (Lincoln, NE: University of Nebraska Press, 2007), 124; Brooks, "'Celtic Pride'," 1, 90–91.

18. "Cellar Celts' Crowds up 1,000 Per Game," *Los Angeles Times*, November 29, 1969.

19. Jeff Greenfield, "Dave Cowens Doesn't Play Hard . . . He Kills Himself," *Sport*, May 1973, 83.

20. Bob Ryan, "Auerbach's Five-Year Plan Puts Celtics at Top Again," *Boston Globe*, May 14, 1974; Greenfield, "Dave Cowens Doesn't Play Hard," 83.

21. Leigh Montville, "Beantown: One Tough Place to Play," *Sports Illustrated*, August 19, 1991.

22. Greenfield, "Dave Cowens Doesn't Play Hard," 83.

23. Peter Carry, "A Matter of Celtic Pride," *Sports Illustrated*, May 20, 1974.

24. For more on the Celtics' history of race-based marketing, see Harvey Araton and Filip Bondy, *The Selling of the Green: The Financial Rise and Moral Decline of the Boston Celtics* (New York: HarperCollins, 1992). On the racial politics of Boston's other sports franchises, see Thomas J. Whalen, *Kooks and Degenerates on Ice: Bobby Orr, the Big Bad Bruins, and the Stanley Cup*

Championship That Transformed Hockey (Lanham, MD: Rowman & Littlefield, 2020); and Howard Bryant, *Shut Out: A Story of Race and Baseball in Boston* (Boston: Beacon, 2002).

25. For more on the NBA's search for and marketing of white stars, see Adam J. Criblez, "White Men Playing a Black Man's Game: Basketball's 'Great White Hopes' of the 1970s," *Journal of Sport History* 42, no. 3 (2015): 371–81.

26. Brooks, "'Celtic Pride'," 78–81; Lane, *Under the Boards*, 115–20. For more on the cultural and political dimensions of the white ethnic revival in the 1970s, see Matthew Frye Jacobson, *Roots Too: White Ethnic Revival in Post-Civil Rights America* (Cambridge, MA: Harvard University Press, 2006); and Richard Moss, *Creating the New Right Ethnic in 1970s America: The Intersection of Anger and Nostalgia* (Lanham, MD: Fairleigh Dickinson University Press, 2017).

27. John Underwood, "The Green Running Machine," *Sports Illustrated*, October 28, 1974; Harvey Araton, "John Havlicek, a Dynamo in Two Eras of Celtics Glory, Dies at 79," *New York Times*, April 25, 2019. See also "Legends Profile: John Havlicek," *NBA.com*, September 13, 2021, accessed March 11, 2024, https://www.nba.com/news/history-nba-legend-john-havlicek.

28. Araton, "John Havlicek, a Dynamo."

29. Araton, "John Havlicek, a Dynamo"; Mark Engel, "John Havlicek Man of the Year," *Basketball Weekly*, January 4, 1979.

30. Underwood, "The Green Running Machine."

31. Larry Whiteside, "Hondo: Like a Bridge over Troubled Waters, He Has Carried the Celtics Through," *Boston Globe*, December 30, 1973.

32. Greenfield, "Dave Cowens Doesn't Play Hard," 79, 80; Jim Haughton, "A Man for All Seasons, Especially This Season," *Basketball Weekly*, January 2, 1975; "1973 MVP Vote in NBA," *Basketball News*, October 15, 1973.

33. Greenfield, "Dave Cowens Doesn't Play Hard," 77.

34. Greenfield, "Dave Cowens Doesn't Play Hard," 78.

35. See Theresa Runstedtler, "Clyde Cool," in *City/Game: Basketball in New York*, ed. William C. Rhoden (New York: Rizzoli Electa, 2020), 136–43; *Black Ball*, 63–66.

36. Greenfield, "Dave Cowens Doesn't Play Hard," 84; Haughton, "A Man for All Seasons"; Peter Carry, "Boston's Perpetual Motion Machine," *Sports Illustrated*, April 2, 1973.

37. Aram Goudsouzian, "From Lew Alcindor to Kareem Abdul-Jabbar: Race, Religion, and Representation in Basketball, 1968–1975," *Journal of American Studies* 51, no. 2 (2017): 450.

38. Jabbar, quoted in Harry Edwards, *The Revolt of the Black Athlete* (New York: Free Press, 1969), 53.

39. John Matthew Smith, "'It's Not Really My Country': Lew Alcindor and the Revolt of the Black Athlete," *Journal of Sport History* 36, no. 2 (2009): 224.

40. Runstedtler, *Black Ball*, 132–34.

41. "Black Journal; 60; Kareem," 1972–05–02, Library of Congress, Ameri-

can Archive of Public Broadcasting (GBH and the Library of Congress), Boston, MA and Washington, DC, accessed June 24, 2024, http://americanarchive.org/catalog/cpb-aacip-512-154dn40k35.

42. Runstedtler, *Black Ball*, 130.

43. Jabbar quoted in Adam Criblez, *Tall Tales and Short Shorts: Dr. J, Pistol Pete, and the Birth of the Modern NBA* (Lanham: Rowman & Littlefield, 2017), 103.

44. Runstedtler, *Black Ball*, 91.

45. For more on these Black-led antitrust lawsuits in the NBA, see part 1 of *Black Ball*, 17–123.

46. Brooks, "'Celtic Pride'," 107.

47. Carry, "They're Centers of Attention."

48. Thomas Rogers, "Milwaukee Awaits Start of N.B.A. Title Playoffs," *New York Times*, April 28, 1974.

49. Bob Ryan, "Won't Someone Please Rid Us of Milwaukee?," *Boston Globe*, April 7, 1974.

50. Dave Begel, "Floorburns: A Pro's Badge of Courage," *Basketball News*, March 21, 1974.

51. Larry Whiteside, "Bucks Realize Jabbar Alone Is Not Enough," *Boston Globe*, April 27, 1974.

52. "Heinsohn's Strategy: Stop the 'Other' Bucks," *Los Angeles Times*, April 28, 1974. See also Rogers, "Milwaukee Awaits Start of N.B.A. Title Playoffs."

53. "Bucks, Celts Open Final," *Washington Post*, April 28, 1974.

54. Rogers, "Milwaukee Awaits Start of N.B.A. Title Playoffs"; "Bucks, Celts Open Final."

55. "Bucks, Celts Open Final."

56. For Game 1, see Thomas Rogers, "Celtics Go 1-up on Bucks," *New York Times*, April 29, 1974; Bob Ryan, "Celtics Dazzle and Bucks Fizzle, 98–83," *Boston Globe*, April 29, 1974.

57. For Game 2, see Thomas Rogers, "Bucks Win in Overtime; Series Even," *New York Times*, May 1, 1974; Bob Ryan, "Warner Spurt Evens Series: Bucks Reply in OT, 105–96," *Boston Globe*, May 1, 1974.

58. "Celtics Stride Away, 95–83," *Washington Post*, May 4, 1974; Larry Whiteside, "Chaney Press Best in Business," *Boston Globe*, May 4, 1974.

59. "Celtics Stride Away"; Bob Ryan, "Celtics Buckle Bucks: Press Wears Down Foe, 95–83," *Boston Globe*, May 4, 1974.

60. Bob Ryan, "Bucks Knock Starch out of Press—and Celtics—97–89," *Boston Globe*, May 6, 1974; Larry Whiteside, "Folks, That Was the Old Oscar—Ball Was His . . . Also the Tempo," *Boston Globe*, May 5, 1974.

61. Sam Goldaper, "Bucks Square Series," *New York Times*, May 6, 1974.

62. Whiteside, "Folks, That Was the Old Oscar."

63. "Celtics Burn Bucks, 96–87, for 3–2 Lead," *Washington Post*, May 8, 1974.

64. Thomas Rogers, "Beat Celtics in 2 Overtimes of 6th Game, 102–101," *New York Times*, May 11, 1974.

65. Will McDonough, "Abdul-Jabbar's Killer Shot Was Forced by Celtics Defense," *Boston Globe*, May 11, 1974.

66. Thomas Rogers, "Celtics and Bucks Battle for Title Today," *New York Times*, May 12, 1974.

67. Roger Kahn, "Lew Alcindor's Life as a Pro," *Sport*, February 1970.

68. Larry Whiteside, "Play Wasn't Meant for Me, Says Jabbar from Cloud 9," *Boston Globe*, May 11, 1974.

69. Michael K. Herbert, "Added Notes," *Basketball Digest*, December 1974. Emphasis added.

70. "Fans Crush Ticket Lines, Sales Halted," *Boston Globe*, May 12, 1974.

71. "Bucks' Tickets Sell out Fast; Fans Unhappy," *Los Angeles Times*, May 12, 1974.

72. "3 Road Hits, and an Oscar," *Boston Globe*, May 13, 1974; "Celtics Won It by Stopping Jabbar," *Chicago Defender*, May 13, 1974; "Boston Makes All the Right Moves: Celtics Switch Strategy and Beat the Bucks, 102–87, for NBA Title," *Los Angeles Times*, May 13, 1974.

73. "Celtics Won It by Stopping Jabbar"; Carry, "Boston's Perpetual Motion Machine."

74. Carry, "A Matter of Celtic Pride," 22.

75. Ulish Carter, "Celtics Spells Teamwork Doom for Bucks," *Tri-State Defender*, May 24, 1974.

76. A. S. Doc Young, "Good Morning, Sports: Winning and Racism," *Chicago Defender*, May 16, 1974.

77. Bob Ryan, "30,000 Cheer Celtic Champs," *Boston Globe*, May 15, 1974.

78. Maria Karagianis, "Living: At Home with the Havliceks," *Boston Globe*, May 18, 1974.

79. Karagianis, "Living: At Home with the Havliceks."

80. Sam Lacy, "More Power to Haywood and Others," *Baltimore Afro-American*, April 3, 1971.

81. Oscar P. Robertson, *The Big O: My Life, My Times, My Game* (Lincoln, NE: University of Nebraska Press, 2013), 307, 309. On the *Robertson* lawsuit's impact on his post-NBA career, see also Runstedtler, *Black Ball*, 208–209.

82. Formisano, *Boston against Busing*, 70.

83. Formisano, *Boston against Busing*, 1–2, 9, 75–77.

84. Richard Rothschild, "Fun Facts about the 1975 NBA Finals," SI.com, 3 June 2015, accessed June 9, 2025, https://www.si.com/nba/2015/06/03/nba-finals-1975-warriors-bullets-rick-barry-jamaal-wilkes-cavaliers; Runstedtler, *Black Ball*, 195.

85. On the NBA's moral panics and mismanagement in the late 1970s, see *Black Ball*, 201–79.

86. Engel, "John Havlicek Man of the Year."

87. Bob Ryan, "Celtics: No Offense, No Defense, No Nuthin'," *Boston Globe*, November 11, 1977.

88. Quoted in Criblez, *Tall Tales and Short Shorts*, 214. See also Lane, *Under the Boards*, 128.

89. John Papanek, "Gifts That God Didn't Give," *Sports Illustrated*, November 9, 1981. See also Runstedtler, *Black Ball*, 282; John Matthew Smith, "'Gifts That God Didn't Give': White Hopes, Basketball, and the Legend of Larry Bird," *Massachusetts Historical Review* 13, no. 1 (2011): 1–30.

90. See Patrick Ferrucci and Earnest Perry, "Double Dribble: The Stereotypical Narrative of Magic and Bird," *Journalism History* 41, no. 2 (2015): 93–102.

4

"I Was Raised on This Sport"

Football and Female Expertise

VICTORIA E. JOHNSON

The 2023–2024 National Football League (NFL) season was rocked by what was dubbed "the Swift Effect." When global pop mega-star Taylor Swift and Kansas City Chiefs tight end Travis Kelce went public with their budding romance, unprecedented public attention was focused on female football fandom, expertise, and involvement in the sport. From game telecast commentary to newspaper op-eds, from social media speculation to expert polling analysis, voices celebrating and condemning the phenomenon raged in debate throughout a season that concluded with a Chiefs Super Bowl victory. Notably, across media, there was remarkably little *neutrality* or measured response where opinions regarding Swift's impact on the NFL were concerned. On the one hand, celebrants praised Swift's ability to drive viewership numbers up, introducing new generations of female fans to the game. According to statistics compiled by the Video Advertising Bureau, "[a]t least one in five Americans" said they were watching the 2024 Super Bowl "because they or someone in their household want to catch [Taylor Swift] at the game. . . . That's 21% of Americans, a staggering stat."[1] And yet, these new fans—and Swift herself—were also castigated for "'taking away from what really happens on the field.'"[2] In an age of skepticism regarding social media, celebrity, and self-promotion, Swift's presence—and the Swifties in her wake—were interpreted to be "casual" fans at best, invested in the melodrama and narrative of off-field romance. At worst, Swift and her fans were pilloried as insincere and emasculating. For such critics, the Swift Effect was equated with unnecessary distraction: the *feminizing* and undermining of the sincere efforts and dedication of the verifiable game on the field.

Critics—and, further, political conspiracy theorists—managed to erase the fact that Swift had grown up a dedicated Philadelphia Eagles fan, even incorporating the team's jersey into her concert costume carousel.[3] Her star persona was, historically, that of a relatable, identifiable "girl next door," typically idealized in such an "All American" sport. And, *beyond* the Swift Effect, female viewership of the NFL was already up "by nearly one-third across the [2023] NFL season."[4] Indeed, discussions of the Swift effect on the male "preserve" of football—whether celebratory or condemning—occurred at the same moment that female presence and influence across the sport was experiencing a surge.[5] On the heels of commemorations of the fiftieth anniversary of the passage of Title IX (1972), the NFL had unprecedented and growing numbers of female executives, and it was energetically promoting the interscholastic and global growth of girls' and women's flag football. Following the bleakness and uncertainty of the COVID-era sports landscape, such invigorated attention to—and consternation about—female expertise and belonging in the realm of football may have seemed to explode out of nowhere, trailing Swift's celebrity supernova. However, this chapter proposes that female inclusion in football and, further, female football expertise—with the accompanying anxieties they provoke—are, instead, historically recurring phenomena amplified particularly in periods of social and political transition in which struggles over women's rights are prominent in broad, popular discourse.

Scholars of US sports and social history have detailed struggles over football, traditional values, and anxieties over gender and social change in key eras of the sport's transformation. Michael Oriard has noted that, in the same era that the game of football became standardized and increasingly embraced as a national pastime (as conveyed in print media of the 1870s to early 1900s), the "New Woman" challenged status-quo ideals. As seen in popular magazine illustrations, figures such as the Gibson Girl explicitly embraced athletic pursuits, including football. Such New Woman icons were sources of both admiration and anxiety, representing "conflicting impressions of beauty and power."[6] Others have detailed the NFL's explosive early growth in popularity through national television broadcasting rights deals and, particularly, the cultural phenomenon of *Monday Night Football* (ABC, 1970–2005; ESPN, 2005-persent). "MNF's" unique "up close and personal" coverage and weeknight, prime-time telecasts were groundbreaking in understanding that much of the game's audience was female and that game coverage could move beyond "x's and o's" to combine "the best elements of both drama and history, intimacy and newsworthiness,"[7] presumed to appeal to a broad audience interested in the stories behind the on-field action. Feminist scholarship in the sociology of sport and in film and media studies has closely analyzed the era from the 1990s onward to assess the powerful yet paradoxical appeals of female sports icons who embody "marketplace feminism" or popular feminism while still remaining emblematic of cis-gendered, heteronormative "ideals."[8] Such work has informed post-2010 scholarship on digital-era streaming and social media that examines the "cool sports girl" in sports talk and sports journalism—"typically a heterosexual and often white woman who possesses significant knowledge while also appealing to hegemonic ideals of femininity."[9]

Between the 1970 premiere of *Monday Night Football* and the 1990s emergence and growing prominence of the "female athlete as cultural icon," however, there emerged a small but notable set of TV series, made-for-TV movies, and theatrical films that featured female protagonists as football team owners, coaches, or players.[10] These mainstream, commercial texts—and the critical and popular discourses surrounding them—each explicitly referenced the feminist movement, linking their heroines to historic understandings of sports as a venue for rights claims, and as an inherent public good. In a period in which debates over Title IX were still prominent in the public eye (though legal challenges to the law have never abated) and the significantly increased professional prominence of women in the workforce triggered new anxieties, these female-centered football narratives imagined the sport to be an idealized level playing field and democratic pursuit. These films capitalized on established conventions by which football narratives operate in a simultaneously melodramatic *and* pedagogical mode, focused on rights discourses. Specifically here, hard-won accomplishment on the football field benefits middle-class *white* women while reinforcing the logic and value of *family*. The following focuses particularly on two of these texts: The made-for-television movie *Quarterback Princess*, starring Helen Hunt, which aired on CBS (December 10, 1983); and the Warner Bros. feature film *Wildcats*, produced by and starring Goldie Hawn, which was released on Valentine's Day in 1986.

I analyze these films' appeals to an imagined, mainstream, "mass" audience as they align participation in football play and coaching with the "possessive investments" of middle-class, white feminism and the resulting benefits that accrue to each of their heroines.[11] Each reinforces thoroughly conventional, dominant patriarchal "ideals" of cis-gendered, heterosexual femininity, while also extending definitions of football and its "commonsense," conventionally-gendered logics. *Quarterback Princess*, *Wildcats*, and related productions in this same period forged a template that is simultaneously calcified in its resistance to change *and* strategically positioned as having empowering and emancipatory value in the present.

Beyond these texts' visual and narrative conventions, their imagination of typically blonde, heterosexual, female football expertise serves to support broader, post-1970 US cultural logics that—both legally and in production practice—aligned network broadcasting, "mainstream" commercial media, and *football* as analogous and linked social institutions in purported service to the public. In other words, by the 1980s, with football narratives already linked to public pedagogy across commercial media, "cool girl" femininity and female expertise were meaningfully mobilized to simultaneously appeal to *progress* in feminist terms while also supporting mainstream conventions as "common sense."[12]

In 1994, Julie D'Acci's foundational study of *Cagney and Lacey* (CBS, 1982–1988, with follow-up TV movies from 1994 to 1996) examined the popular series of the 1980s as a critical site of industrial, textual, social, and historical struggles over the meanings of "woman, women, and femininity" as well as *feminism* in the context of the historically male-dominated police series. Adapting D'Acci, I ask below: "How exactly do" femininity and *football* "come to have various meanings at a specific moment of history and culture? How do these different meanings serve the interests of the people and institutions producing them? . . . How do these meanings help to shape real human beings along particular lines or in particular ways?"[13] How do football's conjoined melodramatic and pedagogical conventions and the articulations of football with female expertise, as established in the broadcast era, remain foundational to the NFL's most contemporary, targeted, cross-media appeals to female participation in league-sponsored flag football—especially as the league casts NFL Play as a global Diversity, Equity, and Inclusion initiative? How is *feminism* invoked to imagine football as a site of unity, citizenship ideals, and community while simultaneously privileging *some* expertise over others, and underscoring the NFL's *market* commitments? Specifically, in a context in which states are aggressively pursuing anti-LGBTQ+ legislation, conventional promotions of "football for all" that are couched predominantly in images of privileged femininity within a "family circle" would appear to merit further discussion and analysis.

Broadcasting's Public Service Ethos and Its Institutional Legacies

In order to examine female-led football narratives of the 1980s and the continued work their conventions do in the present, it is important to consider the ethos of mainstream, commercial media from broadcasting's inception through the early 1990s, when cable TV first became the dominant mode of media reception in US households. While broadcast media addressed a broadly national, demographically diversified audience (generationally, racially, ethnically, and in gendered terms) in a presumptively "shared" address, cable's more "niche," interest-specific capabilities shifted media to more fragmented appeals, with audiences imagined to be conjoined through distinct demographic categories and interests (for example, MTV; the Weather Channel; CNN). From the 2010s onward, the transition to digital transmission and availability of internet-enabled streaming media received on personal devices (tablets, phones) have made media shared in common even more rare. Notably, across these transitions—supported not just by changes in technology but also by concerted policy decisions and market transformations—*sports* media remains the central cultural domain in which the broadcast ethos still thrives.[14] Here, then, I draw a connection between female-led football films' socially engaged discourses and the legal and industrial link that, historically, has connected US sports broadcasting and commercial entertainment media as *pedagogical* texts, in service to the public. Thinking through these connections allows us to consider how broadcast media, televised football, and narrative football fictions have been institutionally and formally linked through conventions that position them as civically minded public goods and how that ethos continues to operate and speak *across* audiences, even in the more atomized present.

The Radio Act of 1927 prescribed that broadcasters, in using the "public resource" that is the airwaves, must serve "in the public interest, convenience, and necessity" and that they would be licensed to operate according to this principle. In the 1960 Programming Policy Statement, the FCC introduced an "ascertainment" requirement for successful licensing. Among fourteen elements identified as necessary to meet public interest requirements was the regular offering of sports programs.[15] From the classic network era through the multichannel era and the connected viewing or digital, streaming era, media law and policy and TV industry negotiations with sports leagues have defined sports as a public good and viewers' access to sports as a necessity and a right.

As ushered by then Commissioner Pete Rozelle in the interest of the NFL, the Sports Broadcasting Act of 1961 further codified the paradox by which the Big Three broadcast networks (ABC, CBS, NBC) and professional sports leagues were linked as for-profit entities that were presumed also to serve as public trustees. One year prior to the passage of the Sports Broadcasting Act, the FCC had, for the first time, "officially acknowledged that *commercial* programming could be considered a public service."[16] Following the quiz show scandals and in light of the Kennedy administration's encouragement of documentary and news production that would activate the American public's engagement in the Cold War era, this acknowledgement encouraged for-profit broadcasters to invest in "pedagogical" programming that could still draw an audience. By the 1970s, each network had pursued such programming in the form of made-for-TV movies of the week.

ABC-TV's *Brian's Song* (November 30, 1971) is *the* touchstone and template not only for such made-for-television "pedagogical" productions but, generally, for football films of the *Monday Night Football*-era. The power of *Brian's Song* and subsequent, lauded TV movies was synonymous with televised football in the form's savvy combination of fact-based newsworthiness with "up close and personal" melodrama. The TV movie brought "public struggles into the intimacy of private spaces," simultaneously enabling debate *and* containing transformation within a familial context.[17] If the TV movie of the broadcast era was often—if certainly not always—hailed as a teaching tool, as a commercial entertainment, it also shared with both football telecasts and football fictions mainstream ideological objectives and their reinforcement. Indeed, movies and TV about football are not, generally, about football at all. *Brian's Song* became a story of friendship, brotherhood, and love. And, in female-centered football fictions, football is "family," modeling sibling bonds through acceptance by the team, and modeling ideal parenting via the "mother" coach's fealty to her father's legacy and in her service as a rare, anchoring presence, guiding otherwise "lost" youth. And this is where *Quarterback Princess* and *Wildcats* enter the picture.

"I'm a *Girl*!" The *Quarterback* (Must Also Be a) *Princess*

Though Title IX became law in the United States in 1972, its three-pronged test clarifying its "equal opportunity" mandate was not finalized until 1979, and the 1980s saw vigorous backlash and legal challenges to the law.[18] In this context, *Quarterback Princess* was broadcast as the *CBS Saturday Movie* on December 10, 1983. In the tradition of *Brian's Song*, *Quarterback Princess* is based on the true story of Tami Maida of Prince George, British Columbia, who played quarterback for the McMinnville, Oregon, Warriors for one season while her father completed a doctorate at Oregon State. While the film places Tami on the "Minnville Grizzlies" varsity team as a sixteen-year-old, off-screen Maida played junior varsity as a fourteen-year-old, alternating games with a second quarterback. Maida had previously played as the only female in the junior bantam division of the Prince George Minor Football Association, after playing three years of organized flag football. Consistent with the TV movie, however, press coverage of Maida's accomplishments always emphasized her "intelligence" and finesse, her femininity (and separate dressing room from the rest of the team), and her equal proclivity for girls-only team sports, including volleyball, track and field, and basketball.[19]

Quarterback Princess helped CBS sweep the ratings for the competitive Christmas-special-filled week in which it aired.[20] Featuring a cast of veterans such as Don Murray, Dana Elcar, and Barbara Babcock, directed by Oscar and Palm d'Or winner Noel Black, and shot on location in Oregon with high cinematic production values, the film had all the markers of "Tiffany Network" appointment-viewing for a Saturday night. With closing titles art by LeRoy Neiman and game sequences reliant upon *Monday Night Football*-established conventions, the movie also overtly allied its address with aesthetic conventions from esteemed sports texts and "event" broadcasts.

During the December 2, 1983, telecast of *Rudolph the Red-Nosed Reindeer*, CBS aired a promotion for *Quarterback Princess*'s "World Premiere! Based on a True Story," to air the next week.[21] The trailer promised a film that would detail the unusual—as a female quarterback, Tami's is "no ordinary dream." Sneak-peak footage portrays her suited up in the locker room, playing quarterback in game action, and being taunted by opposing linemen ("Hey little girl, you're gonna get creamed!"). However, the promotion also promised that the film would meet highly conventional expectations for teen melodrama, as it featured scenes showing Tami being kissed by a handsome male date and basking in glamorous triumph as Homecoming Princess. Promotions for *Quarterback Princess* thus underscored the productive paradox of the made-for-TV movie. As Laurie Schulze and Elayne Rapping have each noted, the TV movie is responsive to topics up for social debate, enabling "us to think and act as citizens in a public social sphere."[22] But these films' responsiveness and topicality are also "domesticated" with debates contained, and largely resolved, within the family circle. Ultimately, the TV movie—as with most successful commercial texts—assures "that all personal problems in a capitalist society may be resolved by individuals who view themselves, essentially, as family members."[23] Thus, the "difference" represented by a girl who quarterbacks a high school football team is tempered throughout the film by Tami's conventionally feminine attractiveness, her evident heterosexuality, and her idealized roles as a dutiful daughter and supportive sibling—both within her family *and* to her coach and teammates. Tami is—and, according to the genre's logics, *must* be—a success at being both a star athlete *and* a princess.

Prior to the opening titles, Tami's father, Ralph Maida (Don Murray) is shown driving past Minnville's football summer camp and introducing himself to head coach Ed Ainsworth (Carmen Argenziano). Ralph is himself established as "different" in relation to the town and team: he is "foreign" as both a Canadian and as an academic, finishing a doctorate in psychology (though his "manly" bona fides are established by his apparent expertise as a big game hunter). Slow to realize that Maida is asking for his *daughter* to be able to try out for her new school's team, the coach is portrayed as skeptical but not obstructionist. The Maidas' home life—prior to packing up for the States—is revealed to be rustic, outdoorsy, athletic, and dominated by women, with three daughters and wife/mother Judy (Barbara Babcock) at home. Though the opening sequence of *Quarterback Princess* sets up the uniqueness of Tami's family and her dream, throughout the film her ability to play is presented as, simply, common sense.

Resistance to Tami's dream to quarterback the Grizzlies comes from two parties that are each portrayed as woefully out of touch with the times: an older generation of townspeople, who fear that the reputation and success of their "boys" will be diminished or neutered by association with a "girl," and the "mean girl" cheerleader contingent at the high school, whose "excessive" femininity is threatened by Tami's mobility between conventional and unconventional gendered realms. The film, thus, never questions Tami's skills and ability to succeed in both unconventional *and* conventional ways. It presents those who would prevent Tami from playing football as not only resistant to modern realities but beholden to such limited understanding of gender roles as to seem embarrassingly archaic.

An early scene in which the Maidas appear before the Minnville school board to seek its approval of Tami's tryout introduces the resistant constituencies at the same time that it instructs the gathered (and viewers at home) about Title IX. Mr. Caine (Dana Elcar) and Mrs. Upchurch (Mary Marsh) represent Tami's harshest critics. Caine explicitly fears his star center son's emasculation at the hands of a female quarterback, stating, "What the hell chance is he going to have for a scholarship if he is snapping the ball to some *girl* reaching down there between his legs?" Upchurch proposes that Tami be made a cheerleader, like her own daughter, Tiffany. Tami makes an impassioned yet humble plea to "at least try. I don't know—maybe I'm not good enough to make the team, but I sure would like to have a shot at it." Immediately after Tami's request to simply pursue equal access through hard work and merit, the school board chair (Michael Currie) educates the collective: "The bottom line is the Oregon State Athletic Association says there's a *federal* regulation—Title IX—which requires equal athletic opportunities for boys and girls. Which means—

which *means*— if we don't have a girls' football team, we have to let her try out for the Grizzlies. That's the *law*!"

While perhaps simplifying Title IX a bit much, within the first fifteen minutes of the film, *Quarterback Princess* establishes the principle of equal access and its clear conformity with the American Dream. Of course, Tami *is* good enough to make the team. Notably, the players and coaches—seeing Tami's evident talent—do not share the elders' or mean girls' qualms. Tami's on-field progress and acceptance as "one of the guys" align her success with conventional football narrative rewards for the underdog's hard work, self-reliance, and resulting reward in the affirmation of American Dream ideology.[24] The dilemma for the remainder of the film, then, is Tami's struggle to resolve her *own* confusion over her sense of self and where she fits in *as* a "girl." The second and third acts of the film thus intersperse on-field success with off-field reinforcements of Tami's conventionally feminine identification, underscoring both her sisterlike bond with her teammates and her heterosexual coupling with Scott (John Stockwell), her classmate and boyfriend. As the film—and the Grizzlies' on-field successes with Tami at the helm—progresses, the "old guard" gradually learns to embrace Tami as one of their own and her trailblazing family as part of the community.

Judy and Ralph Maida's unquestioning support of Tami's dream—while initially underscored as "unusual" through their Canadian-ness and relatively off-the-grid self-sufficiency—positions them as a mediating and reassuring presence that anchors viewers between Tami's exceptionalism and the outdated traditions of the community elders. In two pivotal scenes, Judy, in particular, gives voice to the commonsense logic by which Tami should be allowed to play and, further, to thrive. Early in the film, Judy is accosted by Mrs. Upchurch and two of her friends while shopping in the local grocery store. The three ladies' shopping carts move in lockstep, in staging reminiscent of *Valley of the Dolls* (20th Century Fox, 1967), as they close in on Judy to scold her for Tami's perceived gender impropriety. Framed with canned goods and preserved foods behind her group, Upchurch tells Judy, "We don't want women's lib in Minnville." Judy's fresh perspective, on the other hand, is emphasized by framing her in front of lush produce of vibrant colors. She replies, "My daughter wants to play a *game*. The *law* gives her the right. And God gave her the ability. Who are you to say that she can't?"

Later in the film, Judy and Tami share a late-night chat after which Tami's wavering confidence is restored and her "split" identity is affirmed as a strength rather than a source of confusion and distress. Arriving home

FIGURE 4.1: Screenshot from *Quarterback Princess* (CBS TV, 1983).

to discover Judy watching the conclusion of *It's a Wonderful Life* (RKO, 1946) on TV—perhaps *the* iconic Hollywood tale of dreams deferred and the "blessings" of self-sacrifice—Tami asks whether Judy is happy with her life, "being a woman, being married, having all of us?" Judy mentions having wanted to be a singer, but, she continues,

> then I met your father and suddenly it wasn't important anymore. 'Course, there wasn't any *real* choice then; a woman was expected to marry a man and start having babies and raise a family and live happily ever after. But I'm glad I made that choice. And, yeah, I'm happy. But you know *you* can do anything. You can have everything. . . . The trouble is that attitudes just haven't kept up with opportunities. And some people . . . they're frightened. Because, to them, you represent a world they don't understand.

Systemic resistance or structural impediments (the lack of "*real* choice") are, here, both placed in the past while also underscoring that the real problem is "some people." Given that the Maidas, the coaches, and the team represent the *now*, Tami's future looks bright, with the right *interpersonal* relationships.

Tami's boyfriend, Scott Massey, struggles with his own sense of self and insecurities, given her athletic expertise—which makes her "so *different* from all the other girls"—while recognizing that she *is* a girl. As a competitive lumberjack who drives a vintage Chevy pickup and is clearly popular at school and with the football players, Scott's masculinity and, therefore, Tami's attraction to him, is not in question. Scott's independence from the team allows Tami's relationships with her teammates to be chaste and to remain sibling-like, rather than romantic and disruptive. Though Tami's closest friends on the team—her center and Caine's son, B. J. (Beau Dremann), other quarterbacks, Marvin (Tim Robbins) and Roger (Scott Culbertson), and lineman Brian (Joshua Cadman)—initially fear hurting her and clearly see her as pretty, they quickly integrate her as "one of the guys" due to her undeniable football skills, easygoing personality, and ability to joke in kind. Indeed, she is *better* than the guys. As her most supportive assistant coach and offensive coordinator George Watson (John Wesley) tells her, "You take game pressure better." Notably, Coach Watson is the only African American presence in the entire film.[25] This is significant in that Watson's early, unquestioning, and sustained support for Tami's role on the team conforms with a broader articulation of Black masculinity to blonde expertise in shared community within female-led football narratives, as examined further below.

Tami's worlds converge and her quest finds closure when she leads the Grizzlies to the championship on the same night that she is crowned Homecoming Princess, wearing a dress purchased for her by her teammate "brothers." *Quarterback Princess* thus makes female football achievement "safe" in that Tami's expertise is thoroughly consistent with status-quo ideals. Tami embodies progress within tradition, exercising expertise within the warmth of a family circle.

Wildcats and the Enduring Power of Blonde Mobility

In 2017, Reese Witherspoon inducted Goldie Hawn into the Hollywood Walk of Fame with an emotionally charged recounting of having seen *Wildcats* (Warner Bros., 1986) in the theater with her father. "And that day," she says, "Goldie blew my ten-year-old mind."[26] Witherspoon specifically notes the impression the film made on her in terms of race and gender "norms" of the 1980s, stating, "this was the eighties, guys, and the idea of a petite blonde lady coaching an inner-city football team was *laughable*." In the face of such inconceivability, Witherspoon's new idol "was young and beautiful and hilarious and brave.... It's hard for me to articulate how important this was for me, a tiny blonde girl." Recently listed by *Forbes* as the "world's richest actress," and herself representative of a Sheryl Sandberg-esque mode of corporate feminism and "Mom-lebrity," Witherspoon credits Hawn with inspiring her to become a producer and for changing "the possibilities of what women can do in film."[27] She returns several times to Hawn's star persona's canny and idealized combination of conventional femininity with business acumen in a male-dominated domain. Hawn's *Wildcats* character was "just like me . . . feminine and funny and tough and warm." She states, "It just taught me that feminism comes in lots of different packages and that a woman can be feminine and love fashion and be taken seriously in the world."

Hawn's Molly McGrath wants to coach football—she repeats several times in the film—because she was "raised on it." Her expertise carries forward the legacy of her deceased father, allying her desire to coach and her knowledge of football with patriarchy and its "logical" continuance. This expertise and commitment are established in the film's opening titles with a home movie montage featuring the centrality of football to Molly's childhood with her sister Verna (Swoozie Kurtz) and her dad. Featuring family moments of celebration and play, each home movie clip emphasizes Molly's love of football. At a backyard birthday party, the camera pans away from a group of girls playing pin the tail on the donkey to a five-year-old Molly, in a plaid dress, kicking a football. Clips feature Molly "advising" her dad on the sidelines and surrounded by his players, who lovingly tease her. On her birthday, Molly has a cake decorated like a football field, with plastic players on top. Under a Christmas tree, Verna opens a doll, while Molly instead glows with joy while unwrapping a shiny red football helmet. As the home movie clips unspool visually, the soundtrack features LL Cool J's "Football Rap" recounting a history of "old school" football stars and their renowned grit: "Old-timers, do you remember their names? Like Bronco Nagurski and Night Train Lane? Bulldog Turner, my man Sam Huff, in the snow and the mud they were still real tough." Crucially, here, Molly's childhood passion is *also* allied with the cultural mobility and fluency associated with Blackness. Before the film "begins," the title sequence's home movies, underscored by "Football Rap," immediately conjoin white, female expertise with Black, male expression as presumptively allied interests and shared histories. Indeed, throughout the film, Molly's staunchest support comes from her sister, who—the titles make clear—has always accepted and supported Molly's lifelong dream, and from Ben Edwards (Nipsey Russell), the principal who hires her to coach at Central High. Fully aware and all too familiar with the fact that Molly's gender has meant that his "inner-city," majority Black school is the only opportunity open to her, Edwards addresses Molly's concerns over lack of staffing, resources, and personnel, invoking scarce opportunity and its limits: "If the word got around that you chickened out on *this* job, you think anybody would ever offer you another chance?" Unlike her white former high school colleagues or ex-husband, unquestioned and unwavering support comes first, in the film, from Edwards, as Molly's Black male mentor. The majority of the rest of the film is dedicated to Molly's securing the same support from her team as she coaches them to potentially become future Ben Edwardses.

Throughout, *Wildcats* is thus consistent with Richard Dyer's foundational explication of mainstream Hollywood's limited imagination of Blackness and whiteness, particularly as it is only through Black presence that the white, female protagonist is coded as "defiant" and "independent."[28] In thoroughly stereotypical fashion, Central High is portrayed as prison-like (patrolled by Dobermans and armed guards), with students constantly scuffling or placing wagers. The neighborhood is populated by loiterers, gamblers, hustlers, and thieves. The players—predominantly Black and Latino—are portrayed as lazy, undisciplined, lewd, oversexed, and all about partying. They have "succeeded" in football only on the strength of "natural" athletic ability and other teams' misfortunes. In contrast to Molly's ease with Central's students and facilities, the characters coded as the "whitest" in the film (Molly's ex-husband Frank, his girlfriend Stephanie, and two stuffy private girls' headmistresses) are inflexible, rigidly conservative, and fearful of Central High's students. After winning over her new team through grit (outlasting all of the players in a running challenge), inability to be shocked or embarrassed (giving as good as she gets in profane exchanges and aiding and abetting a team prank), and choreographed conditioning drills (engaging the players through popular music and dance moves), McGrath introduces structure and increasing success to the players' lives. Through her work with Edwards and players Trumaine (Wesley Snipes), Bird (Mykel T. Williamson), Finch (Tab Thacker), Cerullo (Nick Corri), and Krushinski (Woody Harrelson), the Wildcats' "Blackness" licenses, authenticates, and empowers McGrath's white, female experimentation, liberation, and excellence.

In the both/and logic of the star vehicle and Hawn's noted feminine iconicity, her status as "coach"—or potential ascendant to patriarchal authority—is made "nonthreatening" by her endearing klutziness, naïve optimism, and her maternal relationship to her daughters, Alice (Robyn

Lively) and Marian (Brandy Gold), as well as to her team. Unlike Tami, who is a peer, Molly remains a "cool" mom to her supposedly "rough" players, each of whom is proven to simply need her attention, guidance, and structured practices and community to thrive. Indeed, in a pivotal custody hearing scene, Molly's slotback, Krushinski, wishes he "had a mother half as good as" Molly. And yet the film's tension is motivated, throughout, by Molly's potential to lose custody of her daughters due to her facility and intimacy with the players and the team's "inappropriate" behavior around the girls (featuring coarse language, underage drinking, and sexual encounters in the girls' presence). To lead the Wildcats to the championship victory *and* to secure custody of her daughters, Molly must see her coaching dream through in the name of her family, as a mother first, then as a coach. To the growing excitement of fans in the stands and to the thrill of her onlooking Wildcats and daughters, Molly comes to this realization at halftime of the championship game. She tells Frank, "The deal's off! You're not sending our girls to some school they don't want to go to, and you're not taking them away from me. And I'm not quitting my job here, either. . . . I don't want to be a quitter anymore. I don't want our girls to see a quitter. For *them*. Not for me." Molly can, apparently, be coach *and* mother, tough and "cute," embodying white, middle-class heterosexual mobility that is rewarded with an ideal balance of fraternal community, patriarchal tradition, and maternal love. Once again, here, football is *family*, with female expertise carrying on a patriarchal legacy while simultaneously "domesticating" and providing maternal support and structure to a previously undisciplined and comparatively unloved team.

Molly's ability to be mother *and* coach/father to her team apparently requires the absence, or literal sidelining and marginalization, of Black women within the film. The Central High cheerleaders, Trumaine's girlfriend, Marva (Ellie English), and Bird's girlfriend (who remains nameless) each appear in overtly stereotypical roles, respectively characterized by demonstrative physicality, sexual promiscuity, and/or gold-digging and cold dismissiveness. Judge A. Jordan (Royce Wallace) is the lone exception, as she looks kindly upon Molly's custody dilemma but also upbraids the coach's players as unruly "turkeys." As Anne Helen Petersen has written of the "cool girl" in film history, "We'd like to think of 'cool' as connotative of something progressive, even radical. But Cool Girls are neither, at least not precisely[;] to be 'cool' is to tread a fine line between something different, something almost masculine, but never anything *too* masculine, or assertive, or independent."[29] In *Wildcats*, "something different" comes through Molly's association with and acceptance by African American *men*, as a potential challenge to white patriarchy, at the same time that the cool girl retains all of the power to return to and be enveloped within the white, patriarchal status quo. Perhaps this is another reason many critics felt *Wildcats* lacked teeth. While her players have nowhere else to go, Molly's coaching job, in the end, not only holds no risk, but instead represents redoubled benefit—iconic of "masculine" reward (her coaching success is an extension of her father's paternal legacy) *and* "feminine" restoration (through parental custody and maternal ideals).

Indeed, though Hawn was frequently hailed for her work on *Wildcats* as both producer and star, the film was generally panned for its less successful repeat of Hawn's "adorable but goofy" entrée into a male enclave for which she'd received such glowing accolades (including a Best Actress Oscar nomination) in *Private Benjamin* (1980).[30] Female critics were notably kinder to the film, with Janet Maslin calling *Wildcats* "another of the iron-buttercup roles in which Miss Hawn has been specializing since 'Private Benjamin,' films in which her inspired dizziness masks an unexpectedly strong will."[31] Tops at the box office on its opening weekend, the *Los Angeles Times* noted, "'Wildcats' may be a crowd-pleaser, but you wish it were half as provocative as it is eager to please."[32]

And yet, as Reese Witherspoon's adoration suggests, *Wildcats* has remained a touchstone for a generation that came of age post–Title IX. For example, decades since its release, the film is regularly cited in discussions of the increased presence of female-identifying coaches of male football teams in high school, college, and professional ranks. A *Washington Post* essay focused on several female coaches in 2010, for instance, recalls, "Of course, in short shorts and with big hair, Goldie Hawn taught us this lesson almost a quarter-century ago" that coaching is not gender-specific, it's "'about inspiring kids . . . attention to detail and positive self-image.'"[33] And, in a profile of Natalie Randolph of Calvin Coolidge Senior High School in Washington, DC, the author acknowledges, "Randolph is tough, but players still appreciate the novelty of having a woman in charge. During one practice last month, the junior cornerback Ranard Ware chanted, 'Wildcats!' . . . Other players have asked if they could call [Randolph] Mom."[34] Though reporters identify the film as inspirational and a touchstone in feminist terms, Witherspoon's acknowledgement that there are "many types of feminism" is significant. The film itself is arguably representative of second-wave understandings of the right to pursue individual opportunity—particularly for blonde, heterosexual women who also belong in the family circle—a logic shared by *Quarterback Princess*.

In Our Flag Football Era? The NFL as Public Servant

Quarterback Princess and *Wildcats* were both released in an era in which the public service responsibilities of broadcasters were starting to be systematically dismantled. The broadcast media mandate and ethos of service in the public interest that defined industry practice from broadcasting's inception through the mid-1980s was undergirded by a logic of scarcity and corresponding "mass" audience address. With relatively few national network outlets, broadcasters had to reach an audience that would, broadly, feel "invited" into a program while still offering content unique enough to captivate. Criticism of this model points out that commercial media with such "mass," mainstream appeal (such as *Quarterback Princess*) typically defaulted to majoritarian and market-palatable ideals. Conventional, popular Hollywood cinema (such as *Wildcats*) arguably epitomizes these same "consensus" resolutions, even when contentious issues may be raised along the way. Though broadcast television—and the dominance of the "Big Three" national networks of ABC, CBS and NBC—remained the primary way by which the majority of US households received daily media, by the early 1990s this landscape had shifted.

As noted above, by the mid-1990s, cable became the dominant TV provider in most US homes. With the passage of the Telecommunications Act of 1996, understanding of the "public interest" was formally and irrevocably codified away from relatively few broadcast outlets and understanding public service through logics of scarcity with "mass" audience appeal, to a multiplicity of outlets with increasingly atomized appeal. Ideally, in this scenario a multiplicity of "choice" leads to a diversification of media voices and responsiveness to differentiated audiences. Post 2010s, with the enhanced mobility of internet protocol media (for example, allowing streaming video reception on phones and tablets as well as on traditional TVs and computers), à la carte, on-demand media has exponentially expanded, allowing for intensely individuated address and reception (for example, our curated social media feeds). If media providers are now absolved of serving in the broad, public interest, however, other corporate entities have, in this same, post–Telecommunications Act era, been rewarded for establishing "social responsibility" programs and charitable/community service and outreach divisions (particularly through tax benefits). Market actors are presumed to have the public's best interest at heart. Uniquely, in this context, the ethos of broadcasting still remains central to *sports* coverage, with its largely "shared" mass-audience availability and address. This ethos also remains foundational to professional sports leagues in their public outreach initiatives.

For the National Football League, investing in female-centered flag football programs has been one of its most recent "public service" initiatives. Partnered with Nike and Gatorade as well as with youth sports experience business RCX Sports and NFL team's community relations departments, the "Play!" and NFL FLAG initiatives are devoted to the expansion of flag football, particularly for girls at the high school level. Through donations to state athletic associations, camps and scholarship support, the league hopes to assure the future of the sport, particularly through the bodily commitment of women of color. Seeking to expand its *global* footprint, the NFL features stars such as Mexico's Diana Flores in its lobbying for the sport's acceptance into the Olympic Games and expansion of international league play. The NFL's "Run With It" commercial, featuring Flores, was the hit of the annual Super Bowl ad contest of 2023. The ad features Flores evading famous athletes as she runs and parkours from the Super Bowl venue through a mall, rooftops, hotel, pool deck bar, home, and through neighborhoods. Her exceptional athleticism and grace are undeniable. Notably, however, after-game coverage of Flores defaulted to "traditional" explanations of her expertise. In a featurette produced by NFL Films, Flores watches the Super Bowl commercial with her family, placing her—first and foremost—as a dutiful daughter and sister. She fell "in love" with football thanks to her father; she had previously been a ballerina, dancer, pianist, and gymnast; she has the talent (and talent agency behind her) to be a multi-tool star and an "emerging emblem of female empowerment."[35] While "Run With It" and its "family circle" featurette were designed particularly for the Super Bowl's traditionally conceived, mainstream, multigenerational, broad demographic audience, that summer's launch of the "Let's Play" campaign—featuring YouTube and social media influencers together with artists like Quay-Vo and athletes including US women's flag football quarterback Vanita Krouch—was intended for a more youthful, individuated, globally-oriented audience, imagined to be engaged in quick bites for the campaign's rollout across social media. And yet, across these streams, the NFL's Play campaign brings to mind Kristen Warner's theorization of "plastic representation," in which content creators engage "an initiative to remake existing source material with the least amount of changes to attract different audience demographics" while, here, still retaining and resonating with a presumptively "traditional," "mainstream," "broadcast"-based audience.[36]

Arguably, female-centric football narratives are still largely "sourced" from conventional stories of white female expertise and its contradictory duality: its power to be mobile *and* domesticated. There is, in this way, a residue that remains within and across the NFL's address to its audiences. Motifs of white, female expertise are, arguably, a fulcrum at which two streams meet, informing the NFL's address to both an imagined, white, cisgendered, heterosexual, middle-class audience of "broadcast" consumers, and an emergent, diversified youth audience addressed in individuated feeds. Here, the NFL appeals to Diversity, Equity, and Inclusion while "still adhering to" its own NFL Films, tradition-rich, didactic style.[37] All of these decades and new initiatives later, the NFL remains a critical site of resistance to thinking *differently* about race and gender constructs. This is significant in a broader social, political, economic, and mediated context in which—without much scholarly or community discussion—sports leagues increasingly have assumed roles as corporate civic leaders and benefactors, through underwriting youth sports development programs and providing media content rhetorically "in the public interest" in ways no longer mandated or supported by public actors.

In August 2024, the NFL launched its new season's promotional campaign with "This Is Football Country," an advertisement produced by the league's public relations partner, 72andSunny. The campaign's press release explains that it "champions the sport's inclusivity and global impact" showcasing "a diverse range of players" celebrating "football's universal appeal and unity, with appearances by notable figures like YouTube's Deestroying and college player Haley Van Voorhis, alongside NFL stars such as Stefon Diggs and Myles Garrett." It "aims to highlight football's role in connecting communities worldwide."[38] Given these aims— and in the larger context of flag football's explosive 44 percent growth in participation among females aged six to seventeen since 2023, the impending launch of a professional flag football league, and the sport's approaching 2028 Olympic debut[39]—it is striking that the closing images of the kickoff campaign feature a white, fair-featured young girl whose left wrist is adorned with friendship bracelets iconic of Taylor Swift's fan community. Proudly wearing a number twenty-six Philadelphia Eagles jersey in defiance of her entire, multigenerational, New York Giants–outfitted family, the girl—faced with their demonstrative shock and consternation—defiantly stands her ground, saying, "What? I go where Saquon goes!" Adorned in the authentic "on-field" gear of the former Giant, now-Eagle Saquon Barkley, white feminine football fandom is here, again, allied with Black male excellence as it authorizes her expertise and defiant independence and cool in the face of received traditions.

Football is presumed to be a broadly shared, historically revered, mainstream social institution. As such, football narratives are a key, cyclically

FIGURE 4.2: Screenshot from 2024 NFL advertising campaign, "This. Is. Football. Country."

reimagined and revivified site for struggles over questions of identity and social power in dialogue with corresponding social institutions. While these "texts" of football are most often conservative in that they typically resolve to conserve the status quo of patriarchal capitalism and cis-gendered hegemonic masculinity as constitutive of US cultural, social, and political common sense, *within* these narratives themselves, there may be paradoxical and contradictory fissures. In this sense, football is imagined as both an unchanging cultural touchstone *and* as a primary venue for visualizing social progress and change. As football historian Michael Oriard has written, more than any other sport, football embraces "the competing values of the modern and the antimodern" of progress *within* tradition.[40] Most football fictions are concerned with questions of rights, with the sport positioned as a terrain of pedagogical debate and resultant public good. Movies and TV about football are, in this way, not *about* football. Football is "community." And—as seen in *Quarterback Princess, Wildcats,* "Run With It," and in the post-Swift-Effect "This Is Football Country" campaign—football is "family," with white female expertise persistently, cyclically, as its idealized and rewarded heart.

Notes

1. VAB Fast Facts, "After Further Review: . . . Ready For It? Examining NFL's 2023 Season Viewership Growth," February 7, 2024, https://www.thevab.com/insight/After-Further-Review.

2. Jordan Mendoza, "Hall of Fame NFL Coach Tony Dungy Says Taylor Swift is Part of Why Fans Are 'Disenchanted,'" *USA Today*, January 13, 2024, n.p. Mendoza is quoting Tony Dungy.

3. See, for example, Lorraine Ali, "What's Behind the Right's Attack on Swift-Kelce Romance? Fear of a Powerful Woman," *Los Angeles Times*, January 31, 2024. https://www.latimes.com/california/story/2024–01–31/taylor-swift-the-nfl-and-the-conspiracy-to-rig-an-election.

4. VAB Fast Facts, "After Further Review."

5. Between 2020 and the opening of the 2023 season of Swift, women "working full-time coaching [in] football operations roles in the NFL" saw a 141% gain, with 223 employed across the league." See Tom Withers, Associated Press, "NFL's Look Changing as More Women Move into Prominent Roles at Teams Across League," *AP NFL*, November 21, 2023, https://www.apnews.com/article/nfl-women-female-executives-catherine-raiche-sam-rappaport-1a2647bf20489ca80b27f677166e8a1e.

6. Michael Oriard, *Reading Football: How the Popular Press Created an American Spectacle* (Chapel Hill: University of North Carolina Press, 1993), 274.

7. Victoria E. Johnson, *Sports TV* (New York: Routledge, 2021), 56. See also Travis Vogan, *ABC Sports: The Rise and Fall of Network Sports Television* (Berkeley: University of California Press, 2018), and Travis Vogan, "*Monday Night Football* and the Racial Roots of the Network TV Event," *Television & New Media* 18, no. 3 (2017): 235–51.

8. See, for example, CL Cole and Amy Hribar, "Celebrity Feminism: Nike Style, Post-Fordism, Transcendence, and Consumer Power," *Sociology of Sport Journal* 12, no. 4 (1995): 347–69, and Sarah Banet-Weiser and Laura Portwood-Stacer, "The Traffic in Feminism: An Introduction to the Commentary and Criticism on Popular Feminism," *Feminist Media Studies* 17, no. 5 (2017): 884–906.

9. Taylor M. Henry, "'They've Never Played the Game': 'Cool Sports Girls,' Gender Inequality, and *Garbage Time* in Sports Punditry," *Sociology of Sport Journal* 41 (2021): 193.

10. Leslie Heywood and Shari L. Dworkin, *Built to Win: The Female Athlete as Cultural Icon* (Minneapolis: University of Minnesota Press, 2003).

11. George Lipsitz, *The Possessive Investment in Whiteness: How White People Profit from Identity Politics* (Philadelphia, PA: Temple University Press, 1998).

12. For analysis of the "cool girl" persona in film and media, see Henry, above, and Anne Helen Petersen, "Jennifer Lawrence and the History of Cool Girls,"

Buzzfeed, February 28, 2014, http://www.buzzfeed.com/annehelenpetersen/jennifer-lawrence-and-the-history-of-cool-girls.

13. Julie D'Acci, *Defining Women: Television and the Case of Cagney and Lacey* (Chapel Hill: University of North Carolina Press, 1994), 2.

14. It is important to note that broadcasting as a mode of delivery still exists, even if most US households receive broadcast images via internet protocol or cable delivery providers. Sports programming is integral to keeping many broadcast entities viable even as each is part of a larger constellation of media outlets within any given corporate "family." For example, ABC is the broadcast arm of Disney, which owns cable "native" ESPN and is home to streamer Disney+.

15. Johnson, *Sports TV*, 25.

16. Anna McCarthy, *The Citizen Machine: Governing by Television in 1950s America* (New York: The New Press, 2010), 248.

17. Elayne Rapping, *The Movie of the Week: Private Spaces, Public Events* (Minneapolis: University of Minnesota Press, 1992); Laurie Schulze, "The Made-for-TV Movie: Industrial Practice, Cultural Form, Popular Reception," in *Hollywood In the Age of Television*, ed. Tino Balio (New York: Unwin Hyman, 1990), 358. In the transition to the cable and streaming eras, the TV movie has migrated to both "prestige" productions on premium/subscription cable outlets such as HBO or streamers like Netflix and, on a more regular basis, to cable channels targeting audiences that are imagined to be, demographically, more female, rural, and older, reminiscent of the broadcast era's wider scope of address (for example, Lifetime, OWN, Hallmark).

18. Nancy Hogshead-Makar and Andrew Zimbalist, eds., *Equal Play: Title IX and Social Change* (Philadelphia, PA: Temple University Press, 2007).

19. See, for example, Pete McMartin, "Tami Calls the Rams' Signals," *The Vancouver Sun*, September 23, 1980, 1; and "Girl Quarterback Darling of Media," *The Globe and Mail* (Toronto), November 19, 1981, n.p.

20. "It's CBS Six Days a Week," *Broadcasting* 105, no. 24 (December 12, 1983): 90.

21. As of this writing, this promotion is available at https://www.youtube.com/watch?v=scdLOaca-d0.

22. Rapping, *The Movie of the Week*, xii.

23. Rapping, *The Movie of the Week*, xl.

24. On conventional sports film narratives, iconography, and affirmation of American Dream ideology, see, especially, Aaron Baker, *Contesting Identities: Sports in American Film* (Urbana: University of Illinois Press, 2006), and Sean Crosson, *Sport and Film* (New York: Routledge, 2013).

25. Though one Black man is seen in the background at the school board meeting scene, he remains unnamed, with no dialogue, and he is not seen again in the film.

26. Goldie Hawn Hollywood Walk of Fame Induction Ceremony, May 4, 2017, https://www.youtube.com/watch?v=wiYuVA-ELjQ.

27. Madeline Berg and Dawn Chmielewski, "How Reese Witherspoon Became the World's Richest Actress," August 2, 2021, https://www.forbes.com/stories/celebrities/how-reese-witherspoon-became-the-worlds-richest-actress/.

28. Richard Dyer, "White," *Screen* 29, no. 4 (1988): 44–65.

29. Petersen, "Jennifer Lawrence."

30. Jagr., "Wildcats," *Variety*, February 12, 1986, 22. See also Gene Siskel, "The Cutsey Klutz Strikes Again in Tame 'Wildcats,'" *Chicago Tribune*, February 14, 1986, 26.

31. Janet Maslin, "'Wildcats' with Hawn," *New York Times*, February 14, 1986, C5.

32. Patrick Goldstein, "'Wildcats' Doesn't Put Points on Scoreboard," *Los Angeles Times*, February 13, 1986, Calendar, 6.

33. Petula Dvorak, "It Doesn't Matter if the X's and O's are Drawn By Someone with XXs," *Washington Post* (March 12, 2010), B1.

34. Juliet Macur, "A Football Coach Used to Tests Insists Her Players Pass Theirs," *New York Times*, May 10, 2010, D1.

35. Edward Cauich, "Mexican Football Star Diana Flores' Super Bowl Ad Broke Barriers. Can She Empower Women?" *Los Angeles Times*, March 13, 2023, https://www.latimes.com/sports/story/2023-03-13/mexican-football-star-diana-flores-super-bowl-ad-women. Representations of Diana Flores's tight-knit Mexican family and focus on her "traditional" roles conform to Arlene Davila's examination of the marketing industry's cyclical reinforcement and challenge to existing stereotypes of the "Hispanic" family. See Arlene Davila, *Latinos, Inc: The Marketing and Making of a People* (Berkeley: University of California Press, 2012).

36. Kristen J. Warner, "In the Time of Plastic Representation," *Film Quarterly* 71, no. 2 (2017): 32.

37. Warner, "In the Time of Plastic Representation," 35.

38. Audrey Kemp, "Best Ads of the Week: Guinness' Football Fever & Palliative Care's Unique Farewell," *The Drum*, August 23, 2024, https://www.thedrum.com/news/2024/08/23/best-ads-the-week-guinness-football-fever-palliative-care-s-unique-farewell.

39. Tashan Reed, "Why Flag Football's Olympic Inclusion Has Been 'Rocket Fuel' For Growth, Especially Among Women," *The Athletic*, July 17, 2024, https://www.nytimes.com/athletic/5604787/2024/07/17/flag-football-olympics-2028-rising-popularity/.

40. Michael Oriard, *King Football: Sport and Spectacle in the Golden Age of Radio and Newsreels, Movies and Magazines, the Weekly & Daily Press* (Chapel Hill: University of North Carolina Press, 2001), 68–69.

PART II

Athletes and Resistance

5

Women's Distance Running, Disordered Eating, and Sport Autopathography

JAIME SCHULTZ

A small but significant pattern emerged between 2013 and 2023 as six US women distance runners published memoirs that described their struggles with eating pathologies. The pattern grew more pronounced as other runners shared similar experiences in blogs, podcasts, magazine articles, and videos. For decades, scientists had documented connections between disordered eating and distance running, but the post-2013 surge of athletes' narratives signaled both a significant crisis and a growing swell of resistance against the sport's traditional power dynamics.[1]

I read the runners' narratives as "sport autopathographies," or athletes' personal accounts of traumas that are either endemic to or exacerbated by their experiences in sport. This builds on Anne Hunsaker Hawkins's foundational work regarding "pathography," a term she borrows from the neurologist and writer Oliver Sacks, who borrowed it from Sigmund Freud.[2] As Hawkins defines it, pathographies and, alternatively, autopathographies are a form "of autobiography or biography that describes personal experiences of illness, treatment, and sometimes death."[3] The genre differs from other forms of life writing in that "it is the illness itself, and not the writer's life-story, that shapes the narrative," explains scholar Garry Kinnane.[4]

Eight sport autopathographies make up the heart of this chapter: six memoirs and two digital stories. This includes the written works of Amber Sayer, Rachael Rose Steil, and Emily Pifer, who competed at the collegiate level, along with those published by professional and Olympic runners

Alexi Pappas, Kara Goucher, and Lauren Fleshman. Professional runners Allie Ostrander and Mary Cain similarly described their eating pathologies in video testimonials, which add another dimension to this analysis.[5]

There are several benefits to reading these texts as sport autopathographies. First, as Hawkins argues, pathographies reveal "significant truths about the cultures and value systems from which they sprang."[6] Taken collectively, the runners' narratives show the correlations between distance-running culture and their individual illnesses. Rather than asking runners why they choose to overtrain and under-fuel, this perspective situates those choices within environments that make them feel as though they are not really choices at all.

This is not to say that distance running causes disordered eating, but rather that there are aspects of the sport that put athletes at greater risk. By exposing those aspects, autopathographies offer important counter-narratives to the prevailing "sport-health ideology," which is, according to sociologist Ivan Waddington, "the broad consensus that 'sport is good for you.'"[7] Athletes seem to epitomize good health: they appear lean, strong, powerful, flexible, vital, and resilient; they are biomechanically efficient, physiologically fine-tuned, nutritionally optimized, and psychologically honed. But scientists distinguish between "health"—a state of mental, social, and physical well-being—and "fitness"—the quality of being able to perform a specific task. "Too many athletes," they conclude, "are fit but unhealthy."[8]

Olympic and professional distance runner Alexi Pappas provides a similar assessment in her 2021 memoir *Bravey*. As she argues, the "vast majority" of athletic programs "confuse *health* with *fitness*. Fitness is not an indicator of durability and sustainability; it is only an indicator of athletic ability at the present moment." Unfortunately, she continues, "Fitness is rewarded while health is taken for granted."[9] Autopathographies accord athletes the power to "talk back" to the cultural script that sport is a health-giving enterprise.[10]

In the process, autopathographers suggest points of intervention to improve their sport and the experiences of other athletes. "Pathography describes a profoundly destructive experience," writes Hawkins; "at the same time it testifies to the capacity to transform that experience in ways that heal."[11] In *Good for a Girl* (2023), Lauren Fleshman, a two-time NCAA Division I 5,000-meter national champion and professional runner, wonders how something as "ubiquitous" as eating pathologies in distance running can "have no counterattack?"[12] These autopathographies are a counterattack. They are acts of healing, resistance, empowerment, and transformation.

Finally, these autopathographers augment the existing scientific research on the traumas they describe. While science is crucial for understanding the correlates, consequences, prevalence, and effective treatments of disordered eating, autopathographies represent the lived experiences of women who feel the pressures of distance running's "lighter-is-faster" mentality; who know what it means to run far without sufficient sustenance; whose bodies break and mend and break again in the service of the sport to which they devote their lives.[13]

Despite these strengths, there are limits to using autopathographies as primary source material. Scholars of various forms of life writing raise important questions about the fidelity between one's lived experience and its representation. "Writing about an experience—any experience—inevitably changes it," Hawkins asserts.[14] Life does not unfold in narrative form. The narrative comes in fashioning stories out of the mundane; in the telling and retelling; in the omissions, embellishments, and emphases; in making the sequential consequential. Narrative-making is an editorial process.

Still, argues sociologist Arthur Frank in *The Wounded Storyteller*, "even edited stories remain true." He continues, "The stories we tell about our lives are not necessarily those lives as they were lived, but these stories become our experience of those lives. A published narrative of an illness is not the illness itself, but it can become the experience of the illness."[15] It is the experience of illness that matters here—the way it is communicated, disseminated, and understood; the way it shapes public perception, encourages action, and gives meaning to the problems of sport.

The use of life writing as source material is also limited by which women tell their stories. According to scholar G. Thomas Couser, autopathographers "tend to be white and upper middle class."[16] This characterization holds with the women studied here, which is perhaps unsurprising given the demographics of US distance running.[17] Additionally, each woman achieved some degree of athletic success. While this might suggest that disordered eating affects only elite athletes, Ostrander, who won the NCAA Division I steeplechase championship three times before turning pro, tells viewers that "under-fueling doesn't just exist at the top. It trickles down through the entire sport and the repercussions are heartbreaking."[18]

To address some of these shortcomings, as well as to integrate the scientific literature and the autopathographical texts, I engage in what literary scholar Gaston Franssen calls "double reading." In his study of patients' stories of chronic fatigue syndrome, Franssen considers the "literary aspects of the memoirs" with "the ways they can be considered exemplary narratives . . . in light of medical, sociological, and psychological insights into the condition."[19] This interdisciplinary, intertextual approach melds the meaning of trauma with its academic study to offer a more complete picture of eating pathologies in women's distance running.

Eating Pathologies

No segment of the population is immune from eating pathologies, a broad term that includes disordered eating and eating disorders. Disordered eating refers to a spectrum of unhealthy or harmful eating behaviors that may indicate the development of an eating disorder but fall below the clinical diagnostic threshold.[20] Fleshman alludes to this type of behavior in her memoir. In her efforts to lose weight and improve performance, she notes, "I never starved myself or skipped meals. I never threw up or binged in my closet." Although, in her assessment, this behavior did not rise to an eating disorder, she nevertheless recalls "food pushing"—foisting her food on a friend to avoid eating it herself—which she later recognizes as "a sign of disordered eating."[21]

Eating disorders are clinical diagnoses that meet the criteria outlined in the *American Psychiatric Association's Diagnostic and Statistical Manual of Mental Disorders*, including Anorexia Nervosa, Bulimia Nervosa, Binge Eating Disorder, and Other Specified Feeding and Eating Disorders.[22] In contrast to Fleshman, Amber Sayer describes her eating disorder in *PR: A Personal Record of Running from Anorexia* (2013). The former NCAA Division I athlete writes that she was obsessed with "consuming as little food as possible and running as much as I could. . . . By the time I was a junior [in high school], my anorexia had become so severe that I was weak and depleted from a chronic lack of calories."[23]

Compared to their non-athlete peers, athletes exhibit a higher incidence of eating pathologies, although the prevalence varies by sex, level of competition, and sport. Women, elite athletes, and athletes in "lean sports," where low body weight is aesthetically desirable or can improve performance—as it can in distance running—are especially susceptible to eating pathologies.[24] The authors of a 2023 study found that 9 percent of competitive women distance runners were at risk of an eating disorder and another 40 percent "were likely" to exhibit some form of disordered eating.[25] The runner-autopathographers speculate that those calculations vastly underestimate the problem. As Ostrander posits, "about 90 percent of the female distance runners I know have struggled with disordered eating or an eating disorder at some level."[26]

Explanations for the phenomenon abound. Certainly, there are individual factors at play. "The truth is, running often attracts a personality type that gets high off extreme discipline," observes Goucher, a three-time NCAA champion, two-time Olympian, World Champion silver medalist in 10,000-meter race, and accomplished marathoner. "On the upside, this kind of discipline can help us stick with rigorous training, but it can also go hand in hand with the numerology of an eating disorder."[27]

Yet the incidence of eating pathologies in distance running points to larger cultural issues. "These behaviors look like personal choices," explains Fleshman, "but they are made within a particular sporting environment."[28] Too often, however, the sporting environment is discounted in the search for individual etiology. "When a runner breaks after visible decreases in body, the judgment and blame falls on them exclusively," argues Pifer, a former NCAA Division I athlete. Consequently, "the coaches and trainers and people in positions of power and authority over the young athlete are held to no responsibility. It's so normalized to blame the athlete that even the athletes blame the athlete."[29]

Ostrander likewise criticizes the tendency to treat eating pathologies as "isolated incidents."

> When 80 percent of a class fails the exam, we don't ask why did each individual person fail, we ask what made the group fail. We're asking why does this girl have an eating disorder and not why do so many people have them and what can we do to fix this. It's clearly a systemic problem.[30]

Mary Cain, a running prodigy who signed a professional contract at age seventeen, uses similar phrasing in her 2019 video op-ed for the *New York Times*. Once "the fastest girl in America," Cain warns viewers that there is "a systemic crisis in women's sports . . . where young girls' bodies are being ruined by an emotionally and physically abusive system."[31]

Cain was one of those girls, as she chronicles in disturbing detail. In 2017, Alberto Salazar, then "the world's most famous track coach," invited her to join the elite Nike Oregon Project, the corporate initiative to improve US distance running. "When I first arrived, an all-male Nike staff became convinced that in order for me to get better, I had to become thinner and thinner and thinner."[32] Within three years at the Oregon Project, she suffered a series of broken bones and severe psychological distress brought on by the program's consistent and abusive emphasis on losing weight.

Cain's video signaled something of an autopathographical inflection point in women's distance running—only Sayer's memoir predates Cain's op-ed. Within a week of its publication, Cain's video registered more than 3.5 million views and prompted Nike to investigate its once-illustrious, and now-defunct, Oregon Project.[33] Even more, the video emboldened an ensuing cascade of runners to add their own stories to the growing hue and cry.[34] In this, they joined the contemporary swell of women athlete activists who challenged the conditions of sport that disenfranchise, disempower, abuse, and degrade them.[35] As one journalist observed in conversation with Goucher, "It seems as if we have reached a tipping point in the sport with more and more women coming forward to share their stories of abuse or mistreatment. There seems to be this air of 'enough.'"[36] Sport autopathographies are one way of saying "enough."

The Running Body

To critique distance-running culture is not to critique distance running itself. On the contrary, the autopathographers express deep affection for it. "I love to run," writes Pappas. "Because it is a way for me to push on and explore the outermost limits of myself, mentally and physically, in a way that is fundamentally good."[37] Fleshman describes how running "made me inhabit my body like nothing else could."[38] This sense of embodiment is a consistent theme in the women's stories. "I loved everything about running, being a runner," Pifer reflects; "the only way I have ever known how to feel 'the present' as anything more than an abstraction is to go running."[39] For Goucher, running was "where my body and brain found a natural presence." It "has been my source of inspiration, my religious practice, my way of interfacing with the world. It has taught me how to move and how to be in my body."[40]

While the women experience feelings of freedom in distance running, it also requires what Frank calls the "disciplined body-self" that "defines itself primarily in actions of *self-regimentation*."[41] The runner-autopathographers are nothing if not self-regimented. "Because distance runners are often high achievers, they are willing to do anything and make all sacrifices to improve," Sayer explains. "There often becomes a mentality that it *should* be painful and hard, or you aren't doing enough."[42] Yet, for the women in this study, self-regimentation starts to look a lot like obsession. They describe "sneaking" in extra runs when forbidden to do so.[43] They recall "runners, men and women both, who weigh their food by every gram and count their calories multiple times a day."[44] Others weigh themselves compulsively—up to five times daily, in the case of Pifer—and meticulously record their results. "I became diligent about keeping a daily weight logbook," Goucher recalls. "I recorded the date, my weight, the calories I consumed, and sometimes commentary to the side of how I felt about it."[45]

Much of the athletes' self-regimentation correlates with their desire to approximate what Pifer calls "the running body"—the sport's prevailing aesthetic. It is, describes Fleshman, "an ideal weight, an ideal body shape, one that almost nobody achieves without harming themselves."[46] Significantly, Pifer refers to "*the* running body," not "*my* running body," and the disciplined pursuit of the body-as-object eventually fractures the runners' original sense of embodiment. In Frank's words, the "single-minded pursuit of regimens transforms the body into 'it,'" as "the self becomes *disassociated* from this 'it.'"[47]

The autopathographers articulate feelings of disassociation as they chase the running body. "As I disciplined myself down, as I wasted away, I became a spectator of my body," Pifer writes.[48] Fleshman reflects that her restricted diet "was disconnecting me from my body."[49] Rachel Rose Steil, who competed for Aquinas College of the National Association of Intercollegiate Athletics, expresses similar feelings of alienation as her eating disorder consumed her. "I wanted so desperately to run with nature again, to run *with* my body, not against it."[50]

The running body is ubiquitous to the point of being obligatory, and its most prominent advertisement is the sport's top competitors. Sayer tells readers that "girls have posters of their running idols taped to their bedroom walls."

> Constant images of unnaturally thin runners can sink into your brain. As you push during a workout, trying to hammer out another repeat, what comes into your mind is the picture of your emaciated idol. "*If she can do it, so can I.*"[51]

Upon meeting renowned distance runner Shalane Flanagan, Pifer recalls that she "wanted to stop time and tape measure all of her dimensions and compare them all to mine." Pifer later researched "the fastest long-distance runners in history" to determine their body mass indices (BMIs)—the ratio of height to weight that is often, if problematically, used as a proxy for fitness. "I thought if my BMI dipped lower than every competitive runner in the country, and then the world, I would have a chance at matching their abilities."[52]

The culture of distance running reinforces the running body. It manifests in the revealing uniforms women wear, in the expectations of fans and sponsors (Nike is a recurring negative force in several autopathographies), and in media commentary that admires runners' "very thin and very young-looking," "toned," and "striated" bodies.[53] It manifests in popular literature—in books like Chris Lear's *Running with the Buffalos*, which chronicles the University of Colorado's 1998 national champion men's cross-country team, and in John L. Parker, Jr.'s *Once a Runner,* the cult classic that *Runner's World* deemed "the best novel ever written about running."[54] Pifer's favorite line from Parker's book: "gaunt is beautiful."[55] These texts become blueprints for distance runners' success.

Teammates exert additional pressures to pursue the running body.[56] Sayer excoriates the "toxic atmosphere" at Duke University, where she began her collegiate career. Among her teammates, there was "the atmosphere of constant food deprivation and the almost unspoken 'who can eat less than whom' contest, which was otherwise ubiquitous on the team."[57] Fleshman similarly describes a training group whose "culture around food and weight was unsettling. Comments about fellow competitors' bodies, regardless of sex, were sharp and frequent. Bluntness around food restriction made me question my own plate."[58] Consequently, observes Pifer, "disordered eating spread through teams quickly. You could watch it happen throughout a season. . . . The destruction of bodies was the primary narrative of collegiate women's cross country."[59]

Research shows that coaches further endorse the running body in ways that prioritize fitness over health. They regularly advise athletes to lose weight, and praise or reprimand them for successes and failures. Some coaches require regular weigh-ins, often in the presence of teammates, or mandate other methods of body assessment and surveillance.[60] Another tactic is to emphasize runners' "race weight," that is, the optimal weight at which to compete.

When Fleshman's performance flagged while competing for Stanford University's storied program, her coach asked her about her race weight. Fleshman confessed that she was heavier than she had been the previous season, to which her coach vaguely suggested that she should "eat healthy" but not "do anything stupid," which she translated as *"Don't get an eating disorder."*[61] Neither she nor her coach had a specific race weight in mind, but Fleshman looked to world champion Paula Radcliffe, who was the same height as Fleshman but ten pounds lighter. That "immediately became my goal race weight."[62] Soon, however, Fleshman found herself "hanging [her] confidence on appearance instead of function."[63]

Whereas Fleshman's coach did not specify a race weight, it was a different story for Cain. During her time training with the Oregon Project, Salazar "was constantly trying to get me to lose weight," Cain recounts. "He created an arbitrary number of 114 pounds, and he would usually weigh me in front of my teammates and publicly shame me when I wasn't hitting weight." Her career slumped. "I was running terrible during this time. It reached a point where I was on the starting line and I'd lost the race before I'd even started because in my head, all I was thinking about was not the time I was trying to hit but the number on the scale I saw earlier that day."[64]

There is, of course, a correlation between body composition and distance running. Put simply, carrying a lighter load makes for better running economy.[65] And the autopathographers do perform better after they lose weight, but their improvement is short-lived. "The thing about eating disorders in distance running is that, for a window of time, they appear to be effective—until they aren't," observes Pappas.[66] Sayer adds that the "paradigm of having the least amount of body fat possible and running performance improvement is one of the unfortunate truths of the sport."[67] But, as sports medicine experts note, "While weight loss may initially benefit performance, a chronic low energy state prevents the body's adaptation to training, and performance will inevitably plateau or decline."[68] However, a double reading reveals that these findings fail to reach the runners and their coaches. Overtraining and under-fueling is a temporarily successful solution, but the formula is unsustainable and, often, uncontrollable.

The Loss of Control

Frank writes that the most "important action problems" for the disciplined body-self "are those of control."[69] Indeed, the theme of control—over one's training, diet, weight, performance, relationships, and emotions—is stitched throughout all eight autopathographies. "I began to slowly restrict my eating in an effort to control my body and be able to control my results as well," Ostrander tells viewers. "Having control over my body and size made me feel like I was in control of my performance."[70] Goucher's need for control transcended sport. "Controlling my eating seemed like a way to gain control over the ups and downs of life," she writes.[71]

Because control is integral to the formation of the disciplined body-self, it "experiences its gravest crisis in loss of control," Frank argues.[72] In that regard, the runners describe three corporeal crises that erode their feelings of control: maturation, performance decline, and injury. The third crisis, injury, also signals a narrative turn after which the runners begin to reconcile and repair the fractured body-self.

Biologic maturation is the transitional phase between prepubertal childhood and adulthood. For cis girls, maturation is typically marked by anatomical and physiological changes, some of which can be detrimental to performance, at least temporarily.[73] Goucher recalls the dismay of going through puberty during her junior year of high school—the process delayed by high training loads and low body fat, as it is for so many women runners. "Hips appeared, and breasts, too. I felt like I was getting fat, clumsy, and slow. I hated my body. I struggled to adjust."[74] For these reasons, puberty can represent a "death sentence" for women runners, as Pappas puts it. Ostrander calls it the "kiss of death."[75] While research on the effects of puberty on athletic performance is limited, what little there is supports the women's experiences.[76]

For some runners, the answer is to delay maturation as long as possible. As Ostrander shares, "When the media and adults in my life suggested that puberty and the weight gain that often comes with it would slow me down it was a simple decision. I just wouldn't do that. I knew that food was required to gain weight, so I just decided to not give myself the fuel that I needed."[77] Researchers refer to Ostrander's strategy as one that results in low energy availability, "a state in which the body does not have enough energy to support all physiological functions needed to maintain optimal health."[78] One outcome of this is primary amenorrhea, in which cis girls do not have their first periods (menarche) until after age fifteen. Although primary amenorrhea was exactly what Ostrander hoped to achieve, it can affect estrogen production, which can, in turn, compromise bone health and accrual and cause other health-related concerns.[79]

The same is true of secondary amenorrhea, in which a woman who has previously menstruated loses her period for three or more months.[80] Despite the risks associated with menstrual disturbances, several runners regard secondary amenorrhea as a badge of honor that indicates their discipline and approximation of the running body. "It felt freeing," Fleshman muses. "The decision to ignore my absent period felt like taking agency over my performance outcomes."[81] Alternatively, they see the return of menstruation as a sign of defeat. When Steil's period returns after a three-year absence, she confesses, "that blood, more than anything, made the weight gain official, made me a failure."[82]

Low energy availability, menstrual disturbance, and decreased bone mineral density—a relationship known as the female athlete triad—can increase the risk of bone fracture, slow healing, and the likelihood of developing osteopenia and osteoporosis, or weakened, porous bones.[83] When Pifer's period stopped in college, she searched "female athlete triad" on the internet. "I felt pride about what, apparently, was happening inside my body. I ignored the part about bones weakening; red flags flashed green." She later experienced multiple fractures, including one in which her "pelvic bone had split in two."[84]

In fact, each autopathographer sustained multiple bone stress injuries throughout their career that were, most likely, associated with the female athlete triad. Sayer was nineteen years old when she had her first period.

"My delayed menarche further exacerbated my bone loss because estrogen is essential in healthy bone maintenance," she explains.

> [M]y body had to "steal" calcium from my bones for daily routine functions. . . . My bones became so leeched of calcium that by the age of sixteen, my bone density scan showed I had severe osteopenia in my hips and wrists and nearly osteoporosis in my spine. The mineral density of my bones (an indication of their strength) was equated to that of an 82-year old. Practically speaking, this meant my susceptibility to injury, particularly stress fractures, was very high.[85]

Ostrander likewise experienced menstrual dysfunction before "the injury cycle struck. Over the course of five years, I got seven bone stress injuries."[86] When one of Fleshman's Stanford teammates fell off a skateboard, she sustained "two compound fractures and a spiral fracture broke her tibia into hundreds of tiny pieces. The injury exposed that she had osteoporosis and had never gotten her period." Fleshman wonders "if anyone had ever asked her about it or cared."[87]

The same three conditions that characterize the triad have also been theorized along a broader spectrum known as Relative Energy Deficiency in Sport (RED-S), which includes cardiovascular, gastrointestinal, metabolic, psychological, and other disturbances.[88] In addition to compromised bone health, Sayer's eating disorder caused electrolyte imbalances, permanent heart and gall bladder damage, depression, fertility concerns, and alienation from her friends and family. Cain also experienced the effects of RED-S. During her time with the Oregon Project, she sustained five bone fractures, engaged in self-harm, and experienced suicidal ideation.

Pappas managed to stave off injury until she was twenty-seven years old, which she credits to not fighting her body's natural maturation. When she refused to quit high school soccer to specialize in cross-country, the latter coach kicked her off the team. It may have been an advantage:

> The ironic twist is that my forced retirement from high school running became a major advantage in my later growth as an NCAA and then professional athlete. I inadvertently stopped training just long enough for my body to go through puberty without the strain of overtraining, which is exactly the challenge that most girls in distance running face at that age. . . . I rode the puberty wave and then, when the time was right, I gradually increased my training."[89]

While Pappas was able to transition through this crucial stage of development without rebelling against it, the other runner-autopathographers were not. This is, in Pappas's estimation, because "the distance running

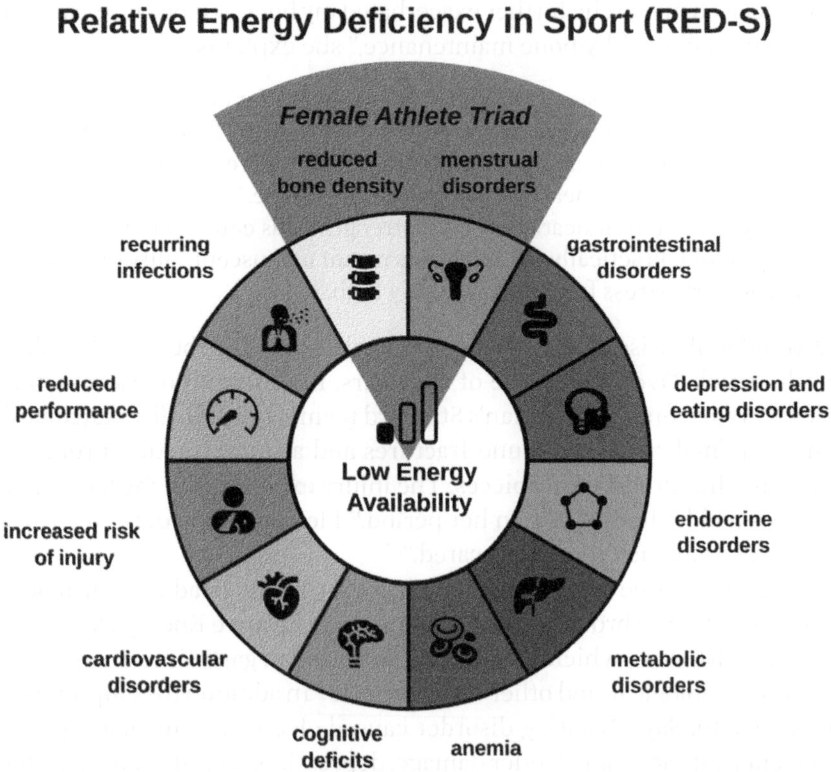

FIGURE 5.1: The Female Athlete Triad is characterized by low energy availability, menstrual disturbance, and decreased bone mineral density. The conditions that characterize the Female Athlete Triad have been theorized along a broader spectrum known as Relative Energy Deficiency in Sport (RED-S), which includes cardiovascular, gastrointestinal, metabolic, psychological, and other disturbances. Image from Wikimedia Commons.

world is not structured to embrace female athletes."[90] Rather, the sport is "designed off of a male model," says Ostrander. "The progression of a male distance runner is generally linear," where boys and men continue to get faster over time. "The same is expected of females," Ostrander elaborates, but it doesn't usually work that way. Instead, the hormonal changes that typical cis boys go through can be advantageous to athletic performance, while it can be the opposite for typical cis girls. "This heightens fear and uncertainty around a changing body, putting pressure on girls to control their performance and therefore their body during a time when fluctuations in body and performance might actually be what's best for their long-term success."[91] Consequently, Pappas explains, "In an effort to please their coaches and keep up with their male teammates . . . many female athletes overtrain and don't eat enough during this critical growth phase instead of allowing puberty to naturally take its course."[92]

We know, at least anecdotally, that female maturation can be associated with performance plateaus and declines in distance running and other sports. But we need data to establish the facts. Ostrander tells viewers that the "lack of research" about the effects of puberty on women's distance-running performance "means that most girls approach it with uncertainty and fear. This leads to disordered eating, relative energy deficiency, limiting beliefs, damage to your self-confidence, and ultimately, fewer women reaching their potential." If researchers could provide runners with a better, data-driven "roadmap" for navigating puberty, it might dissuade them from engaging in dangerous practices to resist maturation.[93] In other words, listening to the stories of women distance runners would forge an important line of research.

Regaining Control

In each narrative, it is only after the crisis of injury that the women begin to rearticulate their body-selves. They all suspect that they are causing themselves harm as they adopt the "elite athlete lifestyle of continual caloric restriction and control," but as long as they can perform, they can hold those suspicions at bay.[94] With injury and other forms of brokenness, however, runners must confront what Pifer calls the "crimes against our bodies" to begin the process of restoring one's health.[95] As such, their stories unfold according to what Frank identifies as "quest narratives," in which the runners eventually "accept illness and seek to use it." Their eating pathologies are "the occasion for a journey that becomes a quest[;] the quest is defined by the ill person's belief that something is to be gained from the experience."[96]

In this respect, the runners express three "somethings" they hope to gain by telling their stories. First, storytelling is part of their own healing process—a therapeutic act that allows them to come to terms with what they have endured and why. They are never entirely free from their pathologies. Rather, they become members of what Frank calls the "remission society," made up of people who "were effectively well but could never be considered cured."[97] As Steil writes towards the end of her memoir, "I was not fixed. The eating disorder lingered, and the desire to lose weight was still there." But in allowing herself to heal, she muses, "I felt stronger, wiser, and yes, heavier, but I still felt the same joy and freedom in running that I had had ever since I first began, before competition, before weight and food had ever invaded my mind."[98] She has engaged in "the process of the self returning to the body" that Pifer describes.[99]

Second, the runner-autopathographers use their stories to help others, a frequent theme in illness narratives. As Hawkins asserts, "In pathography the need to *tell* others so often becomes the wish to *help* others."[100] For example, while Sayer acknowledges that her story is "unique," she hopes that it "can be used as a tool for athletes, coaches, parents, friends, teammates, and peers to help address the pervasive issue of eating disorders in young female distance runners and other athletes."[101]

Third, the runner-autopathographers use their narratives to effect change. For Cain, one solution to the "male model" of distance running is to put "more women in power." As she ruminates, "Part of me wonders if I had worked with more female psychologists, nutritionists, and even coaches, where I'd be today." Cain has since established Atalanta, a professional women's running team that also mentors girls in underserved areas of New York City. "I'm trying to disrupt the current traditional model of professional teams," Cain told *Runner's World*.[102] Fleshman, too, retired from competition and began coaching a team sponsored by Oiselle, the "by women, for women athletic apparel company" that both she and Goucher joined after leaving Nike.[103] Fleshman's approach "started with health," not fitness. "At the center of my coaching was the development of the empowered woman."[104]

With these efforts, Fleshman argues, we can begin to achieve "true equality in sport." To that end, she closes *Good for a Girl* with a list of actions "we need" to further the cause for equality. She asserts that "we need" administrative policies around eating disorders, better research, and the promotion of eating disorder literacy. "We need" certifications for working with female athletes that involve education about physiology, maturation, and development, rules about uniforms, and mandatory reporting systems. "But we also need stories," she concludes. "A flood of them. The invisible and the forbidden. The small stuff that adds up to big change."[105] The stories these eight autopathographers tell open the floodgates for big change. Perhaps the first thing we really need to do, then, is to listen.

Notes

1. There are different opinions about what constitutes "long-distance" running, particularly where it differentiates from "middle-distance" events. In this chapter, long-distance running refers to any event greater than 3,000 meters. Early scientific publications on distance running and eating pathology

include J. D. Norval, "Running Anorexia," *South African Medical Journal* 58, no. 26 (1980): 1024; Alayne Yates, Kevin Leehey, and Catherine M. Shisslak, "Running—An Analogue of Anorexia?" *New England Journal of Medicine* 308, no. 5 (1983): 251–55; James A. Blumenthal, Leslie C. O'Toole, and Jonathan L. Chang, "Is Running an Analogue of Anorexia Nervosa? An Empirical Study of Obligatory Running and Anorexia Nervosa," *JAMA* 252, no. 4 (1984): 520–23; and Lori A. Goldfarb and Thomas G. Plante, "Fear of Fat in Runners: An Examination of the Connection Between Anorexia Nervosa and Distance Running," *Psychological Reports* 55, no 1 (1984): 296.

2. Oliver Sacks, *Awakenings* (New York: Vintage, 1999). In *Leonardo da Vinci and a Memory of His Childhood* (New York: Norton, 1964), Sigmund Freud uses the concept of pathography to explain the relationship between psychoanalysis, history, and biography.

3. Anne Hunsaker Hawkins, *Reconstructing Illness: Studies in Pathography*, 2nd ed. (West Lafayette, IN: Purdue University Press, 1999), 1.

4. Garry Kinnane, "Metaphor, Pathography, and Hysteria: Recent American Writing about Illness," *Critical Review* 40 (2000): 103. The "autopathographic genre" also includes visual culture, social media, graphic novels, and other representational forms. See, as examples, Tamar Tembeck, "Selfies of Ill Health: Online Autopathographic Photography and the Dramaturgy of the Everyday," *Social Media + Society* 2, no. 1 (2016), doi:10.1177/2056305116641343; Linda Nesby and Anita Salamonsen, "Youth Blogging and Serious Illness," *Medical Humanities* 42, no. 1 (2016): 46–51; John Derby, "Accidents Happen: An Art Autopathography on Mental Disability," *Disability Studies Quarterly* 33, no. 1 (2013); Tamar Tembeck, "Exposed Wounds: The Photographic Autopathographies of Hannah Wilke and Jo Spence," *RACAR: Revue d'art canadienne* 33, no. 1 (2008): 87–101; Emily Waples, "Avatars, Illness, and Authority: Embodied Experience in Breast Cancer Autopathographics," *Configurations* 22, no. 2 (2014): 153–81; and Steven Wilson, "Digital Autopathography: Relational Modes of Illness Writing in Marie-Dominique Arrighi's *K, Histoires de Crabe*," *Essays in French Literature and Culture* 58 (2021): 139–55.

5. Amber Sayer, *PR: A Personal Record of Running from Anorexia* (College Station, TX: Virtualbookworm.com, 2013); Rachael Rose Steil, *Running in Silence: My Drive for Perfection and the Eating Disorder That Fed It* (Virginia Beach, VA: Köehlerbooks, 2020); Emily Pifer, *The Running Body: A Memoir* (Pittsburgh: Autumn House Press, 2022); Alexi Pappas, *Bravey: Chasing Dreams, Befriending Pain, and Other Big Ideas* (New York: Dial Press, 2021); Kara Goucher with Mary Pilon, *The Longest Race: Inside the Secret World of Abuse, Doping, and Deception on Nike's Elite Running Team* (New York: Gallery Books, 2023); Lauren Fleshman, *Good for a Girl: A Woman Running in a Man's World* (New York, Penguin Press, 2023); Allie Ostrander, "An Eating Disorder Nearly Ended My Career. I'm Not Alone," streamed live on June 3, 2023, YouTube video, 19:15, https://www.youtube.com/watch?v=W1eGSayIxyE&t=55s; Mary Cain, "I Was the Fastest Girl in America, Until I Joined Nike," *New York Times*, November

7, 2019, https://www.nytimes.com/video/opinion/100000006788354/nike-running-mary-cain.html.

6. Hawkins, *Reconstructing Illness,* ix–x.

7. Ivan Waddington, *Sport, Health and Drugs: A Critical Sociological Investigation* (London: E & FN Spon, 2000), 11. See also Dominic Malcolm, *Sport, Medicine and Health: The Medicalization of Sport?* (London: Routledge, 2017), 1.

8. Philip B. Maffetone and Paul B. Laursen, "Athletes: Fit but Unhealthy?" *Sports Medicine—Open* 2, no. 1 (2016): 24.

9. Pappas, *Bravey*, 68. Emphasis in original.

10. Sidonie Smith and Julia Watson, *Reading Autobiography: A Guide for Interpreting Life Narratives,* 2nd. ed. (Minneapolis: University of Minnesota Press, 2010), 146.

11. Hawkins, *Reconstructing Illness,* xix.

12. Fleshman, *Good for a Girl,* 135.

13. Traci Lyn Carson, Troy Tournat, Kendrin Sonneville, Ronald F. Zernicke, and Carrie Karvonen-Gutierrez, "Cultural and Environmental Associations with Body Image, Diet and Well-Being in NCAA DI Female Distance Runners: A Qualitative Analysis," *British Journal of Sports Medicine* 55, no. 8 (2021): 433–37.

14. Hawkins, *Reconstructing Illness,* 15.

15. Arthur Frank, *The Wounded Storyteller: Body, Illness, and Ethics* (University of Chicago Press, 1995), 22.

16. G. Thomas Couser, *Recovering Bodies: Illness, Disability, and Life-Writing* (Madison: University of Wisconsin Press, 1997), 4.

17. See Alison Mariella Désir, *Running While Black: Finding Freedom in a Sport That Wasn't Built for Us* (New York: Portfolio, 2022); Jay Jennings, "Why Is Running So White?" *Runner's World,* November 15, 2011, https://www.runnersworld.com/runners-stories/a20807821/why-is-running-so-white/.

18. Ostrander, "An Eating Disorder Nearly Ended My Career."

19. Gaston Franssen, "Narratives of Undiagnosability: Chronic Fatigue Syndrome Life-Writing and the Indeterminacy of Illness Memoirs," *Philosophy, Psychiatry, & Psychology* 27, no. 4 (2020): 403–18.

20. Berg Sophia, Pritchett Kelly, Dana Ogan, and Abigail Larson, "Self Reported History of Eating Disorders, Training, Weight Control Methods, and Body Satisfaction in Elite Female Runners Competing at the 2020 US Olympic Marathon Trials," *International Journal of Exercise Science* 15, no. 2 (2022): 721–32; Ryley P. Mancine, Donald W. Gusfa, Ali Moshrefi, and Samantha F. Kennedy, "Prevalence of Disordered Eating in Athletes Categorized by Emphasis on Leanness and Activity Type—A Systematic Review," *Journal of Eating Disorders* 8, no. 1 (2020): 1–9.

21. Fleshman, *Good for a Girl,* 105.

22. American Psychiatric Association, "What Are Eating Disorders?" accessed May 14, 2023, https://www.psychiatry.org/patients-families/eating-disorders/what-are-eating-disorders.

23. Sayer, *PR*, viii, 36.

24. Jorunn Sundgot-Borgen and Monica Klungland Torstveit, "Prevalence of Eating Disorders in Elite Athletes is Higher than in the General Population," *Clinical Journal of Sport Medicine* 14, no. 1 (2004): 25–32; Jorunn Sundgot-Borgen, Monica Torstveit, "Aspects of Disordered Eating Continuum in Elite High-intensity Sports," *Scandinavian Journal of Medicine & Science in Sports* 20 (Suppl. 2), 112–21; Christopher R. Dennison, Lisa Kellar, and Jeff Lucas, "Gender Differences in Eating Disorder Risk among NCAA Division I Cross Country and Track Student-Athletes," *Journal of Sports Medicine* (2019), https://doi.org/10.1155/2019/503587.

25. R.A. Dervish, Laura J. Wilson, and Christopher Curtis, "Investigating the Prevalence of Low Energy Availability, Disordered Eating and Eating Disorders in Competitive and Recreational Female Endurance Runners," *European Journal of Sport Science* 23, no. 5 (2023): 869–76. See also Angela J. Hulley and Andrew J. Hill, "Eating Disorders and Health in Elite Women Distance Runners," *International Journal of Eating Disorders* 30, no. 3 (2001): 312–17.

26. Ostrander, "An Eating Disorder Nearly Ended My Career."

27. Goucher with Pilon, *The Longest Race*, 28.

28. Fleshman, *Good for a Girl*, 89.

29. Pifer, *The Running Body*, 173.

30. Ostrander, "An Eating Disorder Nearly Ended My Career."

31. Cain, "I Was the Fastest Girl in America."

32. Cain, "I Was the Fastest Girl in America."

33. Due, in large part, to Goucher's testimony, Salazar was indefinitely banned from coaching athletics for doping offenses and sexual and emotional misconduct. See Kevin Draper and Matthew Futterman, "Disgraced Running Coach Was Barred for Life for Alleged Sexual Abuse," *New York Times*, January 31, 2022, https://www.nytimes.com/2022/01/31/sports/alberto-salazar-sexual-assault.html#:~:text=Salazar%20was%20first%20put%20on,both%20emotional%20and%20sexual%20misconduct.

34. See Chris Chavez, "Inside the Toxic Culture of the Nike Oregon Project 'Cult,'" *Sports Illustrated*, November 13, 2019, https://www.si.com/track-and-field/2019/11/13/mary-cain-nike-oregon-project-toxic-culture-alberto-salazar-abuse-investigation; Matthew Futterman, "Another of Alberto Salazar's Runners Says He Ridiculed Her Body for Years," *New York Times*, November 14, 2019, https://www.nytimes.com/2019/11/14/sports/olympics/alberto-salazar-nike.html; Talya Minsberg, "'Fat Talks,' an Investigation, and a Reckoning: How Collegiate Runners Forced Reform," *New York Times*, August 12, 2020, https://www.nytimes.com/2020/08/12/sports/women-track-athletes-coaches-abuse.html.

35. See Cheryl Cooky, "Women, Sports, and Activism," *Oxford Handbook of US Women's Social Movement Activism*, ed. Holly J. McGannon, Verta A. Taylor, Jo Reger, and Rachel L. Einwohner (New York: Oxford University Press, 2017): 602–20; Celia Valiente, "Women, Sport, and Activism: An International Perspective," *Routledge Handbook of Sport, Leisure, and Social Justice*,

ed. Stefan Lawrence, Joanne Hill, and Rasul A. Mowatt (London: Routledge, 2024): 59–70.

36. Talya Minsberg, "In Her New Book, Kara Goucher Keeps Running Accountable," *New York Times*, March 25, 2023, https://www.nytimes.com/2023/03/25/sports/running-goucher-longest-race.html.

37. Pappas, *Bravey*, 5.

38. Fleshman, *Good for a Girl*, 9.

39. Pifer, *The Running Body*, 108.

40. Goucher with Pilon, *The Longest Race*, 13, 263.

41. Frank, *Wounded Storyteller*, 41. Emphasis in original.

42. Sayer, *PR*, 154. Emphasis in original.

43. Sayer, *PR*, 31.

44. Goucher with Pilon, *The Longest Race*, 28.

45. Goucher with Pilon, *The Longest Race*, 90.

46. Fleshman, *Good for a Girl*, 82.

47. Frank, *Wounded Storyteller*, 41.

48. Pifer, *The Running Body*, 158.

49. Fleshman, *Good for a Girl*, 117.

50. Steil, *Running in Silence*, 71. Emphasis in original.

51. Sayer, *PR*, ii; 153–54. Emphasis in original.

52. Pifer, *The Running Body*, 14.

53. Pifer, *The Running Body*, 123.

54. David Willey, "A Fan's Notes," *Runner's World*, December 2007, 2020.

55. Quoted in Pifer, *The Running Body*, 7.

56. Justine J. Reel, Sonya SooHoo, Trent A. Petrie, Christy Greenleaf, and Jennifer E. Carter, "Slimming Down for Sport: Developing a Weight Pressures in Sport Measure for Female Athletes," *Journal of Clinical Sport Psychology* 4, no. 2 (2010): 99–111.

57. Sayer, *PR*, 147, 153.

58. Fleshman, *Good for a Girl*, 137.

59. Pifer, *The Running Body*, 174.

60. Dana K. Voelker, Amanda J. Visek, Jordyn L. Learner, and Miranda DiBiasio, "Toward Understanding of Coaches' Role in Athletes' Eating Pathology: A Systematic Review and Ecological Application to Advance Research," *Psychology of Sport and Exercise* 58 (2022): 102059; Peiling Kong and Lynne M. Harris, "The Sporting Body: Body Image and Eating Disorder Symptomatology Among Female Athletes from Leanness Focused and Nonleanness Focused Sports," *Journal of* Psychology 149, no. 2 (2015): 141–60; Anne C. Muscat and Bonita C. Long, "Critical Comments about Body Shape and Weight: Disordered Eating of Female Athletes and Sport Participants," *Journal of Applied Sport Psychology* 20, no. 1 (2008): 1–24.

61. Fleshman, *Good for a Girl*, 80–81. Emphasis in original.

62. Fleshman, *Good for a Girl*, 120.

63. Fleshman, *Good for a Girl*, 138.

64. Cain, "I Was the Fastest Girl in America."

65. Peter G. Weyand and J. Adam Davis, "Running Performance Has a Structural Basis," *Journal of Experimental Biology* 208, no. 14 (2005): 2625–31; Adrien Sedeaud, Andy Marc, Adrien Marck, Frédéric Dor, Julien Schipman, Maya Dorsey, Amal Haida, Geoffroy Berthelot, and Jean-Francois Toussaint, "BMI, a Performance Parameter for Speed Improvement," *PloS one* 9, no. 2 (2014): e90183.

66. Pappas, *Bravey,* 69.

67. Sayer, *PR,* 207–8.

68. Emily Todd, Niall Elliott, and Nicky Keay, "Relative Energy Deficiency in Sport (RED-S)," *British Journal of General Practice* 72, no. 719 (2022): 295–97; Trent Stellingwerff, Ida A. Heikura, Romain Meeusen, Stéphane Bermon, Stephen Seiler, Margo L. Mountjoy, and Louise M. Burke, "Overtraining Syndrome (OTS) and Relative Energy Deficiency in Sport (RED-S): Shared Pathways, Symptoms and Complexities," *Sports Medicine* 51, no. 11 (2021): 2251–2280; Rachel K. Langbein, Daniel Martin, Jacquelyn Allen-Collinson, and Patricia C. Jackman, "'It's Hard to Find Balance When You're Broken': Exploring Female Endurance Athletes' Psychological Experience of Recovery from Relative Energy Deficiency in Sport (RED-S)," *Performance Enhancement & Health* 10, no. 1 (2022): 100214.

69. Frank, *Wounded Storyteller,* 41.

70. Ostrander, "An Eating Disorder Nearly Ended My Career."

71. Goucher with Pilon, *The Longest Race,* 24.

72. Frank, *Wounded Storyteller,* 41.

73. Adam D. G. Baxter-Jones, Angela M. Thompson, and Robert M. Malina," Growth and Maturation in Elite Young Female Athletes," *Sports Medicine and Arthroscopy Review* 10, no. 1 (2002): 42–49.

74. Goucher with Pilon, *The Longest Race,* 18.

75. Pappas, *Bravey,* 70; Ostrander, "An Eating Disorder Nearly Ended My Career."

76. S. Szczesny and J. Coudert, "Changes in Running Speed and Endurance Among Girls During Puberty," in *Kinanthropometry IV: Proceedings of the International Congress on Youth, Leisure and Physical Activity*, ed. William Duquet and James A. P. Day (London: E & FN Spon, 1993), 268–84.

77. Ostrander, "An Eating Disorder Nearly Ended My Career."

78. Paulina Wasserfurth, Jana Palmowski, Andreas Hahn, and Karsten Krüger, "Reasons for and Consequences of Low Energy Availability in Female and Male Athletes: Social Environment, Adaptations, and Prevention," *Sports Medicine-Open* 6, no. 1 (2020): 44.

79. Jarmo Karpakka, Juha Leppävuori, Sakari Orava, and Jorma Heikkinen, "Recurrent Stress Fractures in a Female Athlete with Primary Amenorrhea: A Case Report," *Clinical Journal of Sport Medicine* 4, no. 2 (1994): 136–37; Nikolaos D. Roupas and Neoklis A. Georgopoulos, "Menstrual Function in Sports," *Hormones* 10 (2011): 104–16; Courtney A. Marsh and Frances W. Grimstad,

"Primary Amenorrhea: Diagnosis and Management," *Obstetrical & Gynecological Survey* 69, no. 10 (2014): 603–12.

80. Mitchell J. Rauh, Michelle Barrack, and Jeanne F. Nichols, "Associations between the Female Athlete Triad and Injury among High School Runners," *International Journal of Sports Physical Therapy* 9, no. 7 (2014): 948. Michelle T. Barrack, Marta D. Van Loan, Mitchell Rauh, and Jeanne F. Nichols, "Disordered Eating, Development of Menstrual Irregularity, and Reduced Bone Mass Change after a 3-Year Follow-Up in Female Adolescent Endurance Runners," *International Journal of Sport Nutrition and Exercise Metabolism* 31, no. 4 (2021): 337–44.

81. Fleshman, *Good for a Girl*, 118.

82. Steil, *Running in Silence*, 201.

83. See Mary Jane De Souza, Aurelia Nattiv, Elizabeth Joy, Madhusmita Misra, Nancy I. Williams, Rebecca J. Mallinson, Jenna C. Gibbs et al. "2014 Female Athlete Triad Coalition Consensus Statement on Treatment and Return to Play of the Female Athlete Triad," *British Journal of Sports Medicine* 48, no. 4 (2014): 289. Researchers have also formulated the male athlete triad. See Aurelia Nattiv, Mary Jane De Souza, Kristen J. Koltun, Madhusmita Misra, Andrea Kussman, Nancy I. Williams, Michelle T. Barrack, Emily Kraus, Elizabeth Joy, and Michael Fredericson, "The Male Athlete Triad—A Consensus Statement from the Female and Male Athlete Triad Coalition, Part 1: Definition and Scientific Basis," *Clinical Journal of Sport Medicine* 31, no. 4 (2021): 335–48; Qiang Zhang, Jonathan Greenbaum, Wei-Dong Zhang, Chang-Qing Sun, and Hong-Wen Deng, "Age at Menarche and Osteoporosis: A Mendelian Randomization Study," *Bone* 117 (2018): 91–97; Yimei Yang, Shanshan Wang, and Hui Cong, "Association between Age at Menarche and Bone Mineral Density in Postmenopausal Women," *Journal of Orthopaedic Surgery and Research* 18, no. 1 (2023): 51.

84. Pifer, *The Running Body*, 89.

85. Sayer, *PR*, 186.

86. Ostrander, "An Eating Disorder Nearly Ended My Career."

87. Fleshman, *Good for a Girl*, 96–97.

88. Margo Mountjoy, Jorunn Sundgot-Borgen, Louise Burke, Kathryn E. Ackerman, Cheri Blauwet, Naama Constantini, Constance Lebrun et al. "International Olympic Committee (IOC) Consensus Statement on Relative Energy Deficiency in Sport (RED-S): 2018 Update," *International Journal of Sport Nutrition and Exercise Metabolism* 28, no. 4 (2018): 316–31.

89. Pappas, *Bravey*, 67–68; 70.

90. Pappas, *Bravey*, 72.

91. Ostrander, "An Eating Disorder Nearly Ended My Career."

92. Pappas, *Bravey*, 68–69. See, as examples, Melody S. Plisky, Mitchell J. Rauh, Bryan Heiderscheit, Frank B. Underwood, and Robert T. Tank, "Medial Tibial Stress Syndrome in High School Cross-Country Runners: Incidence and Risk Factors," *Journal of Orthopaedic and Sports Physical Therapy* 37, no. 2

(2007): 40–47; Adam S. Tenforde, Lauren C. Sayres, Mary Liz McCurdy, Kristin L. Sainani, and Michael Fredericson, "Identifying Sex-Specific Risk Factors for Stress Fractures in Adolescent Runners," *Medicine and Science in Sports & Exercise* 45, no. 10 (2013): 1843–51; and Brian J. Krabak, Adam S. Tenforde, Irene S. Davis, Michael Fredericson, Mark A. Harrast, Pierre d'Hemecourt, Anthony C. Luke, and William O. Roberts, "Youth Distance Running: Strategies for Training and Injury Reduction," *Current Sports Medicine Reports* 18, no. 2 (2019): 53–59.

93. Ostrander, "An Eating Disorder Nearly Ended My Career."

94. Fleshman, *Good for a Girl*, 127.

95. Pifer, *The Running Body*, 31.

96. Frank, *The Wounded Storyteller*, 115.

97. Frank, *The Wounded Storyteller*, 8.

98. Steil, *Running in Silence*, 281.

99. Pifer, *The Running Body*, 57.

100. Hawkins, *Illness as a Metaphor*, 25. Emphasis in original.

101. Sayer, *PR*, iii.

102. Sarah Lorge Butler, "Mary Cain Forms a Professional Women's Running Team, with the Athletes as Employees," *Runner's World*, June 28, 2021, https://www.runnersworld.com/news/a36856632/mary-cain-forms-womens-pro-running-team/.

103. Oissele, "Our Story," https://www.oiselle.com/pages/our-story.

104. Fleshman, *Good for a Girl*, 246, 255.

105. Fleshman, *Good for a Girl*, 258. See also Pappas, *Bravey*, 72.

6

In Clemente's Wake

Afro-Latino Players and the Quest for Respect

ADRIAN BURGOS, JR.

Roberto Clemente stands forever at 3,000 career hits. Pass Clemente and join one of baseball's most elite groups. That statistical achievement—which Clemente was just the eleventh player in Major League Baseball (MLB) history to accomplish—has usually meant election into the National Baseball Hall of Fame. Qualifications to be placed on the Hall of Fame ballot include a minimum of ten years playing in MLB and a five-year waiting period after retirement as a player. Candidates are expected to be more than compilers of statistics. They are also supposed to be examples of sportsmanship and high character. Voter guidelines specify, "Voting shall be based upon the player's record, playing ability, integrity, sportsmanship, character, and contributions to the team(s) on which the player played."[1]

Statistical accomplishments only capture part of Clemente's legacy. On the field, he was known for the athletic grace with which he fielded his outfield position, his powerful throwing arm, his galloping running style as he sped around the bases, and his prodigious hitting. Off the field, Clemente earned the respect, even if begrudgingly, for his willingness to speak out against racial and ethnic injustices, and his insistence that everyone (including Blacks and Latinos) deserved to be treated with dignity and respect. These deeply held beliefs guided his interactions with fellow players, team and league executives, and the sporting press and broader English-language media.

Sharing his experience and knowledge with others produced another defining dimension of Clemente's enduring legacy. He actively welcomed and mentored newly arrived Latino players, sharing professional tips and also pointers on how to deal with racism in the United States. Young players were often awed that Clemente was invested in their onfield success, cultural adjustment, and overall well-being. A number of established Latino players would embrace Clemente's example in passing along collective knowledge and wisdom from generation to generation. This approach to mentoring definitely influenced Rod Carew, a Panamanian-born and US-raised player. Clemente sought out Carew at the 1968 All-Star game in Houston. "Tony [Oliva] told me that you're gonna be a great player," Clemente told the young Carew. "I want you to always help the young Latin players when they come to the big leagues."[2] Thereafter Carew endeavored to follow Clemente's example in his interactions with younger Latinos. This peer mentorship, looking out for the next generation, represented Clemente's own idea about what the impact of his time in the game should be for fellow Afro-Latinos.

The tragic manner of Clemente's death elevated his stature from an all-time great baseball player into one of the most revered persons in baseball history. He was gone in an instant on December 31, 1972. The plane he had chartered to carry relief supplies to earthquake survivors in Nicaragua crashed shortly after taking off from San Juan, Puerto Rico. Shockwaves reverberated across the Americas and throughout the baseball world after Clemente's passing. The Puerto Rican people went into mourning at the loss of their native son. People across Latin America likewise mourned. Clemente had spoken out on behalf of all Latinos and especially Afro-Latinos. Clemente had been their "defensor," their advocate.

The proud Puerto Rican had been particularly keen on exposing the misdoings of the English-language media that covered baseball. For him, coverage of US sportswriters was too often written through an imperial frame, conveying ideas of American superiority to Latin Americans and of white superiority to Black people. In addition to describing what happened in game action, Latino players were often derided for their accents, "unwillingness" to assimilate, and perceived un-American-ness.

Once Clemente's main antagonists, baseball writers who covered MLB decided to waive the five-year waiting period for inclusion on the Baseball Writers Association of America (BBWAA) ballot for election into the Hall of Fame. "We feel that Clemente, like Sandy Koufax and Stan Musial, would be a first-ballot inductee, so why wait?" explained BBWAA president Joe Heiling of the organization's 1972 decision.[3] In January 1973, the Hall announced Clemente had earned induction, named on 93 percent of 424 ballots cast. According to Chicago sportswriter Richard Dozer, those who did not vote for Clemente included sportswriters who were more against the precedent of waiving the established waiting period than believers that Clemente did not belong in the Hall.[4] Six months later, Clemente was inducted posthumously in Cooperstown.

Clemente's 1973 induction made him the first Afro-Latino in the Hall and garnered him the recognition he long desired. "The fame Roberto Clemente thought evaded him in life has begun to cascade upon the dead Puerto Rican baseball player with a velocity unparalleled in sports history," declared a *Boston Globe* column.[5] Yet the vote did more. At one level, the baseball writers' decision to waive the waiting period and overwhelming vote for Clemente could be read as an attempt at absolution for their complicity in the racialization of Clemente's on-field performance, his speaking ability, and his persona. At another level, Clemente's wake was created, transforming him into the standard used to gauge the worthiness of other Latino players for recognition and entry into the Hall of Fame. Afro-Latinos thereafter endured similar treatment that African Americans who played in MLB after Jackie Robinson and were judged by the standard Robinson set through his play and conduct.

The work of sports studies scholar Joseph Darda is instructive in better understanding the backdrop to the creation of Clemente's wake and the transformation of professional baseball's racial scene during the 1950s and 1960s. Darda argues that white journalists and the baseball media effectively divorced Afro-Latinos like Clemente from their Blackness and placed them into the category of Latin.[6] This racial schema of Black, White, or Latin had the effect of rendering Afro-Latinos invisible within narratives about baseball's racial integration. Press treatment of Afro-Latinos thus made it more challenging to see how Afro-Latinos encountered racism, individual and institutional, in baseball and in wider US society.

Afro-Latinos endured a peculiar form of visible invisibility within US professional baseball. Initially, as racial integration unfolded in the 1940s and 1950s, Afro-Latinos were lumped in with African Americans when those in baseball circles discussed Black players. Being placed in the same category made Afro-Latinos less visible. Even worse, English-language sources typically rendered Afro-Latinos voiceless in stories about Blacks in baseball's pioneering generation. This was not because they were absent, but rather was due to the language barrier between white journalists and Latinos. And when their voices did appear, the words of Latinos were often presented phonetically, emphasizing their accent, minimizing what they had to say, and suggesting they lacked intelligence.[7] Additionally, the racial schema white baseball men increasingly used in the 1960s, which labeled Afro-Latinos as just Latin, obfuscated their encounters with Jim Crow segregation, anti-Black discrimination, and institutionalized racism. The plight of being Black and Latino in US baseball is what Orlando

Cepeda described as having two strikes: one for being Black, and another for being Latino. Clemente put it even more bluntly: "Here in America, I'm a 'double nigger,' for my skin and my Spanish heritage."[8]

This chapter explores what I have labeled Clemente's wake through an examination of the power sports journalists wielded in shaping the memory of Clemente, and how this memory shaped their treatment of other Afro-Latinos. Multiple meanings of wake are used in this examination. One meaning encompasses the social remembering of a person who has died, of people paying their respects to those affected by the loss. The other meaning, inspired by the nautical process, involves the wave effect produced by a vessel that those who follow must navigate. In either context, this chapter explores the manner in which the baseball world dealt with Clemente and the ripple effects it had on other Afro-Latinos.

The racialization of Clemente is explored to witness how he countered the English-language press treatment of him and other Latinos. Clemente was insistent on being evaluated on his own terms and rejected constant comparisons to Willie Mays. Yet, in Clemente's wake, journalists and baseball historians did to other Latinos what so upset him as a player: they constantly judged Latinos not as individuals or on their own terms. The chapter thus briefly revisits the experience of other Afro-Latinos, specifically Orestes "Minnie" Miñoso and Luis Tiant, as a window into how the English-language press treated Afro-Latinos as different from African Americans. With Clemente as the standard, Afro-Latinos lost their individuality in ways that white American players typically did not. They were never just players, but players in the impossible wake created after Clemente's untimely death.

Home is Not Always Sweet

Clemente made his MLB debut in 1955, in the middle of MLB's racial integration. It took twelve years (1947–1959) for each of MLB's sixteen teams to field their first Black player. By 1960 African Americans and Latinos each represented 8.9 percent of MLB players. The two groups composed over 25 percent of MLB players in the 1968 season. Other parts of baseball changed much more slowly. As teams became more diverse, membership of BBWAA (composed of daily baseball writers) remained overwhelmingly white. "Not only are the vast majority of sportswriters white," a Rand Corporation study reported, "but they are middle-aged; their world view was shaped before Jackie Robinson entered baseball in 1947."[9]

The overwhelmingly white press corps influenced the tone of coverage when it came to Afro-Latinos, as these players' actions on and off the field were typically analyzed through a white American perspective.[10] These writers at times printed quotes from Latino players phonetically, which depicted them as unintelligent or unintelligible. Such depictions mocked Latino players' accents and were part of what I label "intellectual disenfranchisement"—the practice of shifting focus from what was being communicated to an individual's accent, which served to discount Latino perspectives. The manner in which the sporting press did this to Latino players was tantamount to racialization, marking how Latinos spoke as foreign, unintelligent, and unworthy of respect.[11]

Clemente spoke often about the stereotypical and derogatory images sportswriters conveyed through their writing about Latinos. "I blame the writers. They made it look like we were entirely different from the white players," Clemente declared.[12] "The Latin American player doesn't get the recognition he deserves," he complained. Clemente's "greatest satisfaction" came from "helping to erase the old opinion about Latin Americans and blacks." "People never questioned our ability, but they considered us inferior to their station of life," he noted; "[e]ven our integrity was questioned" by the baseball writers.[13]

Coverage of Clemente included praise for his game performance, comparison to other great Black players, especially Willie Mays, and derogatory phonetic quoting of his English. Clemente insisted on being judged on his own terms, in comparison to no one else, no matter how great that player. "Why do they always compare me to Willie Mays," he fumed. "I play like Clemente and not like Mays." As the proud Puerto Rican declared, "I do not hate Mays; he is a good baseball player, but I, Clemente, am also a great baseball player."[14] African American sportswriter A. S. "Doc" Young recalled the Pirates' outfielder's insistence that he was "'the first Roberto Clemente,' not 'the second Willie Mays.'"[15]

White baseball scribes, whether from Pittsburgh or other cities, would occasionally quote Clemente phonetically. "Me like hit weather, veree hot," *The Sporting News* quoted the Puerto Rican star as saying during the 1960 season. "No get warm in cold. No get warm, no play gut."[16] The *Pittsburgh Press* ran the same quote in an article by Les Biederman.[17] The following season an Associated Press story quoted Clemente's description of his contribution in a game: "I get heet and Willie [Stargell] scores and I feel better than good." Another local paper, the *Pittsburgh Post-Gazette*, ran the same quote under the headline "I Get Heet, I Feel Good."[18] This representation of his speaking abilities and intelligence unnerved Clemente. He took as a personal affront the manner in which these English-language sportswriters described and even mocked how he spoke, and how others misconstrued what he attempted to communicate to mean something else.

A twenty-one-year-old Clemente had encountered a disconcerting situation when he first joined the Pirates in 1955, especially when he witnessed African American teammate Curt Roberts not fighting back against those who mistreated the Oakland native. "When I was young," Clemente told *Pittsburgh Courier*'s Bill Nunn, "I couldn't understand why Roberts didn't fight back. They would rub his head and play dirty tricks on him." Such disrespectful behavior would not have occurred in Puerto Rico, Clemente insisted. The racist hijinks that went on in the major leagues were not part of the island's baseball culture; there "they treat a man as a man." The language barrier, however, prevented Clemente and Roberts from communicating effectively: "I couldn't tell Curt my feelings. And he couldn't tell me his." Over time, as he gained more experience and learned more about what African Americans endured in the United States, Clemente came to the realization "that Curt was as frightened as I was. Our skins made us brothers but the language barrier prevents us from fighting back."[19]

Clemente clashed numerous times with sportswriters. The 1960 Most Valuable Player (MVP) vote produced one of the better-known clashes. Clemente felt baseball writers disrespected him and belittled his contributions to the Pirates team that won the National League title and then defeated the New York Yankees to win the World Series. Ballots were cast immediately following the 1960 regular season. Writers voted Pirates shortstop Dick Groat the league's MVP. Groat's leadership and other intangible contributions perhaps swayed the voters. But Groat had an inferior offensive season compared to his Puerto Rican teammate. In traditional statistics, popular among journalists in those days, Clemente boasted a .314 batting average, 16 home runs, 94 Runs Batted In (RBI), and 89 runs scored. Groat, by contrast, batted .325 with 2 home runs, 50 RBI, and 85 runs scored.[20] What really sparked Clemente's ire was that the results placed him in eighth place overall. Even more, three Pirates teammates (Groat, third baseman Don Hoak, and pitcher Vern Law) finished ahead of Clemente in the MVP results. Years later, Clemente declared: "I was very bitter, I am still bitter. . . . I'm a team player [and] winning the pennant and the world championship were more important to me than my average, but I feel I should get the credit I deserve."[21] "He felt he had been terribly overlooked and was very upset about it," observed longtime Pirates announcer Bob Prince. "He would not wear that [1960 World Series] ring."[22] Maury Wills, a teammate on the 1968 Pirates, defended Clemente. Wills believed media coverage swayed fan perceptions about Clemente and Latinos. "Could it be that fans underrate Latinos because the writers don't talk so often to the Spanish-speaking players, and therefore you don't read as much about them?" Wills asked in a 1973 interview with Clemente biographer Kal Wagenheim. "And could it be that the fans don't make heroes out of players from foreign countries because they can't identify with them?"[23]

Clemente was convinced that the media influenced fan perceptions. He spoke out after he homered for his 2,000th career hit in 1966. "The Latin American player doesn't get the recognition he deserves," he began. "Neither does the Negro player, unless he does something really spectacular, like Willie Mays."[24] Monte Irvin, boyhood idol of Clemente, believed he understood how press treatment motivated the Puerto Rican star. Irvin noted the effect on Clemente of finally receiving the respect he long desired following the Pirates' World Series triumph in 1971. "He was so happy, because he was finally getting some recognition for his contribution to the game. It was never money he was after. He wanted recognition."[25]

A cultural issue affected how the English-language press treated Latinos. Sportswriters questioned Latino players' willingness to play hard or through injury. The bias some sportswriters showed was clear to Clemente, who declared, "When Mickey Mantle says his leg is hurt no one questions. But if a Latin or a black is sick, they always say it is in his head!"[26] Dave Concepción, a contemporary of Clemente who played for the Cincinnati Reds, described his own frustration with the English-language press: "We Latins have a lot more patience with North Americans who came to our countries than North Americans have with us here." For Concepción, treating visitors with respect, especially those unfamiliar with a place and their language, was the proper thing to do. This was not the treatment Concepción, Clemente, and other Latinos received from the US baseball media. Rather, sportswriters were at times demanding and other times demeaning in their interactions with Latino players. Monte Irvin observed how sportswriters approached Latino ballplayers. They "acted like Clemente should give them anything they wanted," Irvin told journalist Robert Heuer. "They'd come over to him as if to say, 'You're a Latin and you can't speak English very well so I don't have to be courteous or beholden to you.'"[27]

The press covering the MLB beat continued to be overwhelmingly monolingual until the 1990s. Even though Latinos had surged to nearly 25 percent of MLB players by that decade, few writers spoke Spanish, limiting their ability to secure interviews with those Latinos who felt most comfortable communicating in Spanish. The white American journalist Robert Heuer realized that speaking fluent Spanish enabled him to improve his baseball coverage. Observing how other journalists interacted with Latino players, and their lack of success trying to interview Latinos, led to another realization. "Fluent Spanish has helped me see that Clemente had actually carried a woefully underplayed civil rights issue onto the sports page."[28]

No Longer Black?

A significant change in racial discourse accompanied the growing diversity of MLB player ranks that followed Jackie Robinson's 1947 MLB breakthrough. Joseph Darda compellingly argues that white baseball men, from the press box and front offices, replaced the Black/white binary that had reigned during baseball's segregated era with a Black/nonwhite binary after the civil rights movement (post 1965). These white baseball men also "removed themselves from the racial scene, obscuring white dominance while attributing anti-Blackness to Latinos and Latin Americans."[29] Additionally, white baseball men positioned themselves not as part of the status quo in baseball but rather as knowledgeable race men. From this position they narrated the saga of baseball's desegregation as "objective" observers watching as Black and Brown players figured out how to relate to each other. The new racial binary effectively divorced Clemente and other Afro-Latinos from their Blackness; they were racialized as just Latino and no longer Black.

The notion that the major racial tension in US professional baseball was between African Americans and Latinos proved quite persuasive. It swayed the thinking of the newer generation of Black sportswriters in the 1950s. Gone were the vivid memories of African Americans and Latinos playing side by side in the Negro Leagues that African American sportswriters Sam Lacy, Wendell Smith, and Dan Burley described in their columns. Vanishing also were the experiences of African American players who in the 1940s headed to Mexico, where they enjoyed a kind of freedom playing professionally that was not available in the States. Dozens of African American stars had headed south for the Mexican League during World War II, including Willie Wells, Monte Irvin, and Roy Campanella. Wells explained his decision to play in Mexico to Wendell Smith.

> I am not faced with the racial problem in Mexico. . . . When I travel with the Vera Cruz team we live in the finest hotels, we eat in the best restaurants and can go any place we care to. You know as well as all other Negroes we don't enjoy such privileges in the United States. . . . I've found freedom and democracy here, something I never found in the United States. . . . I was branded a Negro in the States and was told to act accordingly. Everything I did, including playing ball, was regulated by my color.[30]

The "evolution" of baseball's race problem could even be found in the reporting on Clemente's identification as Black in the Black press. Bill Nunn Jr. took over for Wendell Smith at the *Pittsburgh Courier* after World War II. A native of Pittsburgh's Homewood District, Nunn came from a different generation, baseball-wise. Gone were the glory days of the Homestead Grays in the Negro National League. In fact, the Grays had played half (or more) of their home games in Washington, DC, at Griffith Stadium throughout the 1940s before disbanding in 1950. The Pirates became the baseball beat to cover in the *Courier*, and how the paper wrote about Clemente, Latinos, and race in baseball echoed most white dailies.

Clemente's identification as Black was not questioned in his early days with the Pirates. But "the questioning did come," according to Darda. This is not surprising given coverage of racial integration of baseball in the Steel City. The Pirates initially credited Curt Roberts as the team's integration pioneer in 1954, even though Carlos Bernier had played over one hundred games for the Pirates in 1953, and the team had the Puerto Rican Bernier represent them at the dedication of Kennard baseball field in Pittsburgh's Hill District, a Black neighborhood. Bernier appeared alongside three African American players from the Brooklyn Dodgers (Joe Black, Roy Campanella, and Jackie Robinson) at the dedication. Even more, Bernier self-identified as Black, according to family members and biographer Charles F. Faber.[31] However, when it came to writing the team's story about racial integration, Bernier was treated as a "Latin."

The disputing of Clemente's self-identification as Black first appeared not in a sports column but in a 1960 society note in the *Pittsburgh Courier*. The item implied that Clemente "didn't want to be recognized as a Negro" and "preferred the company of white people." Ever critical of racial segregation, Clemente had expressed to a reporter his dislike for how whites treated Black people, including himself and other Afro-Latinos. What appeared in the paper struck a different tone. "The reporter interpreted him as saying that he didn't like being treated as a Black person," Darda observes. "Some readers then took the reporter's paraphrase to mean that Clemente didn't like being Black, that he didn't want to associate with other Black people."[32]

Upset with the paper's depiction, Clemente visited the *Courier*'s office to defend his relationship with the Black community and African Americans. The *Courier* article published a "guest column" based on his visit. However, the paper quoted him phonetically. "Som' co-lored people I understand saying Clemente, he not like co-lored people. This is not the truth at all. Look at me, I am not of the white people. I hav' color the skin." "That is the first theeng I straighten out," he declared, "I like all the people, the co-lored and the white; and since I am co-lored myself, in the skin, I would reely hate myself."[33] Despite his protestations, the notion that Clemente did not want to identify as Black or with the African American community persisted. Even after Clemente's tragic death, a story ran in the leading Black cultural magazine *Ebony* "that dwelled on how the Puerto Rican had resented comparison to Willie Mays, giving the strong impression that he had disliked the comparisons not because he wished to be seen as his own ballplayer, but because he didn't want to be identified with a Black man."[34]

The *Courier*'s coverage of Clemente, Afro-Latinos, and race in baseball was representative of coverage throughout US professional baseball. Two generations of Black sportswriters now reported on the game. The older generation had borne witness to African Americans and Latinos performing together in the Negro Leagues and in Latin American leagues and saw African diasporic connections between Blacks from the United States and the Caribbean. The newer generation was less familiar with that transnational Black baseball scene. They grew increasingly critical of Latinos and Afro-Latinos when it came to racial matters in baseball and beyond.[35]

Even the *Chicago Defender*'s Doc Young wrote about Clemente and other Afro-Latinos as just "Latin" and not Black. Young covered the later years of the Negro Leagues, which overlapped with the start of racial integration in MLB. His 1953 book, *Great Negro Stars and How They Made the Major Leagues,* discussed baseball's integration as "the era of Jackie Robinson, Minnie Miñoso, et al." His 1963 follow-up took a different tack. "Although he continued to celebrate Miñoso," Darda writes, Young's *Negro Firsts in Sports* "shifted from an account in which Robinson and Miñoso had struggled together against Jim Crow into one in which Robinson led a wave of Black players into the major leagues, creating the conditions for a subsequent contingent of Latin American players."[36] A line of delineation emerged where Afro-Latino players who entered MLB before 1955 were Black; those who came after, like Felipe Alou, Cepeda, and Clemente, were "Latin."

Afro-Latino Pioneers and Clemente's Wake

Afro-Latinos felt the impact of Clemente's wake more than any other group in baseball. They were the ones most directly measured by his accomplishments as a player and as an exemplar of humanitarianism. Whether they came before or after Clemente's time playing in MLB (1955–1972), he served as the professional and moral standard by which their worthiness has been considered. Being in Clemente's wake became most noticeable with the assessment of the candidacy of other Afro-Latino candidates for the Hall of Fame. Their career accomplishments were inevitably weighed in comparison to Clemente. Did they model the behaviors on and off the field that had earned Clemente such admiration and respect? Had they been willing to speak out on behalf of others like Clemente? Were they, like Clemente, open in their opposition to racism or injustice?

Among the Afro-Latinos who preceded Clemente in MLB, none shined brighter than Minnie Miñoso. His debut on April 19, 1949, made him MLB's first Black Latino and marked the dawn of baseball's modern era as an integrated and international game. A few racially ambiguous Latinos such as Roberto Estalella and Tomás (Tommy) de la Cruz had previously appeared in MLB because team executives presented them to the public as Cuban and not Black.[37] Lighter-skinned Latinos had performed in MLB even earlier, such as the Colombia-born and US-college educated Luis "Jud" Castro, who played with the Philadelphia Athletics in 1902. But Miñoso's arrival was different. Orlando Cepeda was not being hyperbolic when he referred to Miñoso as "our Jackie Robinson." But the path that Miñoso traveled as an integration pioneer was different from that of Robinson. He was Black and Cuban, both familiar and foreign to Americans. Miñoso's unwavering belief in the dignity of all human beings guided his actions throughout his baseball life and shaped his interactions away from the baseball stadium.[38] However, Miñoso's personality and often jovial demeanor prompted some to ponder why he was not more like Clemente, and why the Cuban was not more outspoken about racial slights and press mistreatment.[39] The Clemente comparison demonstrates that many misunderstood and undervalued the significance of Miñoso's career.

While their MLB careers overlapped, Clemente and Miñoso came from different baseball generations. Miñoso's generation left the Caribbean and entered US professional baseball through the Negro Leagues. His US professional career started with the New York Cubans in 1946, with whom he performed for three seasons, including as a member of the 1947 team that won the Negro League World Series. Clemente signed with the Dodgers in 1954, almost a full decade later. Much changed in that span for Afro-Latinos. Their on-field success and their ability to overcome cultural hurdles cleared the path for talented prospects like Clemente to sign straightaway with MLB organizations.

The extent to which other Afro-Latinos are credited for participating in baseball's racial integration also reflects the impacts of Clemente's wake. As MLB's first Black Latino, Miñoso combatted stereotypes about Latinos and Blacks, such as the Latin's hot-bloodedness, supposed lack of intelligence, and unwillingness to work hard. He combatted such stereotypes by consciously deciding not to retaliate after being knocked down, hit by a pitch, or taunted. The grace, dignity, and humor with which Miñoso handled these challenges allowed Clemente and Felipe Alou to speak more forthrightly as Black Latinos about what they faced in baseball.[40]

Stereotypes about Blacks and Latinos persisted as integration unfolded. Beliefs about racial and cultural difference permeated US professional baseball, influencing decision-making, from team managers to the front office. After the New York Yankees traded away Afro-Puerto Rican Vic Power, general manager George Weiss told fans and the media that "the first Negro to appear in a Yankee uniform must be worth having been waited for."[41] The insinuation was clear: Power wasn't the guy for the Yankees. Performance was not the basis for the trade. Power had been one of the organization's top hitters in the minors, batting .331 in 1952 and .343 in 1953. Power later speculated on the trade. "Maybe the Yankees didn't want a black player who would openly date light-skinned women, or who responded with his fists when pitchers threw beanballs at him."[42]

A controversial 1964 interview with San Francisco Giants manager Alvin Dark provides further evidence of the persistence of racist ideas about African American and Latino players—that they lacked the same mental sharpness, drive, and willingness to sacrifice for the team as white American players. Dark attributed his team's struggles to having "so many Spanish-speaking and Negro players." These players, Dark told *Newsday*'s Stan Isaacs, "are just not able to perform up to the white ball players when it comes to mental alertness." Even worse, Dark believed "you can't make most Negro and Spanish players have the pride in their team that you get from white players."[43] Dark saw the diversity of his team as an obstacle to success. Ironically, the Giants' top brass had placed him in charge of perhaps the most diverse roster of all MLB teams.

Dark's beliefs reflected the general hesitancy of white Americans about the entry of African Americans and Latinos into MLB in the initial decades of integration. Beliefs that the racial and ethnic background of Black and Latino players affected their performance or conduct also influenced management decisions when it came to composing a team's roster or deciding whether players were promoted through the minor league system. Even when a Black or Latino player made a roster, such beliefs could still impact whether they were named to the starting lineup.

Local opposition to integration limited opportunities for African American and Latino players into the 1960s. The Giants organization had to abandon its effort to have Black players perform for its Evangeline League affiliate in Lake Charles, Louisiana, in 1956. Lake Charles city officials rigidly enforced Jim Crow laws, refusing to permit Alou and his African American teammate Chuck Weatherspoon to play at the club's home ballpark. Consequently, the two were forced to leave the Lake Charles Giants.[44] Alou's negative experience prompted a decision to quit professional baseball in the United States and return to the Dominican Republic. He rethought that decision before boarding a flight home. Opting to remain, his route to MLB restarted in Cocoa Beach of the Florida State League, which proved more accommodating than Lake Charles. Two years later he made his MLB debut with San Francisco.

Clemente also dealt with the reality of race in professional baseball as he started his professional career. Part of the Brooklyn Dodgers organization in 1954, Clemente spent his lone season in the minors assigned to the Montreal Royals. The Dodgers sent him to Canada partly to hide the teenage Clemente from other teams seeking to scout and acquire the talented youngster. The strategy, however, proved ineffective, as the Pirates drafted Clemente after the 1954 season. Brooklyn had also hoped to shield the Puerto Rican from the racial hostility that Black players faced in minor league towns across the United States.

Luis Tiant's journey to MLB in the early 1960s illuminated the challenges Afro-Latino prospects continued to encounter in the minor leagues. The Afro-Cuban played three seasons in the Mexican League before the Cleveland Indians purchased his contract for $30,000. Cleveland assigned Tiant to its Charleston, South Carolina, affiliate in the Eastern League. "This was my introduction to the American South," Tiant wrote in his autobiography, *Son of Havana*. "The Black players, including Cubans, faced terrible racism. When we were on the road and stopped to get something to eat, the white ballplayers would have to bring the food to us on the bus because we couldn't go in. We couldn't eat in the same restaurant or stay in the same hotel as them."[45]

No ballpark was a refuge for Tiant, not even Charleston's home field. "And when you got to the ballpark, forget it. They called us niggers, saying they were going to send us back to Africa or hang us. How we looked like monkeys. All kinds of barbarian things; it's amazing what you'd heard, even at home games!"[46] White spectators in the Carolina League engaged in similar behavior when Tiant played in Burlington, North Carolina, the following year. He would often return to his room after games and cry. He did not understand why the fans would hurl racial epithets his way.[47] "They make you feel like an animal—worse than an animal. I think in those days in the South, they [whites] treated animals *better* than they treated Blacks."[48]

Familiarity with US culture and English were key differences between the African Americans and Afro-Latinos who pioneered integration. "It was tough for all the Black players, but at least the American Blacks spoke

English. . . . I couldn't understand anything, and I couldn't even ask for food," Tiant recalled. Not knowing US culture meant potentially getting into dangerous situations, especially if one didn't keep one's composure. "In my country, if somebody called you a nigger, you punched him in the face," Tiant declared. "You couldn't do that in the South in 1962. Whatever happened between you and a white person, if the police came along they'd beat the shit out of you. Then they'd put you in jail. You lose, and then you lose again. So you just tried to keep your cool and look the other way."[49]

Resilience in dealing with the psychic toll involved in pioneering integration and other setbacks proved key in Tiant's long professional career. The Cuban native won 229 games in MLB, was a three-time All-Star, and accrued four twenty-win seasons. He did so after his unsettling experience of being an Afro-Latino participating in integration in the minor leagues, and after suffering a broken shoulder blade early in his major league career that forced him to reinvent himself from a hard-throwing hurler into a crafty pitcher. Tiant's accomplishments, combined with his comeback story, usually garnered serious consideration as a Hall of Fame candidate. However, Tiant, like other Afro-Latinos, was considered in Clemente's wake. His peak support came in his first year on the ballot (1988), when he received 30.9 percent of the baseball writers' vote—75 percent is needed for induction. Increased support over time often followed a solid showing like Tiant's first year on the ballot. Instead, his support declined steadily. Interestingly, three pitchers he was most comparable to in advanced metrics ("similarity scores" as measured in Baseball-Reference.com) were elected to the Hall of Fame: Jim Bunning, Jim "Catfish" Hunter, and Don Drysdale. A key aspect that distinguished Tiant from this trio is his status as an Afro-Latino.

Conclusion

Clemente's wake reflects the different stakes for Black players and white Americans in baseball's integration project. Many whites absolved themselves of the race problem in baseball. Indeed, as Darda demonstrates, whites increasingly pointed to tensions between African Americans and Latinos as the problem within baseball's pioneering generation. The formation of what I call Clemente's wake, the mythmaking around Clemente and its use as a standard to consider the worthiness of other Latinos for inclusion in the Baseball Hall of Fame, points to the power exercised by baseball writers and other baseball insiders as MLB gatekeepers. Even more, revisiting the experience of Afro-Latinos who preceded Clemente, like Miñoso, and those who were his contemporaries, like Tiant, reveals how racial and ethnic stereotypes continued to influence white decision-makers in professional baseball, from the clubhouse to the press box, and from the front offices to scouting and talent development.

Clemente's legacy has meant something different for Latino players than it has for baseball writers and other baseball insiders. Felipe Alou, Clemente's contemporaries from 1958 through 1972, took to heart the example set by Clemente. "He was a vocal defender of Latinos and militant about it. That got him a lot of criticism and even some enemies," Alou wrote, describing Clemente in his 2018 memoir. "As big as Clemente's talent was, the biggest thing about him was his heart. Roberto was not political. He was better than that. He was social. He inspired me on the social side of life, with his care for Latin America."[50] Clemente's legacy also includes a mandate to pass along collective knowledge and wisdom from generation to generation. This peer mentorship, looking out for the next generation, was Clemente's own idea about what the impact of his time in the game should be for fellow Afro-Latinos. It was about making the path less challenging for the next generation. Felipe Alou followed that example, as did Rod Carew. That part of Clemente's legacy even moved beyond those who were his professional contemporaries. Carlos Delgado, who played in MLB from 1993 to 2009, understood the significance of Clemente's legacy. "The reason why I wore 21 is because of Clemente. As a Puerto Rican, you understand how big Clemente was," Delgado stated. "But the legacy, that fight for justice, social justice, I think is more important. As a player, a black player from Puerto Rico, a Latino, getting into the big leagues and hearing the stories of Clemente and Cepeda and Victor Pellot, how hard they had it, when you go in it's much easier," Delgado shared in a 2018 interview.[51]

Clemente's wake within the white American cadre of baseball writers translated into something quite different. Baseball writers who voted in the 1972 Hall of Fame election acknowledged the greatness of Clemente as a player and also participated in creating the standard by which many of them would measure all Latinos, and especially Afro-Latinos. Clemente became the first Afro-Latino elected by baseball writers into the Hall. He remained the sole Afro-Latino from MLB for another decade—Afro-Cuban Martin Dihigo was elected by a Negro League committee in 1977. The path into the Hall proved especially arduous for Afro-Latinos from baseball's pioneering generation. Recognition of their on-field accomplishments and the broader social contexts of the racial and ethnic challenges they overcame to excel became difficult to attain in Clemente's wake. Orlando Cepeda's election occurred in 1999, through the Veterans Committee after exhausting his time on the regular ballot, meaning baseball writers failed to vote him in during his fifteen years on the ballot. Tony Oliva and Minnie Miñoso both earned election in 2022, also through a Veterans Committee. The 2022 election of the two Afro-Cubans can perhaps be read as evidence of voters who were more aware of Clemente's wake and perhaps also had a more nuanced understanding of the challenges Afro-Latinos faced while pioneering integration in MLB. Their election also serves as a more fitting recognition of Clemente's insistence on respecting the dignity of Latinos inside and outside of professional baseball than the veneration of Clemente that is isolated in Clemente's wake.

Notes

1. "Hall of Fame Election Requirement," Baseball Writers Association of America, BBWAA.COM, https://bbwaa.com/hof-elec-req/.
2. "La Vida Voices: The Life of Rod Carew," *La Vida Baseball*, September 8, 2018, https://www.lavidabaseball.com/la-vida-voices-rod-carew/.
3. "Clemente 'One of Greatest'—Nixon," *Washington Post*, January 3, 1973, D2.
4. "Fame Vote Now Could be Disservice to Clemente," *Chicago Tribune*, January 5, 1973, C3.
5. "Hall of Fame Opens Door," *Boston Globe*, January 4, 1973, 57.
6. Joseph Darda, "Roberto Clemente on the Black/Brown Color Line," *Journal of American Studies* (2023): 1–27
7. Adrian Burgos Jr., "Left Out: Afro-Latinos, Black Baseball, and the Revision of Baseball's Racial history," *Social Text* (2009) 27, no. 1 (98): 37–58.
8. Cepeda quote cited in Adrian Burgos, "What Chris Rock Got Wrong," *Sporting News*, May 10, 2015, https://www.sportingnews.com/us/mlb/news/arfrican-americans-baseball-chris-rock-latinos/1spqgzamfumih1eprzkmlfpki7; Kal Wagenheim, *Clemente!* (Chicago: Olmstead Press, 2001), 115.
9. Wagenheim, *Clemente!*, 115
10. Darda, 7. See also Adrian Burgos, *Playing America's Game: Baseball, Latinos, and the Color Line* (Berkeley: University of California Press, 2007); Jennifer Domino Rudolph, *Baseball as Mediated Latinidad: Race, Masculinity, Nationalism, and Performances of Identity* (Columbus: Ohio State University Press, 2020), 3.
11. Burgos, *Playing America's Game*, 261–62.
12. Wagenheim, *Clemente!*, 179.
13. Wagenheim, *Clemente!*, 179.
14. "Sports World Mourns Loss of Clemente," *Cleveland Call & Post*, January 6, 1973, 1A, 4A.
15. "Roberto Clemente," *Los Angeles Sentinel*, January 6, 1973, 1, 8.
16. Robert Heuer, "Clemente's Legacy for Latin Ballplayers," *New York Times* January 2, 1983, S2.

17. Darda, "Roberto Clemente on the Black/Brown Color Line," 17

18. Darda, "Roberto Clemente on the Black/Brown Color Line," 17; Clemente quoted in Markusen, *Roberto Clemente: The Great One* (Champaign, IL: Sports Publishing, 1998), 47.

19. Bill Nunn, "Change of Pace," *Pittsburgh Courier*, January 6, 1973, 25.

20. Groat measured a bit better than Clemente by WAR (Wins Above Replacement), a newer statistic in favor among the baseball analytics community today. Clemente had a 121 OPS+ (Onbase Plus Slugging, league norm is 100) and a 4.0 WAR. Groat's 1960 season included a 110 OPS+ and a 6.1 WAR.

21. Wagenheim, *Clemente!*, 77

22. "Nobody Played the Game Harder: Clemente, a Complex Man," *Los Angeles Times*, January 2, 1973, E1.

23. Wagenheim, *Clemente!*, 127

24. Wagenheim, *Clemente!*, 106

25. Wagenheim, *Clemente!*, 185

26. Peter C. Bjarkman, *Baseball with a Latin Beat: A History of the Latin American* Game (Jefferson, NC: MacFarland, 1994), 10.

27. Heuer, "Clemente's Legacy," S2

28. Heuer, Clemente's Legacy," S2.

29. Darda, "Roberto Clemente on the Black/Brown Color Line," 19.

30. For Negro Leaguer Willie Wells's comment about finding democracy, see *Pittsburgh Courier*, May 6, 1944, 12. On African Americans in the Mexican league, see John Virtue, *South of the Color Barrier: How Jorge Pasquel and the Mexican League Pushed Baseball Toward Racial Integration* (Jefferson, NC: McFarland Publishing, 2007).

31. Thomas Van Hyning, "Carlos Bernier: A Pioneering Pirate," *La Vida Baseball*, September 5, 2018, https://www.lavidabaseball.com/pirates-carlos-bernier/.

32. Darda, "Roberto Clemente on the Black/Brown Color Line," 22.

33. Quoted in Darda, "Roberto Clemente on the Black/Brown Color Line," 22. Roberto Clemente, "Highlights in Baseball Week," *Pittsburgh Courier*, June 4, 1960, 27.

34. Darda, "Roberto Clemente on the Black/Brown Color Line," 24–25.

35. Darda, "Roberto Clemente on the Black/Brown Color Line," 24.

36. Darda, "Roberto Clemente on the Black/Brown Color Line," 25.

37. See Burgos, *Playing America's Game*, 162–76.

38. Orestes Miñoso, personal statement, "Pioneering Latinos: Building a Legacy on and Beyond the Playing Field," Illinois Public Media, Urbana, January 21, 2011, https://ipm-prod.will.illinois.edu/focus/program/focus110120b.

39. Daniel McGrath. "First Latino White Sox Star Gets Another Shot," *New York Times*, December 4, 2011, 37B; Jim Margulis, "Minoso Denied, and This Better Not Be the Reason Why," *Southside Sox*, December 5, 2011, https://www.southsidesox.com/2011/12/5/2613213/minoso-denied-and-this-better-not-be-the-reason-why.

40. This section draws from a eulogy delivered at Miñoso's 2015 funeral service, and appeared as Adrian Burgos, "From the Eulogy for Minnie Minoso," *Sporting News*, March 9, 2015, accessed July 21, 2023, https://www.sportingnews.com/us/mlb/news/minnie-minoso-dead-dies-hall-of-fame-eulogy-obituary-white-sox-indians-election/q5fxgg9tasym1gzbxhpz4tl27.

41. *Washington Post*, October 14, 1953.

42. Richard Goldstein, "Vic Power, 78, Pioneer Latino and First Baseman with Flair," *New York Times*, November 30, 2005, C19.

43. Bjarkman, *Baseball with a Latin Beat*, 138, 229. Dark's comment originally appeared in a 1964 interview with *New York Newsday* sportswriter Stan Isaacs.

44. Felipe Alou, interview by Lawrence Hogan, March 3, 2004, unpublished; Felipe Alou with Peter Kerositis, *Alou: My Baseball Journey* (Lincoln, NE: University of Nebraska Press, 2020).

45. Luis Tiant with Saul Wisnia, *Son of Havana: From Cuba to the Big Leagues and Back* (New York: Diversion Books, 2019), 40–41.

46. Tiant, *Son of Havana*, 41.

47. Tiant, *Son of Havana*, 43–45.

48. Tiant, *Son of Havana*, 41.

49. Tiant, *Son of Havana*, 41.

50. Felipe Alou, *Alou*, 65, 66.

51. Adrian Burgos, "Interview with Carlos Delgado," *La Vida Baseball*, June 8, 2019, https://www.lavidabaseball.com/carlos-delgado-clemente-legacy/.

7

Raising a Glass Helmet

How Black Athletes and Artists Resist Football's Headgear

NOAH COHAN

The plastic safety helmet, developed for use in American football by the sporting goods manufacturer Riddell in 1939, is fundamentally a piece of protective equipment.[1] Originally designed to prevent skull fractures—devastating injuries that resulted in numerous fatalities through the first sixty years of football's history—the new helmet quickly became much more than a means of injury protection.[2] Ensconced in the iconography of the game in a way that its leather predecessor never was, the plastic helmet has gained such prominence as a symbol of the game over the intervening eighty-plus years that it is practically impossible to imagine the modern game of tackle football without it. This is a problem for public health, some have argued, as the inflexible helmet encourages an intensification of football's inherently violent gameplay, resulting in even greater injury risk, especially to the brain.[3]

Such a focus on the football helmet as the crux of the violent sport's larger health and safety issues, while merited, also occludes a different pathology that the technology enables: the problem of the helmet is also a problem of racism. The opaque device obscures the identities of players—most of whom are men of color in the NFL and major college football. It therein intensifies their dehumanization as disposable resources within the political economy of the sport, a broader commodifying dynamic recognized by Thomas Oates, among others, as essential to fan consumerism.[4]

This dehumanization via the helmet has not gone unrecognized, however. After explaining this problem, I highlight two notable forms of resistance that reimagine what the helmet can be. To begin, I examine

"The Glass Helmet Project" and its successor, "The Glass Helmet Experience," a series of videos posted to the YouTube channel of Uninterrupted, the media company headed by NBA legend LeBron James. Collectively, the "Glass Helmet" videos combat what they dub "the Helmet Effect," a dynamic by which players are anonymized and depersonalized by their opaque helmets. The videos imagine a world in which clear helmets allow fans to better see and thereby appreciate the individual men who wear them. With an obvious but unstated focus on Black players as those most marginalized by the helmet's anonymizing opacity, the series urges viewers to appreciate them as "brothers . . . fathers . . . artists . . . creatives . . . thought leaders [and] entrepreneurs."[5]

I then detail and analyze the work of visual artist Esmaa Mohamoud, focusing on her 2019 piece, *Glorious Bones*. In depicting a vibrant field of brightly colored and individually patterned helmets against a black background, Mohamoud imagines an alternative to the helmeted status quo. That alternative, like Uninterrupted's "Glass Helmet" series, emphasizes the individuality of the (mostly) Black men who play the game at the highest level. Unlike "Glass Helmet," *Glorious Bones* overtly celebrates the larger Black cultures that produced these men while also demarcating them as individuals. Importantly, Mohamoud also frames the Black athlete's individuality beyond the bounds of the neoliberal entrepreneurial frame that Uninterrupted's videos impose on each player's personhood. By doing so, Mohamoud more radically reimagines the political economy of football and commercialized sport writ large.

Despite their differences, both pieces recognize that the modern plastic football helmet is much more than a safety device. Furthermore, they demonstrate that the signifying function of team-based helmet logos is not benign. By analyzing "Glass Helmet" and *Glorious Bones* in tandem and building on their messages of resistance to football's status quo, I advocate for a reconception of who and what the helmet represents, such that we can envision a future in which the individual human beings of all races and ethnicities who make up football's precarious labor pool are both better protected and celebrated.

The Allure of Plastic Safety Helmets and What They Obscure

Modern football helmets come in a variety of shapes and sizes, but the basic elements are the same. Beginning just above the eyebrows, interior padding envelopes the forehead, continuing upward over the crown of the head, then across the top and down over the back of the head to the nape of the neck. Both ears and the sides of the head, down to just below the jaw, are also contained within. This padding, whatever its material, is enclosed in a hard plastic shell, with small holes on each side to allow sound to reach the ears.[6] The wearer's face is obscured by a rubberized metal mask that individual players can customize, though they almost always do so in keeping with the design traditions associated with their on-field position. The mask and helmet shell are rendered in team colors, and the sides of the plastic shell are usually adorned with team logos. Sometimes a stripe or two swoops from the center of the forehead just above the facemask over the top of the helmet to the back. Occasionally, particularly in high school and college, small merit stickers adorn the helmet, signifying each player's achievements in relation to benchmarks set by the coaching staff.

The visual combination of the helmet's distinctive material form and aesthetic adornment can be arresting. Whether steeped in tradition or marked by innovation, helmet designs can inspire and excite, regardless of the results of the games played by the athletes who wear them. As objects, these plastic domes have accrued deep cultural resonance as icons and avatars of the communities they represent. But they can also be beautiful: the glistening metallic hue of the University of Notre Dame's "Golden Dome" helmets, the anatomically appropriate positioning of the spiraling yellow horns that emerge from the forehead area of the Los Angeles Rams' helmets, and the simple text iconography of the block "H" and "Y" on the contrasting red and white helmets of Harvard and Yale can stimulate even those who don't care about the games themselves. And a wide swath of collectors, historians, and aficionados have taken pains to document, chronicle, and artistically render helmets from across football's history, forming communities and articulating their own identities via their attention to the aesthetics of these colorful objects.[7]

But the twenty-first-century news media's discussion of the football helmet is understandably dominated by consideration of the equipment's shortcomings as a purported safety device. In particular, this discussion has focused on chronic traumatic encephalopathy (CTE), a brain disorder caused by the lifelong accumulation of concussive and subconcussive hits to the head.[8] Although the rigid shell of the plastic safety helmet effectively protects the outside of the skull upon an on-field collision, it cannot prevent the brain's impact against the inside of the skull. This has led to neurological injury and long-term impairment among an undeniably large swath of current and former football players. Given the participation of millions of American children in tackle football—combined with the especially vulnerable state of their brains—it is no wonder that scholars like Kathleen Bachynski have come to consider the issue of safety surrounding head injuries and the American football helmet a "public health crisis."[9]

The poison pill of CTE, as researchers have made clear, is that it incrementally develops with every subconcussive impact. Such routine impacts appear to be *most* harmful in brains that are still developing, yet the symptoms mostly manifest decades later. Therefore, even if you accept that it is ethically sound for an individual to assume responsibility for the risks of any self-harming behavior, CTE's harms are perhaps most insidious in those who—by virtue of their age and still developing brains—cannot legally assume responsibility for such future risks. And yet, millions of parents sign waivers every year on behalf of their children, exposing them to a harm that those children cannot possibly comprehend.

The helmet plays a vital role in a commonplace notion that football's physiological risks are acceptable. Consistently touting the latest developments in helmet technology and the purportedly enhanced safety brought about by such developments, manufacturers of football helmets, Bachynski argues, effectively "fostered a vicious cycle: equipment innovations enabled greater force and aggression, which created a perceived need for even more equipment."[10] Over the past eighty years, as helmets have kept skulls from fracturing and helmet manufacturers have touted their products' ability to reduce concussions, the sense of protection that helmets provide has exacerbated the routinization of the subconcussive head contact that contributes to CTE.

Yet the media's focus on safety and injury regarding the football helmet and the heads it covers misses something important about the football helmet: the allure of the object in and of itself. The semicircular domed space on the side of the plastic helmet has become, over the last eighty years, a canvas upon which the aesthetic identity of countless American communities has been established. As philosopher Erin Tarver puts it, "sports fandom, far from being inconsequential, is a primary means of creating and reinforcing individual and community identities for Americans today," and the helmet logo is the primary way fans of America's most popular sport recognize the team with which they identify.[11] From the University of Michigan's "winged" helmets to the Dallas Cowboys' star-studded lids, from Florida State's flying spear to the New England Patriots' "Flying Elvis," football helmet logos attract players, fans, and consumer dollars. They are the primary icons of incredibly valuable brands, representing multi-billion-dollar private clubs that carry the trappings of civic and regional pride, as well as massive public universities with tens of thousands of students, hundreds of thousands of alumni, and millions of fans. This powerful communicative function is almost never discussed in considerations of helmet safety, which tend to present the device unadorned and decontextualized. Abstracted as such, the medicalized discourse neglects the massive cultural and economic importance of the helmet, appealing to scientific reason when the object's actual draw—to all but the men who are actively playing the game at a high level—is affective and consumerist.

It is thus no stretch to assert that playing American football without helmets, as some have suggested we ought to do in order to save the game from its own violence, is to lose the very essence of the game.[12] For many—maybe even most—American fans, football would be unrecognizable—and likely not worth saving—if helmets were not a part of it. Fans' very identities are intertwined with the iconic representations that the space of the helmet showcases, as well as the aestheticized violence it fosters in gameplay. One need look no further than the "Jacked Up!" segments that punctuated ESPN's *Monday Night Countdown* from 2002 to 2006—or the fans' uttering of oohs and aahs that accompany big hits even today—to get a sense of the violence's enduring visual appeal.[13]

Besides being an integral part of the on-field product that drives football's popularity, the football helmet is the preeminent symbol of the sport itself. Unlike baseball and basketball—which tend to be represented graphically via an avatar of the ball—football's primary avatar is not the ball, but the helmet. The studio sets of football pregame television shows are often festooned with helmets, usually arranged in accordance with that day's biggest matchups. From 1986 until 2009, *Monday Night Football*'s distinctive opening credits culminated with the crashing together of computer-generated renderings of the participating teams' helmets.[14] Many NFL teams' primary logos—including the Cleveland Browns, Las Vegas Raiders, Los Angeles Chargers, Los Angeles Rams, and Miami Dolphins—either currently or historically have included a football helmet.[15]

It is no wonder, then, that the football helmet is also exceptionally popular as a consumer object. From the game-used helmets of current and former players to the tiny "gumball" helmets long sold in vending machines, the football helmet is a ubiquitous collectible. Though it is impossible to quantify, there is no doubt that collectible helmets of various sizes adorn far more dens, "man caves," and living rooms than locker rooms across the United States. Fans don't just love football, they love football helmets. They love them because football helmets are a fundamental connecting piece between the action of the game and the stories fans tell about themselves about their identities.[16]

Philosopher Gottfried Boehm coined the term "iconic difference" to encapsulate an image's ability to mimic the physical world and yet imbue that which it depicts with new meaning.[17] What I dub "helmetic difference" similarly calls attention to an underappreciated distinction between the plastic football helmet as a piece of equipment with a practical function and its more pervasive cultural role as a consumer object that is both a canvas for symbols and a symbol in and of itself. Inherent in this helmetic difference is a distinction in directional emphasis. As equipment, the helmet's purpose is focused inward: to protect the brain (and, therein, the very personhood) of the athlete. As a symbol, the helmet's purpose points outward: to convey meaning to and attract attention from spectators. While conventional wisdom would suggest that the former protective purpose is the primary function of the helmet, I contend that, in practice, it is just the opposite. The enhanced meaning that the conveyance of team, regional, and branding signifiers provides fans via helmetic difference is a primary means by which they choose to affiliate themselves with the game—forming their fan identity and driving their consumer spending. The aesthetic appeal of the helmet and the team-identifying designs that appear on it, then, are fundamentally dehumanizing to the players who wear them. Understood primarily through the associations fans make with their logos, football helmets obscure the fragility of individual athletes' bodies by cloaking their heads in iconography and subordinating them to the team and its fans. This obscurative function is distinct to American football among its major commercialized spectator sport contemporaries: baseball and hockey's helmets do not cover the face (with the exception of the hockey goalie, to be discussed later in this chapter) and generally feature much less prominent logos, while basketball features no protective headgear at all.

Though the empty space above the ear hole represents the football helmet's most profitable canvas, it is not the only means by which the equipment makes an aesthetic impression and conveys meaning. As developments in face mask design and technology progressed over the twentieth century, the football helmet was transformed such that it enveloped the face as well as the head. Today, with the exception of athletes at the few positions that prioritize vision over protection— kicker, punter, and quarterback—most football players' faces are covered by a lattice of metal bars and, occasionally, a visor. The effect of this covering, though ostensibly protective, adds martial connotations to the equipment. The football helmet is *fierce*, in other words, conveying a violent potential associated with masculinity much like a medieval knight's helmet, with its visor, or a Roman gladiator's helmet, with its grotesque metal visage. Needless to say, this conveyance of ferocity has proven attractive to generations of young men, whether or not they choose to test their own mettle by playing the game. What's more, in covering the players' faces, the modern face mask also obscures, at least to some degree, the personalities of the young people playing the game. More than any other sport, uniform numbers are a necessity in football because without them, apart from the relative difference in body types that separate position groups, most observers would have tremendous difficulty telling the players apart from one another.[18]

To put it bluntly, in such a hyperviolent game, the relative anonymity imposed on players by the helmet inures audiences to tolerate and even celebrate a level of violence and bodily harm they might not otherwise. When a player is writhing on the ground, having torn an ACL or broken a rib, the helmet usually stays on, obscuring his anguish—and, presumably, a masculinity-encoded desire to not be seen in tears. Gameplay is delayed, the player is removed from the field, then whisked to the locker room and onto the next week's injury report. Unless the player is an especially important one to the team's capacity to win games, or plays one of the few offensive positions likely to show up on the roster of a fantasy team, the entire experience is little more than a temporary interruption to most fans. It is only in the most catastrophic circumstances, usually an incapacitating head or neck injury, that the veil of the face mask is lifted, often by unscrewing it while the helmet remains on, revealing the all-too vulnerable human being under the game's imposing armor. This is part of what makes such catastrophic injuries so disconcerting—the forcible recognition of the pain and long-term, potentially life-altering suffering that football imposes on real human beings, who are as vulnerable and fragile as everyone else.

Even when viewed in close-up on TV, unless the player happens to be a quarterback or another "skill" position player with a less obscuring face mask, it is almost impossible to tell one player's head from another. That the quarterback, by far the most important position in modern football and the one most protected, by rule, from the game's violence, is the one whose face is most visible during gameplay has important ramifications that extend far beyond the field. Though the relative lack of bars on a quarterback's face mask has a practical purpose—preserving a clear field of vision for those who pass the ball—it also has the added benefit of making the athletes who play that position almost the only ones who are readily recognizable to fans when they are *not* in uniform. This has meant that legendary quarterbacks like Johnny Unitas, Joe Montana, and Tom Brady have been able to use their likenesses to sell products to a degree that comparatively excellent non-quarterbacks—especially linemen, whose faces are fully obscured—have not.

The problematic nature of this dynamic is especially pronounced with regard to race. Though progress has been made in recent years, the raw statistics still bear out the bias that informs who is developed as a quarterback and who is not.[19] In 2022, white men accrued 70 percent of the NFL starts at quarterback in a league in which the overall player pool is at least 69 percent non-white and 56 percent African American.[20] This discrepancy is the legacy of "stacking," a historical practice wherein white coaches' racist views of Black players' intellectual capabilities led to a developmental emphasis on clustering whites at the "skill" positions thought to require decision-making: quarterback, middle linebacker, and center.[21] The development pipeline for players who play these positions still bears out the legacies of this long-standing racial bias. Stacking, in tandem with the greater degree to which players at non-"skill" positions tend to be obscured by their face masks, further facilitates what Erin Tarver has termed the "mascotting" of Black athletes. Within this dynamic, Tarver asserts that Black athletes are celebrated as athletic symbols of a given community but never considered full-fledged members of that group.[22] White fans might cheer on Black men as Bulldogs or Sooners or Packers, but not welcome them to take their daughters to the prom, join their fraternities, or become members of their neighborhood associations. The picture on the side of the helmet thus plasters over not only the players' humanity, but also their individuality. Whether massed on the sideline, clumped in their position groups, or sequentially numbered on a roster sheet, these young men are effectively always viewed with the helmet on, and thus as anonymous, interchangeable, disposable, and easily stereotyped. Football's headgear, in other words, amplifies the racial alienation of the sport's mostly white fans from its many players of color.

Though millions of white people play American football, I posit that the plastic safety helmet functions as a racist technology in the modern game. Furthermore, in keeping with the NFL's demographics and the larger contours of American history, the helmet is an anti-Black technology. This is not to say that helmet manufacturers, NFL teams, American universities, football coaches, or even fans have racist intentions when it comes to propagating and supporting the use of the helmet as a safety device or consumer object. Rather, it is the material qualities of the device, in conjunction with the way the game functions commercially and as a site of community formation, that accrue historical and cultural baggage. The dehumanization that the football helmet engenders might be a small injustice in the larger scheme of things, but it contributes nonetheless to the larger swath of deindividualizing stereotypes that systemically disadvantage people of color in numerous facets of American life.

The Glass Helmet Project: Uninterrupted's Entrepreneurial Individualism

The football helmet's anonymizing and depersonalizing effects have been noted by the players themselves, as I have explored elsewhere, and their message is also being amplified by select media and cultural producers.[23]

In September 2019, Uninterrupted, the multimedia company cofounded by NBA legend and frequent social justice activist LeBron James, posted a a video to its YouTube channel titled "The Glass Helmet Project."[24] Mallory Chin, of the sports and culture website *HypeBeast,* described the project thusly:

> Seeing as even big league NFL players are constantly covered by the headpiece, essentially making them unrecognizable both as an athlete and the people they are off the gridiron, James and Uninterrupted's Glass Helmet Project [aim] to tackle this problem known as "The Helmet Effect." To combat this, the duo want to give fans the opportunity to connect and appreciate the athletes behind the masks for more than a football player by introducing a see-through iteration.[25]

The Glass Helmet Project video does not feature LeBron James, but it does include his business partner, Maverick Carter, along with former NFL wide receiver Andrew Hawkins and designer Victor Solomon discussing the anonymizing Helmet Effect. Their hope is that the "glass" helmet (which was really manufactured from a clear resin), will make the men who play football more visible and recognizable as human beings with thoughts, feelings, personalities, and life stories that are worth learning.

The video begins with Hawkins, who played six seasons for the Cincinnati Bengals and Cleveland Browns, outlining the relative anonymity he felt.

> I could walk down the street, be the star of a football team and nobody knows who I am. Because people don't recognize you. As players we're kind of looked at as warriors or gladiators. And gladiators aren't people who you remember their names. The Helmet Effect for an NFL player is: you're nameless and faceless. And it's like that by design.

Hawkins's invocation of gladiators is especially telling because it not only highlights the popularized violence of American football by relating it to Roman bloodsport, but also the fundamental disposability of the warriors involved. To be "nameless and faceless . . . by design" is not just to be unrecognizable, it is to be disposable—"gladiators aren't people you remember," because if you did, you might question your role in celebrating the harm that comes to them.

But the Glass Helmet Project isn't a football abolitionist enterprise—far from it. Rather, the transparency of the prototype is meant to reconceptualize the helmet as an "icon of football[,] this physical thing that is so loaded with meaning," to market the players as fully-fledged individuals with interests and lives beyond the gridiron. Hawkins continues:

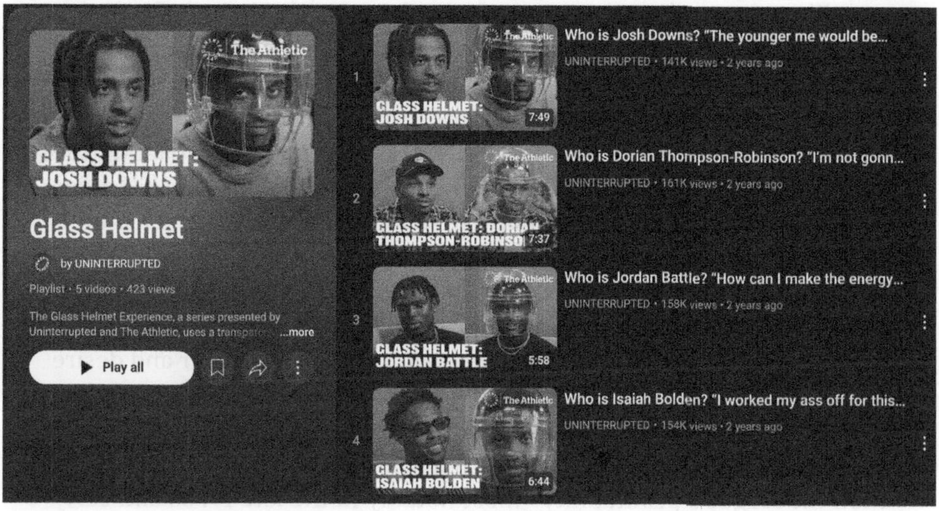

FIGURE 7.1: Screenshot of Uninterrupted's "Glass Helmet Project."

> Your identity is so tied to what you do on the football field. The Glass Helmet for me is showing players that it's OK to show fans and everyone else who you are beyond that. Because that's your real value proposition as a person. And I would also argue that it's going to make you a better player, leaning in to who you are, leaning into your personality and the things that drive you.

Maverick Carter builds on the neoliberal framing implied in Hawkins's use of "value proposition" by emphasizing that not only are these men "brothers . . . fathers [and] artists" but also "creatives . . . thought leaders [and] entrepreneurs." Befitting Carter's own tremendous success in crafting a media empire that capitalizes on the fame and transcendent athletic abilities of his friend and business partner, LeBron James, the glass helmet's potential benefits are framed as monetary as well as humanistic. Solomon similarly asserts that "athletes have evolved to being the kings of culture in a way that everyone is looking to them aesthetically, philosophically, conceptually, and empowering these athletes to embrace that role, I think is super important." To maximize and monetize the public platform that being a professional athlete provides, these men must be visible when the audience looks their way.

While race is never mentioned in the video, the clear implication is that the "kings of culture" that the glass helmet will empower are Black. At the video's end, a selection of athletes are displayed with the glass helmet on. All are Black. Uninterrupted obviously understands that white NFL stars like Tom Brady and Aaron Rodgers, for example, don't suffer from a lack of face time. The "Helmet Effect" is clearly figured as an anti-Black phenomenon. Importantly, as evidenced via the involvement of LeBron James and the media company Uninterrupted—whose catch phrase is "More than an Athlete"—the Helmet Effect's pernicious impact on the Black men who play football is implicitly contrasted to basketball, a game that prominently features the unobscured faces of its players and has built its popularity by marketing their personalities.[26] Of the "Big Four" American men's professional sports, only football and basketball are majority Black. But despite their similar labor demographics, the NBA and NFL have very different histories of dealing with the lenses of fear and desire through which many white fans view their games. While the NBA has struggled through multiple "Dark Ages" of racialized panic surrounding pathologized understandings of Black athletes' behavior that threatened the league's profitability—most notably in the late 1970s and early 2000s—the NFL has not faced similar existential threats, despite its own share of scandal involving African American players. Rather than dealing with audiences' discomfort by marketing other Black stars viewed as more palatable to whites (as the NBA did with Magic Johnson, Michael Jordan, and Tim Duncan), the NFL has largely relied on the subordination of purportedly troublesome individuals to the enduring potency of the team concept. For the latter, the helmet functions as a technology of literal effacement.

After the initial 2019 video, however, the Glass Helmet Project sat dormant until April 2023. Relaunched by Uninterrupted as its own offshoot YouTube channel, called "The Glass Helmet Experience," and reconfigured as a series of individual profiles, "Glass Helmet" featured Josh Downs, Dorian Thompson-Robinson, Jordan Battle, Isaiah Bolden, and Mitchell Agude.[27] All are Black athletes who were rookies in the 2023 NFL season, drafted in the third round or later. Each video begins with a voiceover: "What if the helmet revealed the human underneath it? With questions that peel back the layers of an athlete's true self. Revealing who they are and who they hope to become. Uninterrupted. This is the Glass Helmet Experience." Other than the voiceover, however, no voice apart from that of the individual athlete is heard in each video, nor are any other people pictured on camera. The athletes instead pose a series of pre-scripted questions to themselves, reading them off of note cards before answering. There is some variation in the questions, which are tailored to the individuals' experiences. But the first question, posed once the eponymous glass helmet has been donned, is always simply "Who are you?" Since the athletes are primed to answer this question in relation to their playing career, the follow up question is "Who are you without [the helmet] on?" Rather than "quarterback" or "future NFL star," as Dorian Thompson-Robinson initially describes himself, the athletes are thus prompted to humanize and individualize themselves. "I am still Dorian Thompson-Robinson," the twenty-three-year old asserts. "I'm just a more funny, creative, loving person outside of the helmet."[28] Thompson-Robinson goes on to describe his close relationship to his mother, the childhood blanket that he still sleeps with (which is displayed on set), and his nascent clothing brand, which builds on his artistic practice. In each of the videos, the lesson for the viewer is obvious: if you could see through the plastic safety helmet, you would be forced to reckon with the *individuals* who play football. To "peel back the layers of an athlete's true self," as the intro voiceover puts it, is to first remove the uniform covering the helmet imposes, and to recognize that the prodigious athletic talent these men possess is only a small part of who they are.

LeBron James is well known for supporting Black activism over the last decade, and Uninterrupted has maintained an overwhelming focus on Black athletes across its multimedia productions. Given that background, the "Glass Helmet" series should be considered an act of resistance to the anti-Black racism encoded into the game of American football, broadly, as well as the plastic safety helmet, in particular. But it is worth noting again that "Glass Helmet" never invokes race explicitly. It is up to the viewer to infer that this video series' very obvious point about the opacity of the football helmet is also necessarily about racism. In light of the careful manner in which James has historically managed to balance (some might say temper) his activism with consideration for his corporate supporters, this reticence lessens the critical heft of the series, allowing viewers disinclined to confront the game's racial dynamics—and global capital's role in exacerbating those dynamics for profit—to avoid the discomfort of such recognition.[29]

Glorious Bones: Esmaa Mohamoud Reorients Helmet Design

While the effectiveness of Uninterrupted's critique of the helmet is blunted by its unwillingness to directly call out the racism it seeks to address, visual artist Esmaa Mohamoud's *Glorious Bones* (2019) makes the connection between the football helmet and anti-Black racism explicit. Mohamoud is a Toronto-based artist whose work examines "the gap between contemporary culture's oversimplification and diminishment of Black people, compared to the complexity, richness, and diversity of their actual lived experiences."[30] Her 2021 solo exhibition, *Esmaa Mohamoud: To Play in the Face of Certain Defeat*, toured across Canada, building on this anti-racist ethos by "look[ing] specifically at how the Black body is reduced within the vernacular of athleticism."[31] Several of the pieces focused on football, each using the equipment of the game—cleats, shoulder pads, the chains used to measure first downs—to highlight how Black men are restricted, diminished, deindividualized, and rendered disposable by the sport and its spectators. But *Glorious Bones*, which toured as part of *To Play in the Face of Certain Defeat*, focuses this critique solely on the helmet.

The piece, positioned in the middle of the floor in a large gallery space, consists of three major elements: first, a base of black sand, roughly arranged into a diamond shaped mound about six to eight inches high. Emerging from this mound are forty-six poles, also painted black, about five feet high. A football helmet sits atop each pole. The helmets all appear to be smooth shell Riddell or Schutt helmets of the type that were widely used in the late 1990s and early 2000s. The face masks that adorn the helmets vary in arrangement, from the full cage of a lineman to the three-horizontal-bar models commonly worn by quarterbacks and other "skill" players. All are painted black. But above the monochromatic front presented by the sand, poles, and masks, on the smooth shells of the helmets, is a field of vibrant color.

Rather than being festooned with the usual team logos that adorn the sides of most helmets, or the ubiquitous center stripes, the helmets of *Glorious Bones* are enrobed, from the forehead to the nape of the neck, in patterns inspired by African wax print textiles like Kente cloth. From rectangular geometric shapes to swirling helixes to drawings of eyes peering outward, from magenta to turquoise to electric green to navy, each of the forty-six helmets has its own distinctive decoration. Per sports studies scholar Samantha N. Sheppard, "each customized outer shell highlights the richness of African culture within the context of North American sports and exposes the injurious commodification of Black athletes by racial capitalism for mass entertainment."[32] As Sheppard elucidates, unlike "Glass Helmet," Mohamoud's piece is undeniably critical of the football industry, even elegiac in its heads-on-spikes invocation of the game's brutality. Even so, the piece is also resolute and unabashed in its colorful celebration of the Black cultures from which these helmeted, masked players emerge. As Sheppard further articulates, the players' "magnificent heads are held high in Mohamoud's football fabulation. . . . The installation's sporting spectacle is [thus] multivalent: these are players and totems; this is a gridiron and a burial ground; these heads are on spikes and on pedestals; they are aligned and alienated."[33] Here, as in the Glass Helmet Project, while the helmeted status quo is condemned, the proposed countermeasure is not the abolition of football and football helmets, but rather their repurposing in order to celebrate not just Black athletes, but Black people and their cultures.

Even so, the various patterns that decorate Mohamoud's repurposed helmets provide more than an arresting color palette via their differing designs. As scholar and art critic Charles Reeve puts it, "By covering each helmet with a different pattern of African wax-print textile, she frames brain injury as a trauma experienced by individual players made anonymous by their uniforms. This convergence between the conditions of black athletes and of young black men generally [reveals] the tendency to regard them as social units, without distinct personalities and interests."[34] Like "Glass Helmet," then, *Glorious Bones* celebrates not merely Blackness in football, but individuality within Blackness—battling stereotypes by resisting the anonymizing effect of the opaque helmet and its uniformity. But Mohamoud's piece presents a more radical critique than "Glass Helmet" because it envisions individuality as built on community and culture, rather than neoliberal tenets of personal distinctiveness that prioritize entrepreneurialism. What's more, rather than erasing the helmet by rendering it clear, *Glorious Bones* prompts us to reorient a commonplace understanding of the headgear's signifying function.

The Signifying Helmet

In *Glorious Bones*, Mohamoud demonstrates that revealing the head of the athlete under the helmet is itself a limited vision insofar as it eliminates the communicative possibilities of the space on the side of the helmet. The work asks: rather than let that space be controlled by others' messaging, what if Black athletes could use it to express themselves? In other words, what if football helmets were not totems of team, school, civic, and community identity but instead represented the individual personalities and interests of the athletes who wear them? The idea of variation among helmets on a football team is not so far-fetched. At one time in the game's history, especially during the leather helmet era of the first half of the twentieth century, many college teams experimented with giving different position groups differently colored helmets. Per historian Timothy P. Brown, when rule changes opened up the possibilities for passing the football in 1912, coaches began thinking about adapting the color of the otherwise uniform leather helmets, which to that point were almost always brown or black.[35] Increasing the incentive to differentiate was the fact that "teams did not yet wear home and away jerseys . . . and opponents often shared team colors, so it was difficult to tell friend from foe."[36] To address this problem, numerous teams began outfitting eligible receivers with differently colored helmets so the quarterback could easily identify them. In one particularly evocative instance from the plastic helmet era, Navy head coach Wayne Hardin equipped his eligible receivers in bright orange helmets, rather than the usual gold, for a rivalry matchup against Army in 1961.[37]

But adapting helmet decoration to serve strategic priorities was not the only manner in which early helmets were redesigned to identify and individualize certain players. At the University of Washington in the 1960s and early 1970s, the team captains on offense and defense were each awarded purple helmets, while the rest of the team wore gold. And in the 1980s, Iowa State's football team bestowed a differently colored "award helmet" to reward individual players' previous on-field achievement.[38] Even today, some college programs, most famously Ohio State and Florida State, award merit stickers to players based on reaching individual benchmarks, allowing more senior players to display their personal prowess on an otherwise uniform helmet. All such examples demonstrate that while uniform presentation of team identity in helmet design may be a modern standard, the helmetic difference facilitated by this practice was not inevitable and is not immutable.

None of these precedents from football history, though they present alternatives to the current hegemonic uniformity, truly address Mohamoud's critique. They present differentiation, but only in the service of recognizing individual players' utility, leadership, or past exploits in relation to the game itself. Their personalities—and personhood—are not celebrated in the manner that Reeves highlights as Mohamoud's exhortation in *Glorious Bones*. The different wax-print patterns in her piece suggest individuality *and* Black pride—they signify, as Henry Louis Gates might phrase it, in a resistant modality that is both individual and intertextual.[39]

Even in this mode of symbolizing the individual-within-community, there is some precedent in sporting equipment. If we look to ice hockey, another of North America's favorite contact sports (and one of its whitest), we can find in the goalie helmet an example of plasticized head protection upon which personal expression is not only tolerated, but celebrated. Beginning with Montreal Canadiens goalie Jacque Plante, who adopted a mask for NHL game use in 1959, ice hockey goalies began protecting their faces from the pucks propelled at them at high speed. The masks were adopted league-wide by 1975.[40] Though these masks were initially undecorated, beginning with Gary Cheevers—who had black stitches painted on his white mask where pucks had hit his face—goalies started personalizing their masks, as well as the helmets to which such masks were soon attached.[41] Today, hockey goalies around the world commission artists to paint colorful designs on their helmets.[42] Crucially, while these goalie helmet designs usually include some aesthetic representation of their team's branding, they just as frequently include representation of themes or characteristics that pertain to the individual under the helmet, though sometimes the details of the latter are policed by the NHL.[43] These individual goalie designs are scrutinized but also celebrated by hockey fans, who have come to appreciate the personality characteristics that such designs convey.[44] That almost all of these goalies throughout history, like the vast majority of NHL players, have been white only further elucidates Mohamoud's critique. Through the NHL example, we can see that *Glorious Bones*, striking in its resistance to football's ruling paradigm of helmeted anonymization and highlighting its anti-Black consequences, is not altogether unrealistic in imagining an individualizing alternative.

As with "Glass Helmet," then, *Glorious Bones* demonstrates that a bit of defamiliarization goes a long way toward recognizing that the hegemonic helmeted status quo has pernicious effects on the people who play tackle football, whether or not they ever suffer from CTE or other traumatic brain injury. More hopefully, both also serve as a reminder that resistance is possible, and necessary, if we are to change that status quo. But the differences between the two when it comes to their critiques are meaningful. Since LeBron James, the chief proprietor of Uninterrupted, has made hundreds of millions of dollars positioning himself as "more than an athlete" among the power brokers of corporate spectator sports, it should be no surprise that he attempts to use what Audre Lorde would call "the master's tools" of bootstraps capitalism in his limited attempts to "dismantle the master's house."[45] Mohamoud, by contrast, is an outsider to that political economy as a Canadian woman who is not a professional athlete herself. The result is a more radical defamiliarization and reimagining of the helmet's signifying function.

Still, Black athletes and artists cannot be the only ones raising their voices if meaningful changes to football's culture of harm are actually going to occur. In some ways, we have an unprecedented opportunity in this moment when football continues to be a cultural behemoth even as it faces an existential threat in CTE and an attendant decline in the number of youth players. As Bachynski has convincingly argued, we cannot engineer our way out of brain trauma via the helmet.[46] But we should also follow "Glass Helmet" and *Glorious Bones* by considering the helmet as more than a safety device. The plastic safety helmet will not go away for being an ineffective mode of protection, because it is hugely significant both as a symbol and canvas for symbols. It is a kind of mirror that reflects fans' desires while obscuring the human beings underneath. We must take that importance seriously if we are going to imagine and create a safer, less racist, more humane future for football and for commercialized spectator sport writ large.

Notes

1. "About," Riddell.com. https://news.riddell.com/info/about.

2. Emily A. Harrison, "The First Concussion Crisis," *American Journal of Public Health*, 104, no. 5 (2014): 822–33.

3. Oliver Connolly, "Helmets Don't Eliminate Concussions," *The Guardian*, September 6, 2019, https://www.theguardian.com/sport/2019/sep/06/helmets-dont-eliminate-concussions-its-time-for-the-nfl-to-ditch-them.

4. Thomas Oates, *Football and Manliness: An Unauthorized Feminist Account of the NFL* (Urbana, IL: University of Illinois Press, 2017), 77.

5. Uninterrupted, "The Glass Helmet Project: Tackling One of Football's Most Unique Challenges," September 4, 2019, YouTube video, 4:03, https://www.youtube.com/watch?v=EZcCk5atZMc.

6. Newer helmet models often have other holes that are designed variously to let the helmet "flex" on impact, allow air to cool the head, and serve other ostensible purposes.

7. Noah Cohan, "Whose Helmet? Reconceptualizing American Football's Iconic Equipment," *Kinesiology Review*, https://doi.org/10.1123/kr.2024-0037.

8. Among other sources, see Mark Fainaru-Wada and Steve Fainaru in *League of Denial: The NFL, Concussions, and the Battle for Truth* (New York: Crown Archetype, 2013).

9. Kathleen Bachynski, *No Game for Boys to Play* (Chapel Hill, NC: University of North Carolina Press, 2019), 6.

10. Bachynski, *No Game for Boys to Play*, 69.

11. Erin C. Tarver, *The I in Team* (Chicago: University of Chicago Press, 2017), 2.

12. Connolly, "Helmets Don't Eliminate Concussions.".

13. Aaron Gordon, "When ESPN Cheered Violence," *Salon*, September 13, 2013, https://www.salon.com/2013/09/15/keep_your_helmet_on_espns_jacked_up_in_retrospect_partner/.

14. Katie Thomas, "N.F.L.'s Policy on Helmet-to-Helmet Hits Makes Highlights Distasteful," *New York Times*, October 21, 2010, https://www.nytimes.com/2010/10/22/sports/football/22hits.html.

15. Some helmet designs, most notably the current Raiders and former Dolphins lids, have included this helmet rendering on the side of the helmet itself, creating a kind of infinite regression potential for helmitude.

16. Anecdotal evidence of the passion of aficionados abounds, but, to put numbers to it, when Riddell explored a sale in 2023, it reported annual earnings of $85 million, many times more than could be earned from sales to active

players alone. And Riddell is just one of several helmet manufacturers, though it is by far the largest. See Abigail Summerville, "Football Helmet-Maker Riddell Explores Sale," *Reuters*, November 6, 2023, https://www.reuters.com/markets/deals/football-helmet-maker-riddell-explores-sale-2023-11-06/.

17. Gottfried Boehm, "Indeterminacy: On the Logic of the Image," in *Dynamics and Performativity of Imagination: The Image Between the Visible and the Invisible*, ed. Bernd Huppauf and Christoph Wulf (New York: Routledge, 2009), 226.

18. Football players themselves are not unaware of this dynamic, and many have undertaken to stand out and earn notoriety, either by adding uniform adornments like brightly colored sweatbands and cleats, or by celebrating their on-field accomplishments in distinctive ways. Black players, in particular, have often been recognized for expressive touchdown celebrations, which cultural critics of sport have long linked to a larger tradition of Black male style. The need to be individualized may be felt particularly acutely in football, a dynamic I will detail in greater depth later in this essay.

19. Becky Sullivan, "No Matter Who Wins, the First Super Bowl with 2 Black Quarterbacks Will Make History." *National Public Radio*, February 8, 2023, https://www.npr.org/2023/02/08/1155170993/super-bowl-black-quarterbacks-history-hurts-mahomes. For more on anti-Black racism and the quarterback position, see Louis Moore, *The Great Black Hope: Doug Williams, Vince Evans, and the Making of the Black Quarterback* (New York: PublicAffairs, 2024).

20. Jim Sergent, "Why 2 Black Quarterbacks are Meeting in Super Bowl 57: Opportunity," *USA Today*, February 9, 2023, https://www.usatoday.com/story/graphics/2023/02/09/black-quarterbacks-super-bowl-nfl/11201092002/; "The 2022 National Football League Racial and Gender Report Card (NFL)," The Institute for Diversity and Ethics in Sport (TIDES). https://www.tidesport.org/_files/ugd/ac4087_d74e4aa674334087b6c4506f6d353a48.pdf.

21. D. Stanley Eitzen and David C. Sanford. "The Segregation of Blacks by Playing Position in Football: Accident or Design?" *Social Science Quarterly* 55, no. 4 (1975): 948–59.

22. Tarver, *The I in Team*, 98.

23. Noah Cohan, "Whose Helmet?"

24. "The Glass Helmet Project," https://www.youtube.com/watch?v=EZcCk5atZMc.

25. Mallory Chin, "LeBron James & Uninterrupted Introduce Glass Helmets for NFL Players," *Hypebeast*, September 5, 2019, https://hypebeast.com/2019/9/lebron-james-uninterrupted-nfl-glass-helmets-they-will-be-seen-video-campaign.

26. Mary G. McDonald, "Michael Jordan's Family Values: Marketing, Meaning, and Post-Reagan America," in *From Jack Johnson to LeBron James: Sports, Media, and the Color Line*, ed. Chris Lamb (Lincoln, NE: University of Nebraska Press, 2016), 468.

27. "The Glass Helmet Experience," Uninterrupted, April 28, 2023, https://www.youtube.com/playlist?list=PLXwU4uTVdQIf4iWfsNYh2Gv1HRtGCraEC.

28. "Who is Dorian Thompson-Robinson? "I'm not gonna put a limit on who I could be" | Glass Helmet." Uninterrupted, April 25, 2023, YouTube video, 7:36, https://www.youtube.com/watch?v=0PBQ3uixBbA&list=PLXwU4uTVdQIf4iWfsNYh2Gv1HRtGCraEC&index=2.

29. Here, I'm thinking in particular about James's unwillingness to speak out in solidarity with protestors in Hong Kong in 2019, for which he was roundly criticized and accused of bowing to pressure from Nike, his largest corporate sponsor. See "LeBron Addresses Backlash to Hong Kong Comments," *Reuters*, October 15, 2019, https://www.reuters.com/article/sports/lebron-addresses-backlash-to-hong-kong-comments-idUSKBN1WV01A/.

30. Kavi Gupta Gallery, "Esmaa Mohamoud," https://kavigupta.com/artists/101-esmaa-mohamoud/.

31. Kavi Gupta Gallery, "Esmaa Mohamoud."

32. Samantha N. Sheppard, "*Glorious Bones*: Esmaa Mohamoud's Football Fabulation," *Velvet Light Trap*, no. 87 (2021): 69–72, 69.

33. Sheppard, "*Glorious Bone*," 69.

34. Charles Reeve, "How Artist Esmaa Mohamoud Reveals the Dark Heart of American Athletics," *Frieze*, no. 201 (2019), https://www.frieze.com/article/how-artist-esmaa-mohamoud-reveals-dark-heart-american-athletics.

35. Timothy P. Brown, "How the Forward Pass Changed the Color of Football Helmets," *Football Archaeology*, December 11, 2020, https://www.footballarchaeology.com/p/how-the-forward-pass-changed-the-color-of-football-helmets?utm_source=substack&utm_campaign=post_embed&utm_medium=web.

36. Brown, "How the Forward Pass."

37. Brown, "How the Forward Pass."

38. Paul Lukas, "Hat Trick," *Uni-Watch.com*, January 4, 2013, https://uni-watch.com/2013/01/04/a-look-at-college-football-teams-that-have-worn-mismatched-helmets/.

39. Henry Louis Gates, *The Signifying Monkey: A Theory of African-American Literary Criticism* (London: Oxford University Press, 2014), xxxiii.

40. "History of the Goalie Mask," *USA Hockey Magazine*, https://www.usahockeymagazine.com/article/history-goalie-mask.

41. "History of the Goalie Mask," *USA Hockey Magazine*.

42. The face coverings themselves, once molded fiberglass sheets with eye holes, now take the form of metal bars that are distinct from but not dissimilar to football face masks.

43. Greg Wyshynski, "Wild's Marc-Andre Fleury Dons Native American Heritage Mask," ESPN.com, November 23, 2023, https://www.espn.com/nhl/story/_/id/38970420/nhl-nixes-marc-andre-fleury-mask-honoring-native-americans.

44. Jon Neely, "The 50 Best Goalie Mask Designs in NHL History," *Bleacher Report*, December 20, 2010, https://bleacherreport.com/articles/545279-the-50-best-goalie-mask-designs-in-nhl-history/.

45. Audre Lorde, "The Master's Tools Will Never Dismantle the Master's House," *The Selected Works of Audre Lorde*, ed. Roxanne Gay (New York: Norton, 2020), 39.

46. Bachynski, *No Game for Boys to Play*, 156.

8

"'Bout That Action, Boss"

Signifying and the Cultural Politics of Marshawn Lynch's Sporting Celebrity and Media Persona

SAMANTHA N. SHEPPARD

During Super Bowl XLVIII's Media Day on January 28, 2014, the Seattle Seahawks' elusive running back, Marshawn Lynch, exited his mandatory press conference after only six minutes and twenty seconds of a sixty-minute time slot, to the dismay of reporters and media outlets gathered for the pre-Bowl event at the Prudential Center in Newark, New Jersey.[1] Media Day, as Dashiell Bennett jocosely illustrates, is an "infamous Super Bowl–week spectacle in which every player on both rosters, and the thousands of reporters gathered to cover the big game, assemble on one field in an orgy of self-promotion."[2] Compulsory press conferences are central to this self-aggrandizing spectacle, and Lynch's brief appearance was made only to avoid a potential fine by the National Football League (NFL) for noncompliance with their media access policy, which mandates that players engage in reasonable cooperation with news media during the football season and the playoffs.[3] Lynch's guileful adherence to the rules and subsequent swift retreat from the Media Day frenzy was unsurprising to most reporters, onlookers, and fans. Throughout the 2013 season, Lynch's disdain for these kinds of obligatory interviews had intensified, resulting in the NFL levying a $50,000 fine against the running back for not making himself available to the media for postgame interviews.[4]

Lynch remained at the Prudential Center following his obstinate Media Day performance. Standing at the edge of a step and repeat banner, he surveyed the sports media spectacle around him from behind a pair of black sunglasses. As he took in the scene, Lynch was approached by Deion Sanders, Hall of Fame cornerback turned NFL Network analyst. Known for his media savvy and flamboyant "Prime Time" sports persona, Sanders treaded lightly as he advanced toward Lynch and coaxed the press-averse football star into an informal on-air interview. Sanders placed his arm just above Lynch's shoulder, enclosing him in an intimate near-embrace as they faced the camera. The two shared pleasantries and, despite the camera and microphone's presence, Lynch appeared at ease, the opposite of his tense behavior at the official Super Bowl press event. Making their exchange more conversational than the typically clunky and clichéd press conference format, Sanders compliments Lynch, saying he looks good. In response, Lynch chuckles and drops his head, smiling before he playfully pulls at Sanders's suit to expose the designer tag inside, responding, "Shit, you do too." Sanders's anxious laugh betrays a concern that Lynch's unusual on-camera expressiveness might conflict with FCC rules and regulations. Sander then deftly shifts the conversation to Lynch's preparation and excitement for the upcoming game before explicitly asking Lynch about his shy demeanor and disinterest in press conferences.

SANDERS: You kind of shy?
LYNCH: Nah.
SANDERS: You just don't want to talk really?
LYNCH: I'm just 'bout that action, boss.
SANDERS: You're about to go get it. You just like to do it?
LYNCH: That's what it is. I ain't never seen no talking win me nothing.
SANDERS: Yeah?
LYNCH: Yep. Been like that since I was little. I was raised like that.
SANDERS: Well, I respect it.

Lynch's now-iconic retort—"'bout that action, boss"—epitomizes his "show, don't tell" style of play and sports personality. But his response is more than a trademarkable catchphrase (he actually attempted, unsuccessfully, to file a trademark claim for the expression with the U.S. Patent and Trademark Office); it also gestures toward the Black vernacular tradition of signifying that Henry Louis Gates describes as common rhetorical gameplay in Black communities.[5]

What can be made of Lynch's recalcitrant press conference behavior and rhetorical double-speak? On the one hand, Lynch's refusals to meaningfully engage reporters and his use of evasive strategies and critical redirections have been deemed "unprofessional" by the league, reporters, and some fans who "believe it's the players' responsibility to help promote their own product by cooperating with the media that covers them."[6] In fact, Lynch's Super Bowl XLVIII mutism was explicitly criticized by the Pro Football Writers of America, which released a statement saying they were "extremely disappointed in the lack of meaningful access" and that "several of [their] long-standing and high-profile members were appalled by Mr. Lynch's conduct and refusal to answer any questions."[7] On the other hand, what might it mean to rethink Lynch's perceived unprofessionalism as a deliberate act of Black labor resistance? In explaining his response to Sanders, Lynch breaks down the meaning of "'bout that action, boss," clarifying that talking does not win football games, or anything else for that matter. Unlike sports reporters, Lynch's value is not simply based on what he says, but what he can do on the football field. Furthermore, Lynch's double play on the word "boss" is both a sign of respect to Sanders and also a reminder of how he is required to labor for and within the NFL and sports journalists' economy of exchange. His is a critique of the sports media machine that twists and turns players' words against them, a distortion that can come with personal, professional, and financial consequences.[8] For Lynch, to be "'bout that action, boss" is to control the narrative that surrounds him by redirecting attention back to the gridiron, suggesting that others' assessment of him should come from how well he plays the game on the field, not how well he can play along with reporters who may have dubious intentions.

In *Race Rebels: Culture, Politics, and the Black Working Class,* historian Robin D. G. Kelly describes the "inventive and diverse struggles waged by black workers during the twentieth century," including his own experiences working at a McDonald's in Pasadena, California, where he and his fellow Black and Brown workers "were constantly inventing new ways to rebel, ways rooted in [their] own peculiar circumstances."[9] Kelly describes deliberate slowdowns, acts of carelessness, stealth operations, and both sloppy and stylized work performance as examples of the everyday nature of African Americans' workplace resistance that are often dismissed as "manifestations of immaturity, false consciousness, or primitive rebellion."[10] Kelly uses the term "race rebels" to reference individuals and "forms of resistance—organized and unorganized—that have remained outside of (and even critical of) what we've come to understand as the key figures and institutions in African American politics."[11] To frame Lynch as a race rebel is to recognize how his press conference dissidence is a kind of sporting labor resistance against the NFL's media access policies and the public's consumerist demands for athletic labor beyond the playing field. Lynch's seemingly individualistic acts of refusal articulate a collectivist politics against the commodification of athletes and hyper-commercialized sports media culture. Furthermore, a study of press conferences as sites of working resistance provides the occasion to analyze the form and function of, to borrow from Kelly, these "peculiar circumstances," and to acutely consider what a certain kind of Black audacity and showmanship, as well as self- and community-regard, can affect and make possible in future sports press conferences and the field of sports media more broadly.

In this chapter, I closely attend to Lynch's press conference strategies to account for how race, sports, and media shape the sociocultural and political significance of his refusals to follow sporting and racial scripts. Lynch's sports media persona is complicated by his outsized sporting celebrity, whereby his press conference behavior seems simultaneously at odds with and in service of his superstardom. In this regard, contemporary sports stars occupy roles "as athletic laborers, entertainers, marketable commodities, role models, and political figures, within an increasingly global cultural economy."[12] By assessing these complex and varied expectations on sports stars, I position Lynch's sporting celebrity—a popularity gained by his athletic excellence and his own branding initiatives—in paradoxical synergy with his press conference insubordination. I argue that Lynch's stonewalling, signifying, and telegenic qualities constitute his race rebellion, especially when considered within the genre and attendant protocols of (sports) press conferences. By examining the press conference genre more broadly and by attending to examples of Lynch's recalcitrant strategies more specifically, my analysis shows how Lynch is able to capitalize on his reputation through lucrative media opportunities during and after his playing career. Therefore, I pivot from the podium to the TV and the silver screen to consider how Lynch's commercial endorsements, on-air appearances, and his film debut in Emma Seligman's 2023 raunchy queer comedy *Bottoms* function as a mediatic counterpose to the earlier fixed terms and conditions of his NFL-obligated media exposure. I conclude with a brief turn to David Shields's *Lynch: A History* (2019), a documentary that culls a range of television footage and other media sources to interrogate race, sports, and American media through Lynch's unruly personality and enigmatic media persona. While Shields's unauthorized documentary attempts to critique the spectacle and commodification of Lynch, I argue that *Lynch: A History* reproduces the commoditization and exploitation of the sports media machine that Lynch's press conference behavior and post-football media career resist and subvert for his own and others' benefit.

Beast Mode

Marshawn Lynch was born and raised in Oakland, California, where he played football and ran track at Oakland Technical High School. Prior to being drafted to the NFL in 2007 by the Buffalo Bills, Lynch dominated as a running back for University of California's Golden Bears. As an All-American and Pac-10 Offensive Player of the Year, he dazzled collegiate fans on the gridiron with both his skill and playfulness, including the time he commandeered an equipment manager's training cart for a joy ride on the field after defeating the University of Washington Huskies in 2006.[13] During his professional career, Lynch amassed a number of accolades and distinctions that added to his growing celebrity. He led the NFL in rushing touchdowns in 2013 and 2014, was selected five times as a Pro Bowl player, and, most significantly, won a Super Bowl with the Seattle Seahawks in 2014. Lynch captured sporting acclaim with his unstoppable ability to, in his own words, "run through a motherfucker's face" to get to the endzone. His dominant style of play, nicknamed "Beast Mode," mesmerized fans, and the phrase became a popular moniker for the running back. Perhaps most spectacular among his athletic feats was Lynch's sixty-seven-yard touchdown against the New Orleans Saints in 2011— where he broke nine tackles and strong-armed cornerback Tracy Porter to the ground—which was dubbed the "Beast Quake" because the crowd's celebration registered a small tremor on a nearby seismograph.[14] Lynch trademarked his "Beast Mode" alias, turning the name into a lifestyle and performance brand predicated on "a commitment to attack each day with the same ferocity that Marshawn has when he hits the hole."[15] Throughout his playing days, Lynch gained a loyal fanbase for his telegenic athletic prowess and mixed reactions for his off-the-field mediagenic resistance.

Lynch's sporting celebrity offers an interpretive frame and iconicized trope to evaluate the conjuncture of race, sports, and media culture. While he was playing in the NFL, clips of his athletic feats and his press conferences saturated sports news and social media. Since his retirement, Lynch has become a verifiable media star. Consequently, his fame provides an entry point to dissect "the constitutive meanings and power relations" that broadly encompass sports celebrityhood.[16] As distinctions between sport and entertainment industries continue to collapse, professional athletes are increasingly called upon to be sports and media stars within athletic and popular culture(s). Athletes' celebrity status critically marks them as "multi-textual and multi-platform promotional entities" for their individual benefit as well as the collective benefit of teams, sponsors, and other armatures of the culture industries.[17] Manufactured and molded by sports and media culture, athletes are meant to engage consumers on and off the playing field. Indeed, in a fashion similar to movie stars, athletes are turned into commodities by corporate sport structures, making them "both labour and the thing that labour produces."[18] In other words, sports stars such as Lynch are at once the producers and the products in "the 'unruly holy trinity' of commercial sport, the entertainment media, and late capitalist culture."[19]

The spectacle and drama of sports hinges on the imagistic power of athletes, and sports media and culture industries are especially reliant on Black celebrity athletes' multitudinous symbolic power. As sports sociologist Ben Carrington argues, Blackness and the Black athletic body are a "powerful signifier within contemporary media culture."[20] Perhaps no other athlete in the world represents this paradigm more than "prototypical sport celebrity" Michael Jordan.[21] As David L. Andrews argues, Jordan represents the ultimate player and pitchman, who "enunciates the rhythms and regimes of this late capitalist order" via his malleable, mobile, and transactional celebrity image.[22] "Being like Mike," as the popular commercial/everyman slogan suggests, is less about shape-shifting or taking inspiration from Jordan than about conforming to what "the dominant construction of Jordan's hyperreal image represents [as] a preferred vision of Black masculinity, an identity, against which all *others* are measured."[23] These kinds of calculated comparisons between Jordan and other Black men existed even on his own team. Take, for example, Jordan's former Chicago Bulls teammate, renegade rebounder Dennis Rodman, whose eccentricities on and off the court shaped his mercurial career. Known not only for his basketball skill but also his subversive self-presentation on and off the court, Rodman "radically defied normative convention and conspired, wittingly or unwittingly, to redefine representations of gender, race, and desire within the American cultural imaginary."[24] His countercultural identity, in ways not unlike Jordan's conservative if apolitical one, became highly marketable. As sports studies scholars Mélisse LaFrance and Geneviève Rail attest, Rodman made significant commercial inroads with brands wanting to market the subversive potential of his "bad as I wanna be" persona, turning his countercultural behavior into a consumption practice.[25]

As a sports celebrity, Lynch's athletic and mediatic position zigzags between that of Jordan's and Rodman's professional and emblematic identities. Lynch is both a superior athlete and a "bad boy." His athletic aptitude brings the game of football to newer heights while retaining elements of "the culture" (that is, Black American life, speech, dress, etc.) that are antithetical to the dominant culture and its media apparatus. Mainstream media would not call upon anyone to be like Lynch. However, his "Beast Mode" brand and trademarked phrases are invoked, marketed, and consumed across races, cultures, and media. Lynch's sporting celebrity—like that of Jordan, Rodman, and so many other Black sports stars—is caught up in larger representational structures that shape the visual and cultural politics of contemporary athletics.

"I'm Just Here So I Won't Get Fined"

In 2015, Marshawn Lynch and the Seattle Seahawks returned to the Super Bowl as defending champions to face the New England Patriots. On Media Day, Lynch gave another iconic response to reporters during the mandatory press event. Barraged with reporters' questions, Lynch spent six minutes responding with variations of the statement "I'm just here so I won't get fined." Stating the phrase in both a plain and joking tone, with either verve and dullness, the axiom was repeated twenty-nine times before his timer went off and he stood up to leave. Lynch's obstinate refrain enacts a symbolic and political noncompliance while still meeting the "meaningful" obligation of the NFL's media access policy. His invocation of presence—"I'm just here"—and refusal of access are not only evasive acts but also signifying tactics indicative of his racialized rebellion against compulsory off-the-field labor. The phrase highlights the terms and conditions of his mandated appearance, where the spectacle of the press conference is driven by the league and sports media's economic interests. Lynch's non-answers, with their repeated reference to fines, point to the absurdity of the entire enterprise that penalizes him for not benefitting the NFL and news media by being a personality off the gridiron. Put another way, as *The Atlantic*'s Dashiell Bennett posits of his own journalistic practice: "Try to imagine any other newspaper beat where a reporter can demand that their subjects submit to on-the-record interviews, then go to a person's employer and exact punishment when they fail to do so."[26] In a rare deviation from his canned script, Lynch tells one reporter, "You better make more with your time; you only got three more minutes." Lynch's pushback, in this instance, is a countermove that points out the futility of the reporters' tunnel-visioned pursuits. Moreover, Lynch's repeated refrain acts as a blanket statement, an all-encompassing rhetorical gesture in the tradition of other Black athletes' performative gestures signaling political alignment with Black social justice movements—raised fists (Black Power) and kneeled body (Black Lives Matter)— that use their platforms and resistant posturing to disrupt official ceremony and emit countersignals.[27] To this point, reading Black athletes' press conferences as performances underscores how their acts and postures are intentionally meant to disrupt, to "break through sedimented meanings and normative traditions" by reframing the press conference as a site of transgression against dominant social and sporting practices and rituals.[28]

FIGURE 8.1: Screenshot of Marshawn Lynch telling reporters, "I'm just here so I won't get fined."

While a site of conflict for Lynch, sports press conferences are a particular convention, genre, and metatext within the sports media industrial complex. Pregame and postgame press conferences require athletes to answer questions from a range of journalists about their actions on and off the field. Athletes' answers are meant to provide reporters with "essential information, access, and opportunities fundamental to their role in reporting and storytelling."[29] These rote interview processes are widely understood as mostly "boring, routine affairs."[30] Questions are often unoriginal, impersonal, overly intimate, inane, and/or repetitive. Some athletes, however, use press conferences to reassess their sporting performance or to push back on reporters' framing of their performances.

As sports sociologist Vincent Peña explains, sports press conferences are best understood as "sites for narrative creation, performance, image management, and racialized and gendered interactions between the media and sports figures," where biases and adversarial exchanges are all too commonplace.[31] As a sports media genre, press conferences are so ritualistic that hardly any stand out (that is, circulate beyond sports media), unless they are spectacular in some way and become the subject of sports media discourse within popular culture. Lynch's "'bout the action, boss" and "I'm just here so I won't get fined" moments broke through the mediasphere because his responses were unexpected, provocative sound bites that could be extracted from their context and go viral. Lynch is not alone in breaking press genre convention by saying the unexpected in a way that is meme-worthy. Take, for example, Philadelphia 76er Allen Iverson's notorious 2002 "We talking about practice?" response to reporters who questioned his attendance at the team's practices; or Memphis Grizzlies' head coach David Fizdale's "take that for data" answer about NBA officiating after a 2017 loss to the San Antonio Spurs. These moments breach sporting worlds and enter into popular culture as racialized rebuttals against sports media's controlled narratives.

Press conferences, therefore, can be significant sites for transgression, and Lynch's press conference actions articulate a particular Black refusal of his working conditions. Lynch's resistance in his expression of "Beast Mode" compliance ("just here so I won't get fined") is reminiscent of the kind of Black double voice Zora Neale Hurston describes as "featherbed resistance."

> The Negro, in spite of his open-faced laughter, his seeming acquiescence, is particularly evasive. You see, we are a polite people and we do not say to our questioner, "Get out of here." We smile and tell him or her something that satisfies the white person, because knowing so little about us, he doesn't know what he is missing. The Indian resists curiosity by a stony silence. The Negro offers a featherbed resistance. That is, we let the probe enter, but it never comes up. It gets smothered under a lot of laughter and pleasantries. The theory behind our tactics? The white man is always trying to know into somebody else's business. All right, I'll set something outside the door of my mind for him to play with and handle; he can read my writing, but he sure can't read my mind. I'll put this play toy in his hand and he will seize it and go away. Then I'll say my say and sing my song.[32]

Rather than offer a featherbed, Lynch's "Beast Mode" offers a force-field of resistance. A common tactic across Lynch's press conferences is an agentive and conscious use of brevity. Lynch's clipped, monosyllabic utterances—"yeah," "nope," "I'm grateful," and "thank you for asking"—are additional stonewalling attempts that mimic the pointless platitudes athletes rehearse and deliver to reporters' often canned questions. Lynch's strategies of dissent work to disrupt and openly interrogate televisual logics and racial scripts of Black athletic celebrity as commodity and spectacle.

(In)direct Address: Lynch's Press Conference Monologues

On many televised press occasions, Lynch rejects reporters' questions by responding with short phrases that do not address the inquiry but meet the minimum of his media access obligations. As the *New Yorker*'s Hua Hsu explains, "Lynch was wealthy enough that he could have fun with his choice to opt out and pay the fines as necessary. But a black athlete's insubordination, particularly when it is public, is rarely apolitical."[33] Hsu pinpoints how Lynch's media celebrity is predicated on repeat, deliberate acts of refusal—less a simple contrarian character and more of a structured, marketed, and mediated self-engagement informed by political and cultural analysis, labor dissent, and work site tensions. In many ways, Lynch's televisual performances are a refusal of the sports television industrial complex, a system that mandates telegenic personalities and treats athletes as trained seals who must bark answers at the crowd of journalists. Under the scrutiny of the press, Lynch's radical noncompliance, disgruntled silence, and elliptical curtness enact a televisual politic at once singular and collective, one enmeshed with historical discourses of resistance grounded in the politics of place, race, and sport in (Black) public life and the (non-Black) public's imagination. But Lynch is not always silent, and therefore paying particular attention to two of his press conference monologues can further reveal the politics of his (dis)engagement and how he signifies through his (in)direct address.

In one instance, during the lead-up to Super Bowl XLIX, Lynch not only said his now-iconic retort—"I'm just here so I won't get fined"—but, during another occasion at the podium, he chastised reporters' disregard for his expressed discontent with their continued questions. Ignoring a reporter's attempt to ask him about his popular "Beast Mode" brand, Lynch, clad in sunglasses and his signature Beast Mode hat, proceeds to dress down the media members in attendance. As a man of typically few words, Lynch's verbose response is worth quoting in its entirety.

> Hey, look. I mean, all week I done told y'all what's up and for some reason y'all continue to come back and do the same thing that y'all did. I don't know what story y'all trying to get out of me. I don't know what image y'all trying to portray of me, but it don't matter what y'all think, what y'all say about me. 'Cause when I go home at night, the same people that I look in the face: my family that I love, that's all I really . . . that matter to me. So y'all can go and make up whatever y'all want to make up because I don't say enough for y'all to go and put anything out on me. But I'll come to y'all event and y'all shove cameras and microphones down my throat, but when I am at home in my environment I don't see y'all. [laughs] But y'all mad at me. And if y'all ain't mad at me, then what y'all here for? I ain't got nothing for y'all. I told y'all that so y'all should know that, but y'all will sit here like right now and continue to do the same thing. I'm here preparing for a game, and y'all want to ask me all

> these questions, which is understandable. I could get down with that. But I told y'all I'm not about to say nothing. So for the remainder of my [checks wrist watch]—what's that? Three minutes because I'm here. I'm available for y'all. I'm here. I'm available for y'all. I done talked. All of my requirements are fulfilled, so now for this next three minutes, I'll just be looking at y'all the way that y'all looking at me. Thank you.

Lynch's press conference performance is at once an explanation and obfuscation, a means of chastising a media clamoring to engage with him only on their terms and for their benefit. He scolds reporters who only show a superficial interest in him, lambasting their amnesic behavior to his previous "just here so I won't get fined" response. Lynch is clear in his indictment of sports media's commodifying imperative through his reminders to the press and audience that he is here to prepare for a game. And even as he signals an awareness that press appearances are part of his contract ("I'm available for y'all. I'm here"), Lynch again challenges definitions and expectations of what the NFL's "meaningful access" policy really means. In what might seem like a portrayal of a man disinterested in doing the tedious parts of his job, there is something else at play: principally, a critique of the sports and media industrial complex's compulsory labor demands and attempted claims on his sports fame and racialized celebrity, and how press conferences operate as primary sites of hyper-surveillance and racial commodification. Lynch's reproach of this media scrutiny highlights the league's infringement on his labor and constitutional rights, ones that legal scholar Sohil Shah argues "is a due-process violation of the First Amendment right to freedom of speech."[34] Lynch makes clear how much the press does not actually care about what matters to him despite suggesting otherwise. He refuses the media's desire to create a narrative and reminds press members that they show no real interest in his interior life. While Lynch is talking directly to reporters, within the press conference's televisual framing, the press are sitting or standing off-screen, positioning the viewing audience as the indirect receivers of Lynch's direct address. Accordingly, Lynch extends his criticism to consumers who desire artificial constructions of him produced by sports media. Telling the press and viewers that he does not "see you all at [his] home," Lynch criticizes the televisual and racial scripts of the press conference as extractive, one-way exchanges of his mediated experience for their in-home viewing pleasure, with no benefit to his own communities.

In a follow-up question to Lynch's lengthy monologue, a Black former football player turned journalist tries to appeal to Lynch by discussing a conversation the reporter once had with rapper Tupac Shakur, back when he played for the Jets. "I grew up on the South Side of Chicago.

And I understand. We had a conversation about the inner city and the problems there in the inner city. Is there anything you [Lynch] can tell us about your charity?" The reporter's suggestion of "understanding" Lynch is part of an appeal to sporting and racial solidarity. However, the reporter's question fundamentally misunderstands Lynch's expressed discontent. Looking directly at the reporter, Lynch replies, "When I'm in those inner cities, come holler at me then." Like his earlier monologue, Lynch uses this follow-up to expose sporting and raced pathologies by refusing to engage in public discussions of Black culture for the pleasure of non-Black audiences, especially when such discussions traffic in well-worn racialized tropes. Lynch's invocation of his family and the Black familiar as the locus of his life and one in which the dominant media play no part is his speech's most searing indictment, yet none of the reporters acknowledged the accusation nor even seemed concerned with a world in which they do not figure or matter.

Another of Lynch's press conference monologues disrupted media conventions and went viral in 2020. Unlike his previous acts of refusal and pointed sports media criticism, the twice-un/retired running back used his obligatory media appearances to impart wisdom to his fellow athletes, turning the post-game press conference into a platform for self- and community-regard. After answering a few questions, Lynch provides an unconventional answer to a reporter's query about whether or not the running back planned to return to the league the following year. Instead of directly responding to the question, Lynch addresses his younger, fellow Black athletes about the stakes of their play in terms of their physical, psychic, and financial wellness.

> Look, I'll say like this though, right? This is a vulnerable time for a lot of these young dudes, you feel me? They don't be taking care of their chicken right, you feel me? So if it was me, or if I had an opportunity to let these little young sahobs know something, I'd say take care of y'all money, African, because that . . . don't last forever. Now I done been on the other side of retirement and it's good when you get over there and you can do what . . . you want to. So I tell y'all right now while y'all in it: take care of y'all bread, so when y'all done go ahead and take care of yourself. So while y'all at it right now, take care of y'all bodies, you know what I mean; take care of y'all chicken, you feel me; take care of y'all mentals because, look, we ain't lasting that long. I had a couple of players that I played with that they're no longer here no more—they're no longer—so, I mean, you feel me? So you start taking care of y'all mentals, y'all bodies, y'all chicken, so when y'all ready to walk away, walk away and you'll be able to do what you want to do.

Once more, Lynch takes advantage of press conferences' intimate televisual frame and mode of direct address. Staring directly into the camera, he pleads a case of self-care. Drawing on Black vernacular phrases and meanings, Lynch turns the podium into a pulpit to directly talk to Black players—"Africans"—about taking care of their bread and chicken—their finances—because the reality is that roughly 80 percent of retired NFL players are broke within three years of retiring from the league.[35] Lynch also notes the importance of Black players taking care of their minds and bodies in preparation for life beyond football. This sense of regard for players' struggles is framed in the very real terms of life and death, which constitute football's public health crisis. Lynch notes that some players are "no longer here no more," a fact resulting from the sport's violent, lasting bodily impact after a player's career has ended.

Lynch's "take care of y'all chicken" monologue suggests an awareness of how to break through press conferences' normative traditions. He evades journalists' questions, signifies, and utilizes direct address to create a media moment that will gain traction rather than be quickly forgotten like most post-game press conferences. Lynch's remarks had a wide appeal with many news outlets, which used them to explain Black vernacular to the wider public.[36] This signifying use of Black vernacular is a mode of double-speak and an awareness of double audiences—both the reporters in the room and the Black players Lynch is actually dialoguing with in that moment.

Lights, Camera, Action, Boss!

In many ways, Lynch's press conference behavior set the terms for public understanding of his media persona: witty yet withdrawn, wise yet withholding. Lynch has capitalized on his press conference persona, as have corporate sponsors outside of the NFL. An endorsement deal with his favorite candy, Skittles, for example, included a commercial that recreates a press conference dedicated to the delectable treat. As a spokesperson for Pepsi, Lynch made a commercial poking fun at his dislike of speaking to the press—his voice is dubbed over—that ended with him declaring, "Speech mode, boss!" Lynch reminds sports and popular media audiences that he is self-aware in these commercials and print and television interview exclusives, (re)emphasizing that his silences and viral moments keep people talking about him, and that "despite the fines, it actually helps his personal bottom line."[37]

Lynch is not media averse, even with his press conference antagonism. In fact, Lynch is quite the media darling. Throughout his playing career, he courted endorsement deals with media obligations, was a charismatic guest on late-night talk shows, and even made guest appearances on television sitcoms such as *The League* (FX, 2009–2015) and *Brooklyn Nine-Nine* (Fox 2013–2018, NBC 2019–2021). After retirement, Lynch's star power further ignited as he became a celebrity staple on television, appearing on shows such as the holiday edition of *The Great American Baking Show: Celebrity Holiday* (Roku, 2022). For *Slate* writer Nadira Goffe, Lynch is the best part of the show.

> *The Great American Baking Show: Celebrity Holiday* really, really needed Marshawn Lynch. As it turns out, Marshawn Lynch is not the best baker, but he's the best storyteller out of the special's celebrity contestants. . . . Marshawn Lynch is just astoundingly good on camera. He always says the right things, getting a laugh even out of someone as stoic as Paul Hollywood, and he makes everyone—audience and fellow guests and hosts alike—feel as though hanging out with him is the best use of their time.[38]

As one could argue, Lynch's challenging press conference persona was also very telegenic, even in its recalcitrance. Since retiring, Lynch has appeared in Netflix's murder-mystery improv comedy *Murderville* (2022) and HBO's science-fiction series *Westworld* (2016–2022). The once muted football star lent his voice to video games such as *Predator: Hunting Grounds* and *Call of Duty: Black Ops III*. And while Lynch's open loathing of the NFL's media policies made him a controversial figure, he has become a surrogate for the league as on-air talent for Amazon Prime's *Thursday Night Football* (*TNF*). For *TNF*, Lynch hosts segments under the title "Marshawn Lynch 'N Yo' City," where he visits the cities in which a game is being played, including a visit to Amish Country in Intercourse, Pennsylvania; a boat ride through the bayou in New Orleans; and a tour of NASA headquarters in Houston.

Lynch's diverse media credits form a portrait of a crossover star and his evolving sporting celebrity. They also reestablish that Lynch's press conference performances were not, as Deion Sanders asked during Media Day, about "being shy" but about "that action, boss." In this sense, and through Lynch's signifying, "action" is asserting control over the terms and conditions of one's media exposure and engagement. Lynch's awareness of this imagistic, symbolic, and financial power can be read in his debut film performance in 2023's *Bottoms*, Emma Seligman's high school lesbian coming-of-age comedy. The film stars Rachel Sennot and Ayo Edebiri as two high schoolers on the "bottom" of the social ladder, who devise a plan to have sex with their long-standing crushes by starting a feminist fight club. Lynch was cast in the role of "Mr. G.," a history teacher going through a difficult divorce, who agrees to serve as the club's faculty advisor. Dur-

FIGURE 8.2: Screenshot of Marshawn Lynch as Mr. G in Emma Seligman's high school lesbian coming-of-age comedy *Bottoms* (2023).

ing his time with the club, Mr. G's feminist consciousness evolves and he becomes an advocate for the marginalized girls in the group. Lynch's role in *Bottoms* is more than a "playing against type casting" trope. His excitement about the part was, to a large degree, because he felt his star persona could help redress his own handling of his sister Marreesha Sapp-Lynch's coming out in high school. According to Seligman, "[Marshawn] said he wasn't amazing about it when Marreesha came out in high school and that he felt like this was the universe giving him a chance to right his wrongs."[39] Moreover, Seligman banks on Lynch's celebrity: "Marshawn in the movie, beyond him being a wonderful actor and improviser and a lovely human being, it is wild that it might be seen by so many more people who wouldn't have otherwise seen it."[40] With *Bottoms*, Lynch embraces the power of his media image to reshape expectations of his social politics. Further, he uses film, a media product, to revisit and attempt to repair intimate family relations in a way that (re)affirms the commitments to his people he has stated in sports press conferences.

Unauthorized Media Spectacle

Lynch's sports media stardom is the subject of David Shields's unauthorized 2019 documentary *Lynch: A History*, which details a cultural history of the football player and American society. The documentary is loosely (and I use the term loosely rather *loosely*) based on Shields's 1999 book *Black Planet: Facing Race During an NBA Season*, a controversial work detailing the author's immersion in the Seattle Supersonics during the 1994–1995 season. In *Black Planet*, Shields focuses "on how white people [including himself] think about and talk about black heroes, black scapegoats, [and] black bodies" in professional basketball.[41] In an essay for *The Ringer*, writer Brian Curtis reflects on the impact of Shields's "'monomaniacal' obsession with [Gary] Payton and the Sonics in *Black Planet*," observing that Shields "was gazing in the mirror as much as gazing at court."[42] Curtis draws the reader's attention to Stanley Crouch's 2004 book *The Artificial White Man*, citing that, "among other gripes, Crouch thought Shields picked the wrong heroes: 'This man evidently never read or spoke to Negroes with brains who would challenge his narrow description of black people—all meat, all fantasy, all rhythm, all bad behavior at their most admirable.'"[43] I note this history because the paradoxes that plague Shields's *Black Planet* are also evident in his docu-treatment of Lynch as a means to explore issues of race, violence, nation, and sport. In the film, Lynch becomes a controllable character, ventriloquized by Shields's editing in ways that Lynch has expressly and continuously resisted throughout his career.

Lynch: A History is a study of corporate sport and media culture that appears aligned with Lynch's race rebel, labor refusal politics. The collage film indexes a range of sporting moments specific to Lynch alongside broader ideas of Black athleticism. Social events and sporting events comprise seven-hundred clips from a range of media sources, including interviews with Lynch and others, game footage, television commercials, news reports, film clips, cable news programming, fan videos, and even stills from Dr. Seuss's *The Cat in the Hat*. The documentary also includes haunting footage of state and vigilante murder of Black people; acts of police brutality; and the protest responses that arose during the onset of the Black Lives Matter movement. Examining the politics of place, particularly Oakland as a reservoir of militancy, revolutionaries, radicals, and the birthplace of the Raiders professional football franchise, *Lynch: A History* collates television footage of Black resistance within a wide field of physical struggles and sporting and social movements. Blurring media and sports worlds, the film's style of multi-format visual blitz creates an ecology of US racial history and our contemporary experience of image and information consumption within sport and media's matrices of profit and distribution. In Shields's field of vision, Lynch's mediated sporting and celebrity persona is commanding and defiant, charismatic and intimidating. He is cast within the greater "cultural visibility, acclaim, wealth and significance of US Black athletes in the globalized arena of late capital and competitive sports, cable sports programing, merchandising and branding, and race and the (in)famous sports star."[44] Shields's vexing portrayal of Lynch situates the multihyphenate as an iconoclastic historical contestant, a term I coined to describe "a figure and figuration that participates in and challenges prevailing discourses on sports, history, and Black experiences in American society in ways that, at times, challenge hegemonic norms and convention."[45] Within this unauthorized documentary, Lynch is a cipher and an allegory, athletically moving through televisual and other related media content via montage. The spectacles of sports, media, violence, entertainment, consumerism, white supremacy, police brutality, Black death, geopolitical issues, and sporting celebrity share a sensorium on screen in much the same way they do in our lives.

Shields's documentary uses Marshawn Lynch as totem and metonym for the Black sporting and American body. As a result, Lynch's life becomes the linchpin of the film, a raced formulation that establishes and diffracts meanings and, as the documentary's title suggests, the racial formations of an American history. While compelling, the centrality of embodiment is the problem of the documentary's cultural and journalistic politics. *Lynch: A History* uses a man of *few* and *particular* words to make him say *anything* and *everything* about America. Lynch is thus merely a vehicle for Shields's own fascination with Black existence, rehearsing *Black Planet*'s themes via Lynch's story. Falling into a common pattern and trope of white directors seeing themselves in Black subjects, Shields's unauthorized documentary is not, as Claudia Rankine praises, "a groundbreaking documentary about a silence that isn't really a silence." Instead, the documentary reveals an obsession played out through racial surrogacy. It is, from Shields's field of vision, a sort of profession: "I did not see you, only the availability of your story, your image, your name. Or your body, its shape, its movement."[46] In the end, *Lynch: A History* represents and perpetuates the commodification and exploitation of the sports media machine that Lynch's race rebel behavior in press conferences and agentive post-football media career resists.

"I Ain't Got Nothing to Say" (Or, a Lynch-ian Conclusion)

In 2014, Lynch told NFL Network's Michael Robinson: "I ain't got nothing to say. I just want to play football." Throughout his playing career, Lynch explicitly maintained that rebellious position in his press conference appearances. Even as he has transitioned into a media star, Lynch maintains that his media exposure and engagement will be on his own terms. His earlier acts of refusal and rebuke signal to the press and viewing audiences that the sports media industrial complex desires him, not football, to be the product. Therefore, Lynch's embrace of the media—on his own terms—is part of his longstanding awareness of the power of his image and its profitability on screen, one he did not want sports journalists or anyone else to control and manipulate. He has made it clear that he has nothing to say; he's just about that action, boss.

Notes

1. Lyle Crouse, "Marshawn Lynch Exits Session Again," *ESPN*, January 29, 2014, https://www.espn.com/nfl/playoffs/2013/story/_/id/10370155/super-bowl-marshawn-lynch-seattle-seahawks-leaves-media-session-second-straight-day.

2. Dashiell Bennett, "Marshawn Lynch Doesn't Need to Talk to Anybody," *The Atlantic*, January 29, 2015, https://www.theatlantic.com/entertainment/archive/2015/01/marshawn-lynch-doesnt-need-to-talk-to-anybody/384946/.

3. 2014 NFL Media Relations Policy, *Pro Football Writers of America*, May 23, 2014, https://www.profootballwriters.org/2014/05/23/2014-nfl-media-relations-policy/.

4. Dashiell Bennett, "Marshawn Lynch Doesn't Need to Talk to Anybody." That fine was later suspended on the condition that he would cooperate thereafter. However, Lynch would run afoul of these terms during the 2014 regular season, missing scheduled press appearances, which resulted in the league doubling the fine to $100,000.

5. Henry Louis Gates, *The Signifying Monkey: A Theory of African-American Literary Criticism* (New York: Oxford University Press, 1988).

6. Bennett, "Marshawn Lynch Doesn't Need to Talk to Anybody."

7. Pro Football Writers of America, quoted in Crouse, "Marshawn Lynch Exits Session Again."

8. The interview between Sanders and Lynch went viral. For many, their exchange highlighted Lynch's palpable mediagenic personality and panache for creating popular sound bites (that he later monetized via merchandising).

9. Robin D. G. Kelly, *Race Rebels: Culture, Politics, and the Black Working Class* (New York: The Free Press, 1996), 3.

10. Kelly, *Race Rebels*, 3.

11. Kelly, *Race Rebels*, 3.

12. David L. Andrews and Steven J. Jackson, eds., *Sports Stars: The Cultural Politics of Sporting Celebrity* (New York: Routledge, 2001), 9.

13. Ted Miller, "Hey, Remember that Time Marshawn Lynch Took an Injury-Cart Joyride?" *ESPN*, November 1, 2016, https://www.espn.com/blog/pac12/post/_/id/105507/hey-remember-that-time-marshawn-lynch-took-an-injury-cart-joyride.

14. John Vidale, "One Year Ago, Seattle Seahawks 12th Man Earthquake," *Pacific Northwest Seismic Network*, December 31, 2011, https://www.pnsn org/blog/2011/12/31/one-year-ago-seattle-seahawks-12th-man-earthquake.

15. See "Beast Mode, A Fanatics Experience," https://www.beastmodeonline.com/.

16. Mary G. McDonald and Susan Birrell, "Reading Sport Critically: A Methodology for Interrogating Power," *Sociology of Sport Journal* 16, no. 4 (1999): 238. For more on sport celebrity and media culture, see David L. Andrews and Steven J. Jackson, eds., *Sports Stars: The Cultural Politics of Sporting Celebrity* (New York: Routledge, 2001); David Andrews, *Michael Jordan, Inc.: Corporate Sport, Media Culture, and Late Modern Capital* (Albany: State University of New York Press, 2001); Susan Birrell and Mary G. McDonald, eds., *Reading Sport: Critical Essays on Power and Representation* (Boston: Northeastern University Press, 2000); Aaron Baker and Todd Boyd, eds., *Out of Bounds: Sports, Media, and the Politics of Identity* (Bloomington: Indiana University Press, 1997); Garry Whannel, "Sports Stars, Narrativisitation and Masculinities," *Lesure Studies* 18, no. 3 (1999): 249–65; and Garry Whannel, "Individual Stars and Collective Identities in Media Sport," in *Sport, Popular Culture and Identity*, ed. Maurice Roche (Achen: Meyer & Meyer Verlag, 1998), 24–36.

17. David L. Andrews and Steven J. Jackson, "Introduction: Sports Celebrities, Public Culture, and Private Experience," in Andrews and Jackson, *Sports Stars*, 7.

18. Richard Dyer, *Heavenly Bodies: Film Stars and Society* (New York: Routledge, 2004), 5.

19. Whannel, "Sports Stars, Narrativisitation and Masculinities," 258; Andrews and Jackson, "Introduction," 9.

20. Ben Carrington, "Postmodern Blackness and the Celebrity Sports Star," in Andrews and Jackson, *Sport Stars*, 103.

21. Mary G. McDonald and David L. Andrews, "Michael Jordan: Corporate Sport and Postmodern Celebrityhood," in Andrews and Jackson, *Sport Stars*, 20.

22. David L. Andrews, "Introduction: Michael Jordan Matters," in Andrews, *Michael Jordan, Inc.*, xv.

23. McDonald and Andrews, "Michael Jordan: Corporate Sport and Postmodern Celebrityhood," 33. Emphasis in original.

24. Mélisse LaFrance and Geneviève Rail, "'As Bad as He Says He Is?': Interrogating Dennis Rodman's Subversive Potential," in Birrell and McDonald, *Reading Sport*, 74.

25. LaFrance and Rail, "'As Bad as He Says He Is?'" in Birrell and McDonald, *Reading Sport*, 102.

26. Bennett, "Marshawn Lynch Doesn't Need to Talk to Anybody."

27. Examples include Black Olympic sprinters Tommie Smith and John Carlos, and 49ers quarterback Colin Kaepernick.

28. Jim Denison and Pirkko Markula, "The Press Conference as a Performance: Representing Haile Gebrselassie," *Sociology of Sport Journal* 22 (2005): 313.

29. Vincent Peña, "Press Conferences: Sports Journalism," in *How to Watch Sports*, ed. Adam Rugg and Benjamin Burroughs (New York: New York University Press, 2026).

30. Peña, "Press Conferences," in Rugg and Burroughs, *How to Watch Sports*.

31. Peña, "Press Conferences," in Rugg and Burroughs, *How to Watch Sports*.

32. Zora Neale Hurston, *Mules and Men* (Philadelphia: J.B. Lippincott Co., 1935), 2–3.

33. Hua Hsu, "The Profound Silence of Marshawn Lynch," *New Yorker*, June 14, 2019, https://www.newyorker.com/culture/cultural-comment/the-profound-silence-of-marshawn-lynch.

34. Sohil Shah, "Free Speech, Football, and Freedom: Why the NFL Should Not Compel its Players to Speak to the Media," *Texas Review of Entertainment & Sports Law* 16, no. 1 (2014): 43.

35. Leigh Steinberg, "5 Reasons Why 80% of Retired NFL Players Go Broke," *Forbes*, February 9, 2015, https://www.forbes.com/sites/leighsteinberg/2015/02/09/5-reasons-why-80-of-retired-nfl-players-go-broke/.

36. Along with typical sports media outlets such as ESPN, publications ranging from the *Los Angeles Times* to the *Washington Post* to *Fox Business* shared stories about this press conference. Clips of Lynch's advice went viral on social media.

37. Bennett, "Marshawn Lynch Doesn't Need to Talk to Anybody."

38. Nadira Goffe, "The One Person Who Can Save Celebrity Baking Shows from Themselves," *Slate*, December 5, 2022, https://slate.com/culture/2022/12/marshawn-lynch-great-american-baking-show-roku.html.

39. Emma Seligman, quoted in Devan Coggan, "Marshawn Lynch Starred in *Bottoms* to Honor His Queer Sister," *Entertainment Weekly*, September 1, 2023, https://ew.com/movies/marshawn-lynch-starred-in-bottoms-to-honor-queer-sister/.

40. Seligman, quoted in Coggan, "Marshawn Lynch Starred in *Bottoms*."

41. See David Shields, *Black Planet: Facing Race During an NBA Season* (Lincoln, NE: University of Nebraska Press, 1999), back cover.

42. Bryan Curtis, "The Original Bad Boy," The Ringer, May 8, 2018, https://www.theringer.com/nba/2018/5/8/17325524/black-planet-david-shields-seattle-supersonics-gary-payton-sportswriting.

43. Curtis, "The Original Bad Boy." See Stanley Crouch, *The Artificial White Man: Essays on Authenticity* (New York, Basic Civitas Books, 2005).

44. Samantha N. Sheppard, *Sporting Blackness: Race, Embodiment, and Critical Muscle Memory On Screen* (Oakland, CA: University of California Press, 2020), 23.

45. Sheppard, *Sporting Blackness*, 42.

46. Claudia Rankine, quote from https://www.lynch-a-history.com/. Jared Sexton, "Black Box," *Docalogue*, January 2019, https://docalogue.com/january-minding-the-gap/.

PART III

Political Activism

9

Transgender Participation in Sport

The Fight for Inclusion in Public Space

TRAVERS

On June 14, 2023, *CBC News*[1] reported that a nine-year-old cisgender girl was harassed at a Kelowna, British Columbia, track meet by two adults who wrongly assumed she was transgender. In Utah, a cisgender teenager was misgendered by a state education official, subjected to cyberbullying, and required police protection. As sportswriter Frankie de la Cretaz reports, "Following the incident, the girl's parents described their daughter as a tomboy with a muscular build and short hair who favors baggy clothing, who is now being subjected to severe cyberbullying and harassment."[2] These incidents are not anomalous and reflect the collateral impact of anti-trans harassment campaigns on gender-nonconforming women and girls. They exemplify the broader climate of anxiety, gender surveillance, and moral panic surrounding women's sport—a panic fueled not by evidence, but by ideological investments in binary gender categories, male superiority, and a deeply racialized system of sex policing.

Cases of girls who wear their hair short, appear "too athletic," or fail to conform to stereotypical gender norms being subjected to gender surveillance and harassment are not new—the policing of "female masculinity"[3] predates debate and policy related to transgender inclusion in sport.[4] Incidents of cisgender girls being "accused of being trans" in Canada and the United States since 2020 can be traced directly back to the anti-trans backlash deliberately engineered by conservative groups. Not only are anti-trans campaigns harmful to trans people, but, as the above cases make clear, they also result in the increased surveillance and harassment of cisgender women and girls and gender-nonconforming people of all ages. Anti-trans policies and laws punish people, particularly those assigned male at birth, who fail to conform to cisgender heteropatriarchal norms.

In this chapter I argue that contemporary efforts to police and exclude transgender women and girls from sport must be understood not as isolated policy decisions, but as manifestations of a broader cultural project rooted in heteropatriarchal, white supremacist, and colonial ideologies. These efforts are underpinned by persistent anxiety about gender nonconformity, an unquestioned belief in male physical superiority, and what I term "testosterone panic"—the fixation on testosterone as a proxy for athletic unfairness, despite a lack of scientific consensus or empirical support.[5] While these ideologies predate the current anti-trans backlash, their intensification in sport policy reflects a convergence of fascist, conservative, and trans-exclusionary feminist agendas.

Modern Sport and the Policing of Gender

Despite its association with play and fairness, modern sport has long served as a conservative institution reinforcing binary gender norms. From its emergence in nineteenth-century Europe as an elite, white, male domain, sport has policed the participation of women and racialized people. Sport historically excluded women under the guise of protecting competitive integrity and female frailty.[6] The inclusion of women has always been conditional and surveilled, with participation governed by norms of femininity and white heteropatriarchal ideals.

Modern sport is characterized by a long history "sex testing" for women athletes on the basis of the assumption that, on average, men are stronger and faster than women, and that male impostors need to be screened out. Discourse and policy related to transgender women cannot be understood without attention to this broader "female eligibility" landscape of surveillance and suspicion. In what follows, I chart the historical and contemporary landscape of "female eligibility" policies, demonstrate the scientific and ethical flaws in sex-testing regimes, and expose the cultural logic that sustains these policies under the guise of fairness. I argue that sport, rather than being a neutral or protective domain, is a central institution in the maintenance of binary gender and racialized power, and that current policies targeting trans athletes both reinforce and expand this regime of control.

The fraught history of "female eligibility" reveals how anxieties about race and gender shape sporting norms. Sex testing was introduced ostensibly to prevent male impostors from competing, but in practice, it targeted women seen as "too masculine" or insufficiently feminine. These regimes of testing and exclusion have disproportionately impacted athletes from the Global South and those whose bodies do not conform to Eurocentric ideals of femininity. Such athletes have been subjected to a host of invasive and humiliating procedures based on pseudoscientific assumptions about unfair advantage.

Scientific Critiques and Policy Evolution

The introduction of the International Olympic Committee's (IOC) 2004 "Stockholm Consensus" was heralded as a step toward transgender inclusion, but it reinforced medical and legal gatekeeping by requiring surgery, legal recognition, and hormone therapy. This policy relied on the unverified presumption that hormone levels were an adequate marker of gender authenticity and athletic capacity. Among the critics of the Stockholm Consensus, Pat Griffin and Helen Carroll made different recommendations for trans athletes in high school settings than for college athletes. In *On the Team: Equal Opportunity for Transgender Student Athletes*, they recommended gender self-determination, without any requirement of medical treatment, as a basis for high school participation. And for transgender women to be eligible to compete at the college level, Griffin and Carroll recommended immediate eligibility for transwomen who had been able to access hormone blockers as girls to avoid "male" puberty, and after one year of hormone therapy for transgender women who had undergone natal "male" puberty. In 2011, the National Collegiate Athletic Association (NCAA) adopted these guidelines for college athletes, granting immediate eligibility to transwomen who had accessed hormone blockers and requiring one year of hormone therapy for transwomen athletes for whom this had not been possible—again tying eligibility to testosterone suppression.[7]

However, science has consistently failed to establish a clear causal link between testosterone levels and athletic performance. Scholarship to date[8] indicates that what is considered a "fair" vs. an "unfair" advantage in athletic competition is a social rather than a biomedical decision. Structural advantages such as access to facilities, coaching, and nutrition often go unacknowledged in these debates. Leading endocrinologists and human rights advocates have condemned testosterone-based eligibility thresholds as unscientific and unethical. As Mia Fischer argues, the obsession with testosterone distracts from these broader inequities and reproduces eugenic, racist, and colonial frameworks of athletic normativity.[9]

Anti-Trans Mobilizations and the Strategic Deployment of "Protection"

The growing influence of anti-trans campaigns reflects not simply backlash to social progress but a strategic political project. Far-right actors, religious conservatives, and trans-exclusionary feminists have coalesced around the purported need to "protect women's sport."[10] This coalition cloaks its efforts in the language of fairness and safety, even as it promotes a vision of gender that is static, binary, and rooted in racialized and heteropatriarchal norms.

It was not until many years after the introduction of the Stockholm Consensus that an openly transgender woman competed in the 2020 Olympic Games (held in 2021), when Laurel Hubbard from the United States competed in weightlifting. But given the current climate of anti-trans social movements and policies targeting transwomen and girls for exclusion from "female" sport, Hubbard may be the last transwoman to compete at this level for some time.

Within days of his inauguration, President Trump produced a series of executive orders, with devastating impacts on transgender people in general, that include specific prohibitions surrounding sport participation. These executive orders include the claim that that there are only two, unchangeable sexes,[11] the defunding of affirming healthcare for transgender minors,[12] and a ban on transgender women and girls competing in girls' and women's sport in elementary, high school, and post-secondary institutions.[13] Trump confirmed the intended impact of these executive orders—to push transgender people back out of public life—by banning transgender people from military service and announcing that his administration will deny visas to transgender athletes participating in the 2028 Olympic Games, scheduled to take place in Los Angeles.

While the NCAA played a leadership role in transgender inclusion by adopting *On the Team*'s recommendations for transgender athletes in 2011, backlash to transgender woman Lia Thomas winning a Division I swimming championship in 2022 produced a shift in policy to a "sport-by-sport approach" for determining transgender eligibility. On February 6, 2025, the NCAA responded to Trump's ban on transgender women in sport by declaring transgender women ineligible to compete in all NCAA women's events.

Anti-trans initiatives reflect backlash to the significant social change achieved by LGBTQ+ social movements in general over the past five decades and specifically attempt to reverse "the transgender tipping point" regarding visibility and acceptance that occurred in the United States and Canada around 2014.[14] While homophobia and transphobia continue to be relatively pervasive, queer and trans people who are otherwise privileged have experienced significant inclusion in public life. Anti-trans laws and policies and executive orders from the White House denying the existence of trans people have reversed some of these gains, with trans people in many states in America experiencing increased harassment and violence.[15]

As with other "anti-gender" legal efforts to deny trans people access to appropriate bathrooms, and trans kids and young people access to recognition and affirming healthcare, bills and laws seeking to prevent trans girls and women from participating in "female" sport rely on fearmongering to exclude and delegitimate transgender people and shore up Eurocentric heteropatriarchal sex and gender systems.

Anti-trans movements are composed of an alliance between white supremacist, conservative, and heteropatriarchal organizations and movements and so-called "gender critical feminists," who view transwomen and girls as "male interlopers."[16] In the past several years, laws designed to delegitimize and exclude trans people in various ways have been passed in many American state legislatures.[17] Following a wave of anti-trans policies the United States, including those preventing transwomen and girls from participating in "female" sport, first the premier of the Province of Alberta, Canada, and then the leader of Canada's United Conservative party, announced their intention to prevent transwomen and girls from competing against cisgender women and girls.[18] As Fischer notes, this rhetoric often centers the protection of white, cisgender girls, invoking paternalistic logics of vulnerability and danger. In doing so, it obscures the actual harms facing girls and women in sport—underfunding, harassment, unequal access, and institutional sexism—while weaponizing gender panic against trans and gender-nonconforming people. As Sharrow et al. explain,

> Proponents claim that women's sports require "protection" from transgender athletes, even as they are unable to cite examples of trans athletes competing in their states. Research identifies many significant threats to women and girls in sport— including lack of funding and sponsorship, pay inequities, a decreasing proportion of female coaches and administrators, unequal access to participation, underrepresentation in the media, vulnerability to sexual harassment and abuse, hostile climates, and insufficient implementation of Title IX. Yet the Republican lawmakers now rallying to "save" women's sports do not appear to be tackling these problems.[19]

In previous work, I refer to anti-trans sport policies as evidence of "testosterone panic," wherein fearmongering propaganda is used to target and exclude trans people and mobilize a conservative political base to secure state power.[20] In "Bathroom Battlegrounds and Penis Panics," Schilt and Westbrook describe conflicts relating to bathroom access for transgender people as "penis panics," within the context of "gender panics" more broadly.[21] Schilt and Westbrook define "gender panics" as "moments where people react to a challenge to the gender binary by frantically asserting its naturalness" and the need to keep women-only spaces penis-free.[22] Efforts to prevent trans people from using appropriate bathrooms rely on rhetoric about the need to "protect" cis women and girls from "male predators." According to Schilt and Westbrook, penis panics are not really about bathroom access at all but rather work to resist any challenge to cisgender heteropatriarchy. Anti-trans campaigns use inflammatory language and misinformation that are effective in mobilizing populist sentiment and political backlash.[23] Anti-trans rhetoric has been used by new fascist movements as a dog whistle to build and mobilize their base and have frequently succeeded without having provided any evidence to support their claims of transgender usurpation of athletic success in female sport.[24] The threat of harassment and violence by organized vigilantes, as in the case of the two adults who accosted the nine-year-old in Kelowna, is punishing and terrifying for the people whom it targets.[25]

In the current context, the surveillance of trans and gender-nonconforming bodies through sporting policy is being used as both punishment for transgender visibility and a wedge issue for conservative movements. At the institutional level, we have seen World Rugby, the NCAA, World Aquatics (formerly FINA), and most recently, USA Climbing adopt policies to exclude transwomen. Except for trans-exclusionary radical feminists, the supporters of anti-trans measures in girls' and women's sport who bankroll these campaigns do not otherwise support gender justice in sport or any other sphere of society. Rather, these are fascist organizations that are anti-feminist at their core, and their opposition to trans participation in sport is part of their commitments.

Scientific Critiques and Policy Evolution

Since the 2004 IOC "Stockholm Consensus," some progress was made in adapting these policies for high school and college athletes—notably, through Griffin and Carroll's 2010 recommendations. However, eligibility continued to hinge on testosterone. However, science has consistently failed to show a reliable causal link between testosterone levels and athletic performance. Access to resources such as coaching and nutrition have a far more significant impact on performance but is rarely discussed in eligibility debates. Fischer argues that the obsession with testosterone obscures these inequities and reanimates colonial logics of bodily classification.[26]

Sex testing in elite athletic events began in the 1950s, purportedly to screen for men posing as women to take advantage of "lesser competition," although there is no record of this ever happening. Instead of discovering "male cheaters," however, a succession of unscientific tests identified women athletes with physical or chromosomal "anomalies" for exclusion from women's sport and/or coercion into "treatment" to neutralize the "male advantage" these anomalies supposedly conferred. This had devastating consequences for the women athletes who were prevented from competing and for those who were coerced into unnecessary and harmful medical interventions.[27] Leading scientists of sex development have raised doubts about the scientific veracity of every form of so-called "sex testing" ever used, and feminist criticism has drawn attention to the practice as a violation of human rights.[28]

While the IOC and the International Amateur Athletics Federation (IAAF)—World Athletics (WA) as of 2019—responded to feminist criticism by suspending the imposition of sex testing for all women athletes in 2000, the practice continued selectively: women who appear "too masculine" or perform "too well'"—both of which are social rather than empirically based assessments—continue to be subjected to sex testing.[29] Many scholars note that selective sex testing has been disproportionately deployed against Black and Brown women from the Global South.[30] As Fischer observes, "Black women athletes, especially those who are successful, trans or not, are often intensely scrutinized for being 'too manly' and 'masculine' compared with their white competitors because they transgress, or are perceived as transgressing, dominant ideals of femininity grounded in whiteness, as exemplified by the sexist and racist media portrayals of Serena Williams."[31]

Some of the athletes who have "failed" sex tests are women diagnosed with hyperandrogynism (a condition wherein the body naturally produces higher levels of testosterone than the "female norm"). One of these athletes is South African runner Caster Semenya, and the prurient publicity surrounding her has contributed to a climate of "moral panic" around female eligibility.[32] When Semenya won an 800-meter race in Berlin in 2009, she was subjected to media scrutiny and selective sex testing because some people involved in the sport saw her as "too masculine." In violation of her right to privacy, the results of a gynecological exam Semenya was forced to undergo were "leaked" to the media: Semenya was diagnosed as "intersex," or, in the nomenclature of the *DSM-IV's* updated diagnosis, as having a "Disorder in Sexual Development."[33] Because Semenya's testosterone levels were higher than that deemed "normal" for women, she was ruled ineligible to compete unless she underwent testosterone suppression therapy, typically administered in the form of a birth control pill.[34] From 2011 to 2021, testosterone levels were used by the IOC, IAAF/WA, and affiliated sport organizations to determine female eligibility. These policies rest on scientifically unsupported claims that higher average levels of testosterone among men when compared to women are the basis of unfair advantage. According to these policies, women diagnosed with hyperandrogynism—and transgender women—were required to submit to medical treatment to reduce testosterone levels to compete. That the mandated threshold for testosterone changed during this period did little to inspire confidence in the science behind sex testing.

Two key legal cases of athletes diagnosed with hyperandrogenism—those of Dutee Chand (2015) and Caster Semenya (2019)—exemplify the scientific and human rights challenges to these policies. In 2014, Chand, an Indian woman, was barred from competition by the International Amateur Athletic Federation (IAAF), now World Athletics (WA). In a 2015 case before the Court of Arbitration for Sport (CAS), Chand achieved a temporary measure enabling her and other women with hyperandrogenism to compete while the IAAF was provided with a two-year window to present satisfactory evidence about the connection between higher levels of testosterone and sport performance. Chand's victory temporarily suspended the testosterone rule, allowing Semenya to compete without suppression and raising hopes for a more just standard. However, a 2019 ruling by the CAS reinstated the limit, and subsequent appeals by Semenya to higher courts failed. These rulings reinforced an arbitrary threshold and legitimized the idea that certain bodies pose an intrinsic threat to fairness.

The failure of legal challenges to sex testing paved the way for new, more expansive forms of surveillance. This was despite the 2021 public statement by the IOC finally acknowledging that sex testing has no scientific basis, and the significant harm done to athletes barred from competition and/or forced to undergo medically unnecessary—and often harmful—treatment.[35] Rather than play a leadership role in imagining sporting structures beyond the cultural norms of binary sex distinction, however, the IOC announced a new policy for transgender participation in the same statement, one that relies on sport-by-sport, evidence-based decision-making about the extent to which transgender women purportedly have an unfair advantage.

While the new IOC policy is partially in response to the failure of science to support sex testing and compliance measures in high-stakes court cases undertaken by athletes who failed sex tests, it has been profoundly influenced by anti-trans movements.[36] The influence of anti-trans social movements in shaping sport policy was first seen in 2020, when many American states passed laws and policies preventing transgender girls and women from competing,[37] and at the international level, when World

Rugby announced a ban on transgender women competing in international women's competitions. Organizations such as the UK's Fair Play for Women have influenced sport policy in the United Kingdom and beyond—with World Rugby as the first example—but the language of "gender-affected" sport in the IOC's 2021 announcement reflects this influence as well. The new IOC policy was preceded first by the World Rugby policy in 2020 and then by the *Guidance for Transgender Inclusion in Domestic Sport*, produced by the United Kingdom's National Governing Bodies and the Five Sports Councils in 2021. The influence of the UK-based Fair Play for Women, an anti-trans group of self-professed "gender critical feminists," can be clearly seen in this document. The document makes a distinction between sports that are "gender affected," wherein transwomen purportedly have an unfair advantage over cisgender women, and sports that are "skill based," where trans and cisgender women may compete on an equal footing.[38] According to Fair Play for Women, an organization dedicated to the exclusion of transgender women from sport,

> many US states allow high school *boys* [my italics] who self-identify as a girl to compete in female categories. As they are under 18, these "transgirls" will usually have had no medical intervention. Here in the UK many sports clubs now allow *males* [my italics] to compete as female if they can show a doctor's note confirming that they have lowered testosterone into the "female range."[39]

As House observes, the United Kingdom's Fair Play for Women "sprang up at least initially, with a primary focus on contesting trans rights reforms, and particularly changes to the GRA [2004 Gender Recognition Act]."[40]

The new IOC policy retrenched a heteropatriarchal, two-sex system by offloading the oppressive work of surveillance and exclusion to lesser bodies—national and international governance bodies for each sport. In a heightened context of anti-trans moral panic, and despite scientific and human rights objections, many international and national sport organizations are returning to policies requiring sex testing for all women athletes and banning transgender women outright from women's competition. In 2025, World Athletics introduced a DNA testing requirement for women athletes, despite widespread criticism of its scientific validity and ethical basis.[41] This marks a dangerous return to biologically essentialist frameworks that seek to "protect" women's sport by regulating who counts as female.

In examining bills and laws barring transwomen and girls from sport participation in many American states, Fischer documents "how the deployment of a white feminist rhetoric of "protecting women's sports" works to shield these bills and their proponents from accusations of transphobia and bigotry while masking their white supremacist underpinnings.[42]

> Obscuring the white supremacist underpinnings of these bills, a coalition between anti-LGBTQ Christian conservative forces (represented primarily by policy groups and Republican lawmakers) and trans-exclusionary radical feminist (TERF) women's sports advocates are strategically mobilizing under the deceptive banner of "protecting and saving girl's and women's sports" to pursue these legislative efforts.[43]

However, the Center for American Progress finds that including trans high school athletes does not reduce cisgender girls' involvement in sports.[44]

Testosterone Panic and Moral Regulation

Policies targeting transgender women athletes replicate and intensify earlier sex-testing regimes. Framed as fairness, they are in fact moral projects, governed by affective reactions to gender ambiguity and an underlying fear that the sex/gender binary is collapsing. This testosterone panic echoes the "penis panics" described by Schilt and Westbrook: moments of cultural crisis wherein gender nonconformity is coded as deviance and discipline is justified as protection. The harm that such "assessments" produce has already been materialized with bans on the participation of transgender women by World Rugby in 2020, FINA in 2022, and USA Climbing in 2023. These anti-trans policy changes are based on the unverified claim that transwomen retain vestigial strength that makes their participation unsafe or unfair for their cisgender counterparts.

In September 2023, USA Climbing announced a change to its transgender participation policy by requiring transwomen and girls on the national and international competition track to reduce their hormone levels to 5 nmols/L for twelve months prior to competition. The policy announcement sparked outrage from trans and nonbinary climbers who had been shut out of the process. According to Trans Climbers Belong, an organization that emerged to contest the new policy,

> USA Climbing's new policy focuses predominantly on transfemme athletes undergoing hormone replacement therapy. As is often the case with policy like this, it is shortsighted, lacking context, and fixated on testosterone levels. USA Climbing has cited studies while ignoring the context of their inconclusive results regarding the impact of medical transition to physical capabilities and left out that no studies have ever been completed on the impact of hormone replacement on climbing ability or on

> athletes in any sport in the context of competition conditions. Beyond this, many of the requirements stemming from USA Climbing's new adherence to the US Anti-Doping Agency's Therapeutic Use Exemption Requirements for Transgender Athletes are harmful to trans athletes. They are invasive and demeaning to trans climbers while also having little to no connection to a goal of fair competition. Furthermore, no trans voices were considered or listened to in the creation of these policies.[45]

Trans Climbers Belong asked members of the climbing community to refuse to support all USA Climbing events until these policies are rewritten. The campaign was successful to a degree in that USA Climbing suspended the policy to allow for further deliberation.[46] While a formal policy has yet to be released, USA Climbing recently announced that it is conforming to the International Federation of Sport Climbing's policy on transgender inclusion,[47] a policy that is consistent with the 2015 International Olympic Committee's requirement that transgender women reduce their testosterone levels below 10 nmols/L to be eligible to compete.

Sport is a challenging space for resisting anti-trans campaigns because of commonly held beliefs about male athletic superiority. Even among strong supporters of transgender rights are many who believe "fairness" requires that transwomen and girls be prevented from competing against cisgender women and girls. The characteristic debate about the inclusion of transwomen involves questions as to the extent to which hormone therapy effectively achieves "physiological equivalency" by changing biological characteristics associated with an assumed male athletic advantage.[48] Campaigns against trans participation in women's sport rely on "the frailty myth," whereby cisgender women and girls are viewed as in need of protection from "biological males."[49] The recent change to international rules related to the women's category in swimming provides an illuminating example. When Lia Thomas became the first transgender woman to win a Division I NCAA swim championship in 2022, she became the subject of virulent anti-trans campaigning.[50] As evidence of the influence of anti-trans campaigns and the damage the IOC has done in terms of establishing regressive female eligibility policies, World Aquatics responded to the moral panic around Lia Thomas by producing policy barring transwomen who had transitioned after the age of twelve from women's competition, stating that a third—and yet nonexistent—gender category is the appropriate arena for transwomen to compete.[51] This move, in tandem with bans on youth access to hormone therapy, effectively eliminates any viable path to eligibility for most transwomen, while intensifying scrutiny of all athletes deemed gender nonconforming.

Conclusion: Challenging the Logic of Exclusion

The intensified policing of trans and gender-nonconforming athletes reflects a moral panic rooted in deep cultural anxieties about gender, race, and power. It reflects a refusal to reckon with the nonbinary realities of sex, the complexity of athletic performance, and the enduring influence of colonial gender regimes. As anti-trans laws, policies, and surveillance practices proliferate, they harm not only trans people but also cisgender athletes who do not conform to narrow ideals of femininity.

What none of these policies related to "female eligibility" consider is the extent to which the sex segregation of sport is problematic.[52] Sex segregation in sport is grounded in a vision of sex as a binary system that conforms to Eurocentric norms, emphasizing sex-based difference despite the significant degree of overlaps in performance between male and female athletes.[53] Despite evidence of overlapping performances, mainstream sporting policies reinforce Eurocentric cultural norms about female frailty and male athletic superiority.[54] Trans athletes and women athletes who do not conform to female norms challenge these taken-for-granted beliefs that there are only two sexes, that sex can be scientifically determined, and that men as a group are superior to women as a group. These beliefs were used to justify and impose colonial relationships based on the view that heteropatriarchal gender and sexuality regimes are marks of "civilization" and continue to shore up heteropatriarchal and racial capitalist/colonial systems of power and privilege.[55] Sport is central to this "civilizing" project, and female eligibility policies are a key component.[56]

The combination of this shift in international policy and testosterone panic–fueled policies and laws barring transwomen and girls from participating in "female" sport in the United States and, most recently, in Alberta, Canada, is having alarming consequences.[57] Such policies and laws signal lack of acceptance to trans people in general and will make it even less likely that transwomen and girls will participate in sport. Barriers to sport participation for queer and trans youth were significant prior to anti-trans campaigns, and anti-trans policies, bills, and laws will decrease participation further.[58] Anti-trans measures signal to trans girls and women that they are not welcome in sport and that their privacy may be violated if they attempt to participate. The impact of this, particularly for transgender young women wishing to compete in high school or youth sport, will be that many will decide not to participate at all. This should be unthinkable, given the benefits of sport and physical recreation participation for girls and women and the already concerning drop-off in participation from this population during adolescence.[59]

Sport is not a neutral terrain, and debates about fairness and safety must be situated within broader struggles over bodily autonomy, scientific legitimacy, and social justice. Policies that claim to protect women's sport often do so by reinforcing the very systems of oppression that feminist movements have long sought to dismantle. To move forward, we must reject the false choice between inclusion and fairness and instead confront the ideological foundations of the sport binary itself. By doing so, we resist not only the exclusion of transgender athletes, but also the deeper cultural logics that seek to punish all forms of gender nonconformity under the guise of fairness.

Notes

1. Winston Szeto and Brady Strachan, "9-Year-Old's Gender Questioned in 'Gobsmacking' Track-and-Field Incident, Family Says," *CBC News*, June 13, 2023, https://www.cbc.ca/news/canada/british-columbia/kelowna-short-hair-girl-gender-identity-1.6875738.

2. Frankie de la Cretaz, "How the World of Competitive Climbing Was Rocked by Transphobia," *The Nation*, February 2, 2024, https://www.thenation.com/article/society/usa-climbing-trans-athletes-rules/.

3. J. Halberstam, *Female Masculinity* (Durham, NC: Duke University Press, 1998).

4. See Susan Cahn, *Coming on Strong: Gender & Sexuality in Women's Sport* (Chicago: University of Illinois Press, 2015); Pat Griffin and Helen Carroll, *On the Team: Equal Opportunity for Transgender Student Athletes*, Women's Sport Foundation and National Center for Lesbian Rights, 2010, https://www.nclrights.org/wpcontent/uploads/2013/07/Transgender StudentAthleteReport; and Helen Lenskyj, *Out of Bounds: Women, Sport & Sexuality* (Toronto, Ont: Women's Press, 1986).

5. Travers, "Female' Sport and Testosterone Panic," in *Justice for Trans Athletes: Challenges and Struggles*, ed. Ali Greey and Helen J. Lenskyj (Toronto: Emerald Publishing, 2022), 43–60.

6. Tony Collins, *Sport in Capitalist Society: A Short History* (New York: Routledge, 2013).

7. A. Travers, "Sport, Transgender Athletes, and Nonbinary Experience," in *The Oxford Handbook of Sport and Society*, ed. L. Wenner (New York: Oxford University Press, 2022), 924–48.

8. Travers, "Sport, Transgender Athletes, and Nonbinary Experience."

9. Mia Fischer, "Protecting Women's Sports? Anti-Trans Youth Sports Bills and White Supremacy," *Communication and Critical/Cultural Studies* 20, no. 4 (2023): 397–415, https://www.tandfonline.com/doi/abs/10.1080/14791420.2023.2267646.

10. Jaime Schultz, Anna Baeth, Anne Lieberman, Lindsay Parks Pieper,

Elizabeth A. Sharrow, "The Future of Women's Sport Includes Transgender Women and Girls," in *Justice for Trans Athletes*.

11. Federal Register: The Daily Journal of the United States Government, https://www.federalregister.gov/documents/2025/01/30/2025-02090/defending-women-from-gender-ideology-extremism-and-restoring-biological-truth-to-the-federal.

12. Federal Register: The Daily Journal of the United States Government, https://www.federalregister.gov/documents/2025/02/03/2025-02194/protecting-children-from-chemical-and-surgical-mutilation.

13. Federal Register: The Daily Journal of the United States Government, https://www.federalregister.gov/documents/2025/02/11/2025-02513/keeping-men-out-of-womens-sports.

14. Fischer, "Protecting Women's Sports?"

15. Advocates for Trans Equality, "As Anti-Trans Policy Attacks Increase, So Does Violence," November 21, 2022, https://transequality.org/news/anti-trans-policy-attacks-increase-so-does-violence.

16. Serena Bassi and Greta Lafluer, "TERFs, Gender-Critical Movements, and Postfascist Feminisms," *Transgender Studies Quarterly* 9, no. 3 (2022): 311–33; Judith Butler, "Why Is the Idea of 'Gender' Provoking Backlash the World Over?," *The Guardian*, October 23, 2021; Claire House, "'I'm Real, Not You': Roles and Discourses of Trans Exclusionary Women's and Feminist Movements in Anti-Gender and Right-Wing Populist Politics," *DiGeSt Journal of Diversity and Gender Studies* 10, no. 2 (2023): 14–32.

17. Elizabeth A. Sharrow, "Sports, Transgender Rights and the Bodily Politics of Cisgender Supremacy, Laws," *Laws* 10, no. 63 (2021): 1–29, https://doi.org/10.3390/laws10030063.

18. On February 21, 2024, UCP leader Pierre Pollievre announced that his party would seek to prevent the access of transwomen to women-only spaces, such as bathrooms, changerooms, and sporting activities (Peter Zimonjic, "Poilievre Backs Banning Trans Women from Women's Sports, Change Rooms and Bathrooms," *CBC News*, February 21, 2024). His party did not win the subsequent federal election; indeed, Pollievre lost his own electoral riding.

19. Elizabeth Sharrow, Jaime Schultz, Lindsay Pieper Parks, Anne Lieberman, and Anna Baeth, Monkey Cage, "States Are Still Trying to Ban Youth Sports. Here's What You Need to Know, *Washington Post*, July 26, 2021, https://www.washingtonpost.com/politics/2021/07/26/states-are-still-trying-ban-trans-youths-sports-heres-what-you-need-know/.

20. Travers, "'Female' Sport and Testosterone Panic," in *Justice for Trans Athletes*, 43–60.

21. Kristen Schilt and Laurel Westbrook, "Bathroom Battlegrounds and Penis Panics," *Contexts* 14, no. 3 (2015): 26–31.

22. Schilt and Westbrook, "Bathroom Battlegrounds and Penis Panics."

23. Fischer, "Protecting Women's Sports?"

24. Butler, "Why Is the Idea of 'Gender' Provoking Backlash?"; Sharrow, "Sports, Transgender Rights."

25. De la Cretaz, "How the World of Competitive Climbing Was Rocked by Transphobia."

26. Fischer, "Protecting Women's Sports?"

27. Phyllis Ellis, *Category: Woman: Who Gets to Decide,* directed by Phyllis Ellis (2022; Orama Filmworks & Proximity Films), DVD; Anne Fausto-Sterling, *Sexing the Body: Gender Politics and the Construction of Sexuality* (New York: Basic Books, 2020); Rebecca Jordan-Young and Karina Karkazis, *Testosterone: An Unauthorized Biography* (Boston: Harvard University Press, 2019); Lindsay Pieper, *Sex Testing: Gender Policing in Women's Sports* (Champaign, IL: University of Illinois Press, 2016).

28. Cassandra. J. Wells, "On the Resiliency of Sex Testing in Sport" (PhD dissertation, University of British Columbia, 2020.)

29. Mia Fischer and Jennifer McClearen, "Transgender Athletes and the Queer Art of Athletic Failure," *Communication & Sport* 7, no. 1 (2020): 21; John Gleaves and Tim Lehrbach, "Beyond Fairness: The Ethics of Inclusion for Transgender and Intersex Athletes," *Journal of the Philosophy of Sport* 43, no. 2 (2016): 311–26; Kathryn Henne, *Testing for Athlete Citizenship: Regulating Doping and Sex in Sport* (New Brunswick, NJ: Rutgers University Press, 2015).

30. Shari L. Dworkin, Amanda Lock Swarr, and Cheryl Cooky, "(In)Justice in Sport: The Treatment of South African Track Star Caster Semenya," *Feminist Studies* 39, no. 1 (2013): 40–69; Fischer and McClearen, "Transgender Athletes and the Queer Art"; Henne, *Testing for Athlete Citizenship*; Madeline Pape, "Expertise and Nonbinary Bodies: Sex, Gender and the Case of Dutee Chand, *Body & Society* 25, no. 4 (2019): 3–28.

31. Fischer, "Protecting Women's Sports?"

32. Schultz, Baeth, Lieberman, Pieper, and Sharrow, "The Future of Women's Sport."

33. Alice Dreger, "Sex Typing for Sport," *Hastings Center Report* 40, no. 2 (2010): 22–24; Fausto-Sterling, *Sexing the Body;* Cordelia Fine, *Testosterone Rex: Myths of Sex, Science, and Society* (New York: Norton, 2017); R. M. Jordan-Young and K. Karkazis, *Testosterone: An Unauthorized Biography* (Boston: Harvard University Press, 2019); Roger Pielke, "Bombshell: World Athletics Admits its Research Underpinning DSD Regulations is 'Potentially Misleading'," *Honest Broker Newsletter*, August 17, 2021, https://rogerpielkejr.substack.com/p/bombshell-world-athletics-admits.

34. T. Nyong'o, T., "The Unforgivable Transgression of Being Caster Semenya," *Women & Performance: A Journal of Feminist Theory*, 20 (2010): 95–100.

35. Ellis, *Category: Woman*; Pieper, *Sex Testing*.

36. Alice Dreger, "Sex Typing for Sport"; Fausto-Sterling, *Sexing the Body*; Fine, *Testosterone Rex;* Jordan-Young and Karkazis, *Testosterone,* Pielke, "Bombshell"; House, "'I'm Real, Not You'."

37. Sharrow, "Sports, Transgender Rights."

38. Sport England, *Guidance for Transgender Inclusion in Domestic Sport*, 9, 2021, https://movingtoinclusion.co.uk/wp-content/uploads/2023/07/Guidance-For-Transgender-Inclusion-In-Domestic-Sport-2021.pdf.

39. "Sport," n.d., https://fairplayforwomen.com/.

40. House, "'I'm Real, Not You'," 25.

41. Tariq Panja, "Track and Field to Be First Olympic Sport Requiring DNA Sex Tests for Women," *New York Times*, March 25, 2025, https://www.nytimes.com/2025/03/25/sports/olympic-track-female-sex-tests.html.

42. Fischer, "Protecting Women's Sports?" 398.

43. Fischer, "Protecting Women's Sports?" 398.

44. Shoshana Goldberg, "Fair Play: The Importance of Sports Participation for Transgender Youth," *Center for American Progress*, March 18, 2021, https://www.americanprogress.org/article/fair-play/.

45. "Why Was the Original TAPP Harmful?" Trans Climbers Belong, 2023, accessed February 16, 2024, https://www.transclimbersbelong.org/, 2023.

46. De la Cretaz, "How the World of Competitive Climbing Was Rocked by Transphobia."

47. International Federation of Sport Climbing, "Policy Statement: Gender Identity and Transsexuality," *International Federation of Sport* Climbing, November 27, 2018, https://images.ifsc-climbing.org/ifsc/image/private/t_q_good/prd/gdgpugkpnyw60tnqxoq3.pdf

48. J. Gleaves and T. Lehrbach, "Beyond Fairness: The Ethics of Inclusion for Transgender and Intersex Athletes," *Journal of the Philosophy of Sport* 43, no. 2 (2016): 311–26.

49. Collette Dowling, The Frailty Myth: Redefining the Physical Potential of Women and Girls (New York: Random House, 2000).

50. Charles Odum, "Lia Thomas Becomes 1st Known Transgender Woman to Win NCAA Swimming Title," *CBC News*, March 17, 2022, https://www.cbc.ca/sports/olympics/summer/aquatics/lia-thomas-first-known-transgender-ncaa-swimming-championship1.6388994.

51. Haley Yamada, "FINA Decision on Transgender Athletes May Have Ripple Effects on Other Sports' Governing Bodies," *ABC News*, July 6, 2022, https://abcnews.go.com/International/fina-decision-transgender-athletes-ripple-effects-sportsgoverning/story?id=85532366.

52. A. Travers, A, "The Sport Nexus and Gender Injustice," *Studies in Social Justice Journal* 2, no. 1 (2008): 79–101; Travers, A, "Sport, Transgender Athletes, And Nonbinary Experience"; Travers, "'Female' Sport and Testosterone Panic."

53. Anima Adjepong and Travers, "The Problem with Sex Segregated Sport," *Engaging Sports*, December 9, 2022, https://thesocietypages.org/engagingsports.

54. Dowling, *The Frailty Myth*; Mary Jo Kane, "Resistance/Transformation of the Oppositional Binary: Exposing Sport as a Continuum, *Journal of Sport*

and Social Issues 19 (1995): 191–218; Eileen McDonagh and Laura Pappano, *Playing with the Boys: Why Separate is Not Equal in Sports* (New York: Oxford University Press, 2008); A. Travers, "Thinking the Unthinkable: Imagining an 'Un-American,' Girl-Friendly, Women and Trans-Inclusive Alternative for Baseball, *Journal of Sport and Social Issues* 37, no.1 (2013): 78–96.

55. Sarah Carter, *The Importance of Being Monogamous: Marriage and National Building in Western Canada to 1915* (Edmonton: University of Alberta Press, 2008).

56. Fischer, "Protecting Women's Sports?"

57. Michelle Bellefontaine, "Danielle Smith Unveils Sweeping Changes to Alberta's Student Gender Identity, Sports and Surgery Policies," *CBC News*, January 31, 2024, https://www.cbc.ca/news/canada/edmonton/danielle-smith-unveils-sweeping-changes-to-alberta-s-student-gender-identity-sports-and-surgery-policies-1.7101053.

58. Alex Kulick, Laura J. Wernick, Mario Alberto V. Espinoza, Tarkington J. Newman, and Adrienne B. Dessel, "Three Strikes and You're Out: Culture, Facilities, and Participation Among LGBTQ Youth in Sports," *Sport, Education and Society* 24, no. 9 (2019): 939–53; Marion Doull, Ryan J. Watson, Annie Smith, Yuko Homma, and Elizabeth Saewyc, "Are We Leveling the Playing Field? Trends and Disparities in Sports Participation Among Sexual Minority Youth in Canada," *Journal of Sport and Health Science* 7 no., 2 (2018): 218–26.

59. Efrat Abadi and Diane L. Gill, "The Role of Socializing Agents on Drop-out and Continuing Participation of Adolescent Girls in Masculine-typed Sports," *International Journal of Kinesiology in Higher Education* 4, no. 3 (2020): 77–90; Doull, Watson, Smith, Homma, and Saewyc, "Are We Leveling the Playing Field?"; Kulick, Wernick, Espinoza, Tarkington, Newman, and Dessel, "Three Strikes and You're Out"; R. Storr, L. Nicholas, K. Robinson, and C. Davies, "'Game to Play?': Barriers and Facilitators to Sexuality and Genderdiverse Young People's Participation in Sport and Physical Activity," *Sport, Education and Society* 27, no. 5 (2022): 604–17; Travers, K.J. Reed, S. Patel, and T. Zakaria, "The SPIRIT Project: LGBTQ2S+ Youth and Inclusion in Physical Health and Education," *Physical & Health Education Canada* 41, no. 3 (2021): 213–23.

10

Weaponizing Sport Ideology

OutKick's "Anti-Woke" Brand and Women's Sports

JASON KIDO LOPEZ

In 2011, sports personality Clay Travis founded the sports media outlet that came to be called OutKick. Acquired by the Fox Corporation in 2021, the company makes a name for itself in a crowded sports media marketplace by branding itself as "fearless, authentic, and wokeless." This mandate is reflected on its website, through its social media posts and in its streaming shows, as commentators like Clay Travis, Tomi Lahren, Dan Dakich, and Curt Schilling trade in alt-right talking points about sports, culture, and politics. To be distinguished from mainstream sports companies like ESPN, OutKick frames itself as a sports-centered media outlet willing to "tell it like it is" against the ideologies of the Left, thereby also alleging that most other sports media companies inauthentically cave to the demands of woke politics.

To build its brand, OutKick employs ideologies common to sports that are consistent with alt-right politics. This chapter explores how OutKick's brand wields two ideologies found throughout sports—that men are better suited for athletics than women, and that sports are apolitical meritocracies. It builds on these foundations to support the alt-right tenet that white masculinity is under attack and needs protecting. There is, of course, a logical tension in OutKick's use of the notion that sports are apolitical to further alt-right politics. For OutKick, politics only emerge in a problematic way when athletes speak in favor of diversity, inclusion, and social justice. Sports are therefore represented as yet another domain in which white masculinity is in danger of being marginalized by activist athletes, woke media companies, and even the simple presence of athletes who are not white men. OutKick brands itself as standing against it all.

The demand to protect sports as the domain of men means that women's sports are usually marginalized by OutKick. For example, in a random selection of fifteen days of OutKick content, about 8 percent of the site's posts included any mention of women's sport, even if the coverage ignored the actual games (such as stories reporting on the Women's National Basketball Association's (WNBA) finances or the legal battles of swimmer Lia Thomas). In fact, most posts were *not* about women's competitions, but focused on issues pertaining to women in sports.[1] OutKick's usual marginalization of women makes sports seem exclusively for men.

However, in the summer of 2023, the company broke from this pattern to comment extensively and repeatedly on three stories involving women athletes and women's sports: (1) Brittney Griner's imprisonment in and release from Russia; (2) transgender women's participation in women's sports; and (3) the United States Women's National Team's (USWNT) run through the 2023 FIFA Women's World Cup. The site posted forty-three separate times about transgender athletes (from May 3 to August 17) and twenty-one times about the USWNT's involvement with the World Cup (from June 9 to August 23). They followed Brittney Griner's imprisonment (the news became publicly available March 5, 2022) and eventual release (December 8, 2022), but continued to opine about her throughout the summer of 2023, posting about Griner over one hundred times from March 5, 2022, to May 21, 2023. These three stories garnered by far the most attention on the OutKick site.

I considered all stories on OutKick that appeared using the search function on OutKick.com, using related terms like "Griner," "USWNT," and "transgender." Relevant links in the found posts were also followed and used as inspiration for other search terms. All posts related to the three stories were analyzed for their overarching themes while searching for answers to the following questions: How were women and women's sports portrayed on OutKick? What, beyond athletics, was discussed and how was it treated? What ideologies and politics were being conveyed and were they connected to tropes found commonly in sports and sports media? The analysis of the posts reveals how OutKick uses messages common to sports to interpret the three widely popular women's sports stories and support its alt-right brand. In its coverage, OutKick leverages the notions that men are better suited for athletics and that sports are apolitical in order to send the message that gender and racial inclusiveness is "ruining" sports. In this way, OutKick uses women's sports to construct its alt-right dictate that sports—as one part of a wider social and political concern—remain under the control of white men.[2]

Sports Branding, Sports Ideology, and Alt-Right Ideology

The marketplace of sports media is increasingly crowded. It is important, especially for smaller sports media companies, to brand themselves in novel ways to stand out. Brands convey values and associations and, therefore, lay out expectations of the company and its products to its audience, producers, and partners.[3] While large companies like ESPN can use their reach to brand themselves as *the* place for sports, those with fewer resources need to find a more niche space.[4] OutKick does this by explicitly branding itself as an alt-right and anti-woke brand. To aid in this branding project, OutKick contrasts itself with sports media companies like ESPN, which it characterizes as liberal and woke. OutKick presents sports leagues like the National Basketball Association (NBA) and WNBA similarly. In this way, the company's political bent is inextricably tied to sports. Its brand—both what it is and what it is not—is formed through sports. Correspondingly, to make sense as a sports brand, OutKick associates itself with meanings commonly found in sports and sports media. OutKick needs to appeal to them to be read as a sports brand, and adapt them for their own branding goals.

Among the most common and consistent messages conveyed through sports is that sports are apolitical meritocracies. According to this trope, sports are pure competitions, and the most capable, fit, and prepared tend to win. In the realm of sports, therefore, social categories that might unfairly hinder people in other contexts—like race, economic standing, and gender—are irrelevant to the outcome of competitions.[5] The best and most deserving will tend to succeed without any outside social or political considerations having an effect, because every athlete supposedly starts the game on an equal footing.[6] The sporting world is taken to be the archetype of a meritocracy, in which "individuals tend to get ahead and earn rewards in direct proportion to their individual efforts and abilities."[7]

Any insertion of politics into this allegedly meritocratic sports is an irrelevant and inappropriate incursion worthy of censure. Athletes who use sports to speak out about political or social topics are often critiqued by media, punished by sports organizations, and attacked by fans. Imagining sports as apolitical meritocracies supports the "pervasive and nearly unshakable belief in the inherent purity and goodness of sport," which Jay Coakley has termed "the Great Sports Myth."[8] The purity of sport supposedly affords a retreat from the messiness of everyday life, society, and politics.[9] The mandate that sports remain free of politics, therefore, protects its competitive purity and its ability to offer escapism.

Of course, sports and sports media aren't purely meritocratic and are rife with social and political meanings. But the Great Sports Myth powerfully normalizes regularly appearing ideologies and renders them invisible. It follows that not all political expressions are critiqued, only those that are usually foreign to sports and sports media. For example, an athlete's support of the military, its personnel, and its interventions wouldn't result in controversy even though it is clearly a political message. Due to the pervasiveness of the presence of the military, those political messages no longer seem political.[10]

When, on the other hand, National Football League (NFL) athletes like Colin Kaepernick knelt to protest social injustice and the oppression of Black people, they were routinely criticized.[11] Unlike pro-military politics, this is a topic usually foreign to sports and it was accordingly viewed as a violation of the apolitical space and a breach of sports' escapism. Additionally, the outcry against athletes using sporting contexts to comment on racism or any other kind of social injustice can be more ardent in an international context. Athletes who use events like the Olympics and the World Cup to speak out on these topics are portrayed by some as being unpatriotic and undeserving of American citizenship.[12]

Sports' claim to be an apolitical meritocracy can support hegemonic ideologies about gender and sexuality. Athletic competitions have the appearance of being semi-scientific proving grounds in which the best and most talented tend to win.[13] The lack of representation of women and gay athletes in mainstream sports can be used to "demonstrate" that sports are spaces best suited for straight men. By doing so, sports are regularly represented as the domain of hegemonic masculinity, and those who don't perform according to hegemonically masculine scripts are marked as not belonging in sporting spaces.[14] Women's sports are often symbolically annihilated and demeaned.[15] Any deviation from cis-gendered heterosexuality is also difficult for conventional sports to include.[16] Finally, the notion of hegemonic masculinity is also built on a picture of gender that is essentialist and binary, reinforcing sexual hierarchies.[17]

The invisible ideologies regularly found in sport form the foundation from which politicized sports brands can build. Relaying these messages, first of all, makes brands legible as a sports brand and, therefore, distinct from other entertainment options. However, whether they are leagues, teams, or media companies, sports-based brands must stand out from one another. Therefore, each sport brand must shape the meanings common to the sporting realm in seemingly novel ways. Jennifer McClearen offers a helpful example of a brand constructing its own picture of sports ideology with her analysis of the Ultimate Fighting Championship (UFC).[18] In order to build what McClearen terms "branded difference," the league promotes the diversity of its fighters.[19] This difference is a crucial part of constructing the UFC's "millennial sports media brand," in which the millennial generation is targeted partially through appealing to the value of diversity.[20] The diversity of the fighters allows the UFC to communicate that "everyone is different" and therefore has to overcome their own individual obstacles to succeed both in and outside of the octagon.[21] In this way, the UFC connects its branded difference to the notion that sports, fighting, and the UFC instantiate the meritocratic American Dream.[22]

While the UFC bent meritocratic ideology toward values that appeal to millennials, OutKick constructs a different commodity audience by referencing alt-right politics. Particularly, it wields the general notion that white men are in crisis, which is a cornerstone of far-right politics exemplified by Trumpism and the Proud Boys.[23] One kind of crisis white men face is from women and, particularly, feminists.[24] A response to this alleged crisis is "popular misogyny," an anti-feminist stance intended to preserve masculinity and patriarchy.[25] A second, related crisis is based on the post-racial premise that white culture is under attack and needs protection.[26] When these crises are combined with the perception that white male culture *is* popular culture, the unwelcome people of color or women are framed as constituting an incursion that needs to be defended against.[27]

OutKick is not the first or only sports media company to mix alt-right and "anti-woke" ideology into its brand. Barstool Sports offers a case in which sporting ideology becomes intermixed with white male grievance politics.[28] Christopher Garcia and Jennifer Proffitt explore how—in response to the "threat" that women journalists play to the homosocial space that is sports—Barstool and its founder Dave Portnoy use harassment guised as humor "to silence feminist storytelling and counter-hegemonic narratives."[29] Kyle Kusz and Matthew Hodler investigate how Barstool reacts to a cultural and political period of "political correctness, feminism, diversity, and inclusion"[30] with white fratriarchy: "a form of male rule operating through fraternal relations and bonds among a select group of men[,] usually to the exclusion of all others."[31] As with Garcia and Proffitt's examination, Kusz and Hodler find humor to be one of the main mechanisms used by Barstool to protect the white male sporting space. This is important, as humor allows Barstool management and personalities to deflect claims of racism or misogyny by claiming they were just joking.[32]

While OutKick occasionally attempts to use satire and humor, it centers its political bent in ways that Barstool does not. OutKick wears its ideology on its sleeve and weaves it explicitly throughout the fabric of its brand. Threats to white masculinity are named and targeted. In its political coverage, those take the form of Joe Biden, Kamala Harris, Barack Obama, and—during the COVID pandemic—Anthony Fauci. OutKick's political heroes, such as Elon Musk and Joe Rogan, are led by Donald Trump. This political leaning is reflected in its sports content generally but becomes most apparent in its coverage of women's sports. This is because, as Richard Mocarski and Andrew Billings note of a different case, "well-hidden discourse comes into conflict with groups that the discourse marginalizes" in OutKick's coverage.[33] In Mocarski and Billings's example of LeBron James, they argue that hegenomic masculinity is implicitly coded as being reserved for white men, but that fact becomes more apparent when the concept is applied to someone who isn't a white man. The same is the case for OutKick; its already explicit alt-right and anti-woke brand rises even more to the forefront in its coverage of women's sports.

OutKick's Use of Women's Sports for Alt-Right Branding

Like mainstream sports media outlets (for example, ESPN and ESPN+),[34] OutKick's homepage rarely represents women athletes or women's sports. There are no links that take visitors directly to information about women's sports and leagues, as there are for their men's equivalents. The easiest way to find OutKick's coverage of women's sports is to use the search option. While useful for research on the site, the fact that this is the central way of locating coverage of women's sports effectively demonstrates how little focus they get.

The following subsections analyze OutKick's coverage of these cases, examining how ideologies common to sports are leveraged to normalize and justify the alt-right tenet that white men are under attack and need to be protected from "wokeness."

The Cost of Griner's Un-American Activism

On February 17, 2022, Brittney Griner was detained in Russia by airport security for having vape cartridges in her bag that officials said contained cannabis oil.[35] Griner's arrest occurred in the lead up to the Russian invasion of Ukraine. According to a US State Department official, during this period, there was a "surge of arrests of Americans," suggesting that Griner was a pawn in the political struggle between the United States and Russia.[36] Nevertheless, within the United States, Griner was relentlessly criticized in alt-right media, which rushed to question whether Griner deserved to be negotiated out of imprisonment and, once released, whether she should have been. Doubts about her worthiness turned on her political activism. It was frequently (and incorrectly) stated that she disrespected the nation by refusing to take the court during the playing of the national anthem and questioning whether it should be played before games.[37] Doubts were also raised about the United States' trading of the Russian arms dealer Viktor Bout for her release in a prisoner exchange.[38] OutKick mimicked this line of commentary, but grounded it in the notion that sports are apolitical and that women's sports and athletes are unimportant.

Much of OutKick's Griner-focused content highlighted her activism and equated it with anti-Americanism. While Griner was imprisoned, Tomi Lahren pontificated.

> I can't figure out why Brittney Griner would be clamoring to get back to a nation she finds so unworthy of her patriotism. If the woman can't even drag her sorry behind out of a locker room in cushy Phoenix, Arizona long enough to stand and salute our flag for the under 2-minute duration of our national anthem, well then maybe the USA isn't really where she wants to be. And maybe after sitting in a Russian prison for a bit, she'll understand what a privilege it is to be born in America and be grateful for the USA: the greatest nation on the face of the earth.[39]

These opinions are found throughout OutKick's commentary on Griner's case: by taking the time in a sporting context to honor Breonna Taylor and support Black Lives Matter, she disrespected the country. By wanting to come home, it is argued, Griner exposed her own hypocrisy: she knows (or learned in prison) that the United States is a peerless country and, therefore, her calls for reform are invalidated.

Upon Griner's release, OutKick commentators frequently argued that she should now stand publicly for the national anthem.[40] This highlights the expectation that athletes play particular roles in sports' usual political spectacles. Normalized due to their regularity, ideological expressions like the national anthem become a part of the athletes' expected performance while on the job. Kneeling, or even not participating, as Griner had done, is worthy of censure, and this expectation was used to further bolster the idea that it is inappropriate to raise political issues through sport.

OutKick regularly evaluated the exchange of prisoners—Griner for Bout—as a lopsided one. They excitedly reported that Boomer Esiason (ex-NFL quarterback turned media personality) called the swap "pathetic" on

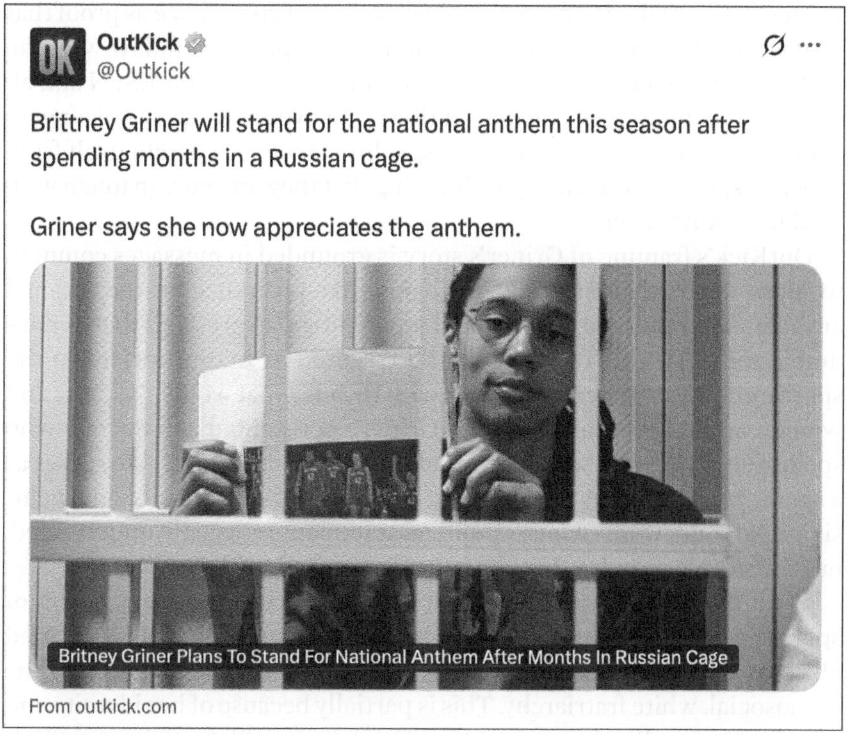

FIGURE 10.1: Screenshot of post promoting OutKick's story on Brittney Griner's release from a Russian prison.

his radio show, for instance.[41] Other voices criticizing the terms of Griner's release were similarly amplified. OutKick would pull quotations from a diverse group, ranging from Will Cain of Fox News[42] to Instagram model Rachel Bush (whose connection to sports is her spouse, NFL player Jordan Poyer).[43] The commentary, however, was largely the same: trading Griner for the so-called "Merchant of Death" was embarrassing for the United States. Griner's freedom was not valuable on its own.

Finally, OutKick used the Griner case to set itself apart from other sports entities by deeming them "too woke." The NBA and WNBA were commonly a target. Steph Curry was mocked for calling Griner a hero[44] and Angel McCoughtry was scolded for not wanting to play in Russia after Griner's ordeal.[45] OutKick separated itself from ESPN by alleging that a "total of 20 people showed up" to Griner's homecoming in Waco, Texas (the location of Griner's alma matter, Baylor University).[46] OutKick celebrated the lack of turnout and mocked "MSESPN" by declaring that "the city of Waco and Baylor weren't, and still aren't, all that accepting of

Griner."[47] OutKick interprets the allegedly low of attendance as proof that ESPN is pushing a liberal agenda that most people don't follow with the following proclamation: "Public service announcement for ESPN and all other left-leaning legacy media out there: not everyone has to talk or care about Brittney Griner."[48] OutKick uses this stance to separate itself from "liberal" sports companies by insinuating that they are more in touch with "ordinary Americans."

OutKick's framing of Griner's story is grounded in messages common to sport. Regularly appearing ideologies—like reverence for the national anthem—are rendered natural, and any political expression that is non-dominant—like anti-racism—can be targeted as inappropriate to the sporting context. When connected with the idea that women's sports and women athletes are unimportant, Griner is presented as someone who spoke out of turn and was appropriately punished. Griner's tale serves as a sports-based allegory representing the failure of social justice and inclusivity. Not only were Griner's political statements allegedly undermined, but the simple premise that she matters is questioned.

With these maneuvers, OutKick seeks to secure the social realm of sports for white masculinist, alt-right politics. Griner and her purported allies of ESPN, the NBA, and the WNBA represent an incursion to the homosocial, white fratriarchy. This is partially because of her identity and popularity. As a Black, gay, and female celebrity athlete, Griner symbolizes the supposedly shrinking space for straight white men, both inside and outside of sports. In OutKick's framing, ESPN and the professional basketball leagues are complicit in giving Griner, and women's basketball generally, more attention than they deserve. This is coupled with Griner's outspokenness about social justice, which also represents an incursion into white, male dominance. Griner, therefore, is a challenge to this hierarchy, and OutKick's rebuke of her separates its sports brand from others.

Transgender Athletes and Protecting (Women's) Sports

Another exception to the usual paucity of OutKick's coverage of women's sports is the issue of transgender women playing women's sports. Like many mainstream conservative media outlets, OutKick has sought out instances in which trans women—at any level—have found athletic success and wrung their hands about the future of sports for women and girls. This has become such a tentpole issue for OutKick that the platform started a podcast in July of 2023 largely centered on the issue: *Gaines for the Girls with Riley Gaines*, starring the former collegiate swimmer and current political activist Riley Gaines. The show regularly frames trans women as an existential threat to women's sports. The podcast supports OutKick's three-part argument against trans women's participation in sports: (1) there are only two essential genders; (2) men are superior to women in the sporting realm; and therefore, (3) any transgender women participating in women's sports are actually men and thus have an unfair advantage over women. This argument allows OutKick to take up an apparently feminist mantle of "protecting" women's sports while also demeaning them as inferior to men's.

In order to validate this argument, OutKick surveys the wider sports world to find cases in which trans women have competed or even say they *will* compete in women's sports. A particularly telling instance of this occurred in a post focused on British cyclist Emily Bridges.[49] OutKick reported that Bridges "will race biological female cyclists this weekend just after beating fellow biological males during a university event."[50] Before Bridges had competed in a single women's race, the post railed against the fact that she *could* potentially earn a spot on England's women's cycling team, which will "come at the expense of a biological female who has worked her ass off for her entire life to get a shot at the 2024 Olympics."[51] Without one race being contested, the post bemoans the hypothetical loss of a spot on the Olympic roster of an imagined athlete. (Bridges ended up quitting because she felt as though she was being pushed out of women's cycling.)[52]

OutKick also amplifies instances of people criticizing the inclusion of trans athletes, framing them as brave truth tellers. For example, when professional boxer Carl Froch claimed on an obscure British sports betting website that "it would be ridiculous for a trans woman to fight a cis woman in the boxing ring or [mixed martial arts] octagon,"[53] OutKick amplified the interview in a post that contained an extended quotation from the boxer stating that trans women are stronger and more powerful than cis women and that, therefore, they shouldn't compete in women's sports.[54] By reporting Froch's opinions, OutKick normalizes its view.

OutKick also takes pains to locate cases in which trans women compete and succeed in women's sports. This requires them to survey the sporting world and cover sports and places they normally ignore: British cycling, collegiate American swimming, and American high school cross-country are all examples.[55] The majority of posts about cycling, 76 percent, focused on trans issues. Searching for posts about "swimmer," I found that 77 percent were about trans athletes. Given how few trans athletes actually compete in high-level competitive sports, OutKick must be seeking examples far outside of its normal areas of coverage.

OutKick highlights stories about trans athletes because they are a perfect opportunity for their brand to communicate the tie between their politics and their sports coverage. By targeting transgender women, OutKick also grounds its commentary in messages common to sport: there are two essential genders, women's athletics are worse than men's, and all of this is "proven" in the meritocratic realm of sports. OutKick gathers only a few actual cases of competition to support a gendered hierarchy in athletic performance, instead presenting its position as common sense and grounding it in a wider sports media context in which women's sports and athletic ability are regularly demeaned. Therefore, it can be asserted as "obvious" that women essentially have less athletic merit than men.

It is for this reason that conservative and alt-right outlets use sports to gain a toehold for their anti-transgender agenda. OutKick, as a sports-focused media platform, positions itself as an expert on the topic. On August 27, 2023, the Fox News Channel broadcast a special intended to "slam transgender ideology in schools," called "OutKick on Fox."[56] The show, featuring Clay Travis, Tomi Lahren, and Charly Arnot, was focused on schooling but was intertwined with OutKick's sports specialty. The strategy was to use sports to weaken sentiment for transgender rights in education.

OutKick's posts about transgender athletes in women's sports accord with its alt-right agenda. Using scripts common to sports about merit and gender, OutKick takes a "principles" stance against inclusion. A core premise is that cisgender women naturally have less athletic capacity, which is leveraged as a reason that they need protection from transgender women (who are transphobically held to be men). Women's sports are thus used to reaffirm the dominance of men and argue against the call of the woke Left for more inclusive (sporting) spaces.

The USWNT: Too Out of Touch to Represent the USA

In the summer of 2023, the Women's World Cup was held in Australia and New Zealand. The USWNT had a turbulent experience in the tournament. Despite being the favorite, the team won only one out of three group stage games and was eliminated from the tournament in the sixteenth round. Just as when any usually dominant team underperforms, there were legitimate questions to be asked, but OutKick instead took the team's shortcoming as an opportunity to pontificate about the perils of "wokeness." In particular, OutKick highlighted the USWNT's fight for equal pay to "wokeness" and argued their loss represented the failure of the team's politics.

One component of the team's defeat was its purported lack of patriotism. Before their first game, OutKick "questioned" whether rooting against the team is un-American.

> That's something that I, personally, wrestle with. At first glance, it seems that yes it [is]. You should root for your country to be successful in everything. That's how almost every country's citizens feel. Except, the USWNT has such a complicated history with the United States that it muddles things a bit.[57]

The "complications" included kneeling during the anthem, protesting a policy that they must stand during the song, fighting for equal pay, and supporting trans athletes. Even in this post focused on women's soccer, space was taken to reference their regularly found transphobic argument: supporting trans women playing in women's soccer "would displace ALL of the actual women on the team."[58] The author unsurprisingly concludes that it isn't unpatriotic to root against them due to their politics and that, in fact, doing so might actually demonstrate patriotism. The OutKick account created a poll that asked readers, "Who are you rooting for in the Women's World Cup?" and 75.8 percent of the respondents selected "Any Other Team" instead of the USWNT.[59] OutKick then used the results to argue that the American public dislikes the team's "pushing a radical, far-left political agenda."[60]

The site was largely silent about the team during their first two group stage games (a win and a draw), but it came to life once the USWNT ended the stage with a nil-nil draw, a result that saw the team qualify for the knockout stage. After the game, Carli Lloyd—a former member of the team and a commentator on Fox's World Cup coverage—criticized the USWNT for dancing and smiling after a disappointing draw.[61] OutKick amplified and supported Lloyd's position, contending that "[y]ou can celebrate when you win" and "[u]ntil then, keep your mouth shut, stop the smiling and get in the locker room."[62] The team was alleged to be too cocky and out of touch with sporting norms; they hadn't won the tournament and couldn't express joy until they did so.

Once the team lost in the knockout round, OutKick's coverage increased. After the loss, eleven posts analyzed the team and pontificated about their exit from the tournament. OutKick predictably took an "I told you so" attitude about the team's performance. Most of the content mentioned and linked to posts about Carli Lloyd's criticism. They also amplified Netherlands player Lineth Beerensteyn's comments, which fit this narrative:

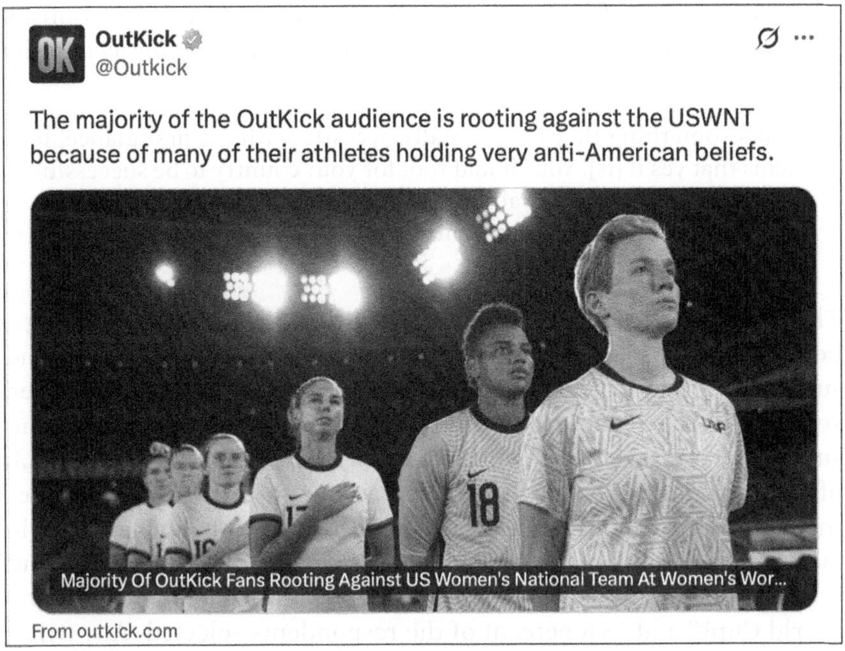

FIGURE 10.2: Screenshot of post promoting OutKick's story on fan support for USWNT.

> From the start of this tournament, they had already a really big mouth—they were talking already about the final and stuff. I was just thinking: "You first have to show it on the pitch before you are talking."[63]

The team was also repeatedly cast as too political. Megan Rapinoe was regularly targeted specifically as the epitome of violating both imperatives: both her politics and on-field behavior were unacceptably progressive, and hence in violation of the "apolitical" space of sports. A post blaming Rapinoe for the United States' tournament exit noted that she "used her platform to speak out on controversial topics through often disagreeable perspectives."[64]

In its coverage of the USWNT's participation in the World Cup, OutKick rehashes some maneuvers used in its coverage of Griner and transgender women's participation in women's sports. OutKick's coverage highlighted famous people who appear to agree with them[65] in order to reinforce the notion "woke" politics have no place in sports. What gets targeted as "woke" might shift and can include a wide set of political stances about equality, social justice, and inclusion, but they are all marked as an unwelcome and unnatural intrusion. Just as with Griner, the fact that the USWNT's political messages deviated from sports' usual politics was an opportunity to mark the former as violating a realm in which the latter are normalized and seem apolitical. And, also like Griner's case, the USWNT's misfortune is framed as a parable explicating the failure of wokeness. Woke politics, therefore, are framed as contradicting common sense. Just as Griner was obviously wrong for "disrespecting" the United States, and just as transgender women are clearly a danger to women's sports, the USWNT's political statements are framed as unpopular and unwelcome.

OutKick promotes its conservative common sense to market itself as different from other sports media. After ESPN aired a tribute to Rapinoe, OutKick critiqued its rival for making "politics the center of attention," which ESPN "delivered . . . in its typical left-leaning way."[66] OutKick argues that the video marks Rapinoe as a patriot, which is a "make-believe reality that only its liberal audience will agree with, while the rest of the country will recognize it for what it is, which is a lie."[67] OutKick, therefore, presents itself clearly as not only different from companies like ESPN by being willing to fight against liberal politics, but as expressing an opinion that most people will agree with. In this way, OutKick frames itself like many alt-right entities in which "White Americans are the overwhelming majority and the normative affect is antipathy toward political correctness and progressive values and ideas."[68]

Conclusion: Sports Ideology and Alt-Right Sports Branding

At the time of this writing, OutKick has moved its focus from Griner and the USWNT to Caitlin Clark. It still covers transgender stories. After a 2024 season in which women's collegiate basketball received historic attention and Clark broke records her senior year,[69] Clark was drafted to the WNBA.[70] OutKick has used the attention on women's basketball and Clark to reinforce most of the maneuvers described above. Over fifteen days, it covered Clark disproportionally more than other stories about women's basketball. Clark (who is white) was the center of 82 percent of the posts, with an additional 13 percent focusing on criticism of her perceived foil, fellow WNBA rookie Angel Reese (who is Black). Very few of the posts are about the games themselves. Instead, OutKick amplifies grievance, claiming that Clark was being treated poorly in the league because she is a successful white and straight player. The title of one post is "WNBA Mean Girls Won't Accept Caitlin Clark until She Apologizes for Being White and Straight."[71] In a familiar pattern, OutKick highlights those who appear to agree with their commentary. It quotes Shaquille O'Neal claiming that WNBA players are jealous of Clark,[72] and repeats Bill

Maher's statement that Clark is disliked because she's white and straight.[73] That OutKick is willing to report this openly marks them as different from other media outlets like ESPN, who, in OutKick's rendering, instead push diversity and inclusion rather than the truth.[74]

This mode of selectively addressing women's sports will continue to be a crucial maneuver for OutKick. The increasing popularity of women's sports will necessitate commenting on them. However, for OutKick, women's sports cannot be covered simply as sports, since that would acknowledge the validity of women in the sporting realm and correspondingly undercut the notion that sports should be dominated by men. In response, women's sports are covered as politics, which—as a corollary—means they provide opportunities to reify OutKick's alt-right brand. Under the guise of protecting women's sports, OutKick supports the notion that sports are and should be the dominion of white men.

Anointing itself itself as the protector of women's sports allows OutKick to call upon ideologies common to sports to fulfill its alt-right brand identity. Presenting sports as a meritocracy "proves" the athletic dominance of men. Progressive women athletes like Griner and Rapinoe can be demeaned for violating the commonsense norms of sport. The notion that sports are apolitical normalizes regularly appearing ideologies while making less common political claims—like those of social justice and inclusivity—seem inappropriate and worthy of censure. In these ways, the alt-right view that sports is a domain that belongs to white men is grounded in meanings familiar to sports fans.

The importance of this is increasingly clear, as politicians and other media companies have sought to gain political traction from sporting narratives. OutKick's maneuvers can be used in other contexts for the same ends. For example, Barstool sports founder and owner David Portnoy has spoken out against trans girls and women participating in girls' and women's sports, reinforcing Barstool's own alt-right brand. In politics, Trump and Trumpians, like former South Carolina Governor Nikki Haley, have taken stances against trans inclusion in women's sports to gain support from Christian conservatives, which demonstrates the growth of these strategies.[75]

Matt Sienkiewicz and Nick Marx argue that right-wing comedy is part of "a networked structure of conservative . . . shows, podcasts, streaming media, and websites that work together, directing viewers to each other and circulating them throughout intertwined ideological spaces."[76] A similar complex is partially constituted through Fox's ownership of OutKick, which enables content and ideology to be shared synergistically and uniformly. Through this complex, alt-right politics gain the appearance of being widely held and commonsense, and can be imported into non-sports media outlets and into the platforms and policies of politicians. However, this ideological complex doesn't necessitate corporate cooperation. OutKick happily amplifies messages that buoy its positions, whether they come from Fox or not. For example, OutKick covered Jason Whitlock's (previously employed by OutKick and currently by Blaze Media) war of words with ESPN celebrity commentator Stephen A. Smith. It also followed Aaron Rodgers's interviews on Pat McAfee's ESPN show, during which the NFL quarterback pushed conspiracy theories and misinformation. Both cases were interpreted by OutKick as black eyes for its media competitor's woke politics,[77] and this was enabled by the complex of linked ideologies and shared content.

OutKick's specific mix of alt-right messages and ideology common to sport helps us understand both components of its anti-woke sports brand. Sports are not just another sphere in which alt-right political positions can be advanced. Sports offer a set of ready-made ways of making sense of the world that seem to be verified and obvious, and a distinct context from which alt-right political actors can operate.

Notes

1. I excluded posts that involved women but were devoid of references to athletes and sports, which included stories about women who aren't athletes having affairs or romantic relationships with men, about sexualization of women attending live sporting events, or about women journalists and media personalities.

2. See, for example, Clay Travis's recently published book *Balls: How Trump, Young Men, and Sports Saved America* (Nashville: Center Street, 2025).

3. Catherine Johnson, *Branding Television* (London: Routledge, 2012); Adam Arvidsson, *Brands: Meanings and Value in Media Culture* (London: Routledge, 2006); Celia Lury, *Brands: The Logos of the Global Economy* (London: Routledge, 2004).

4. Travis Vogan, *ESPN: The Making of Sports Media Empire* (Champaign: University of Illinois Press, 2015).

5. Andrew Grainger, Joshua I. Newnian, and David L. Andrews, "Sport, the Media, and the Construction of Race," in *Handbook of Sports and Media*, ed. Arthur A. Raney and Jennings Bryant (London: Routledge, 2009).

6. Stephen J. McNamee and Robert K. Miller Jr., *The Meritocracy Myth* (Lantham, MD: Rowman & Littlefield Publishers, 2009), 4.

7. McNamee and Miller, *Meritocracy Myth*, 4.

8. Jay Coakley, "Assessing the Sociology of Sport: On Cultural Sensibilities and the Great Sports Myth," *International Review for the Sociology of Sport* 50, no. 4–5 (2015): 403.

9. Michael Serazio, *The Power of Sports: Media and Spectacle in American Culture* (New York: New York University Press, 2019), 230.

10. For just a few examples, see Michael Butterworth, "Militarism and Memorializing at the Pro Football Hall of Fame," *Communication and Critical/Cultural Studies* 9, no. 3 (2012): 241–58; Mia Fischer, "Commemorating 9/11 NFL-Style: Insights into America's Culture of Militarism," *Journal of Sport and Social Issues* 38, no. 3 (2014): 199–221; Sue Curry Jansen and Don Sabo, "The Sport/War Metaphor: Hegemonic Masculinity, the Persian Gulf War, and the New World Order," *Sociology of Sport Journal* 11, no. 1 (1994): 1–17.

11. Jason Kido Lopez, "Rewriting Activism: The NFL Takes a Knee," *Critical Studies in Media Communication* 38, no. 2 (2021): 183–96.

12. Sarah J. Jackson, *Black Celebrity, Racial Politics, and the Press: Framing Dissent* (London: Routledge, 2014), 77.

13. Jason Kido Lopez, *Redefining Sports Media* (London: Routledge, 2023).

14. Nick Trujillo, "Hegemonic Masculinity on the Mound: Media Representations of Nolan Ryan and American Sports Culture," *Critical Studies in Media Communication* 8 (1991): 290–308.

15. Pamela J. Creedon, "Women, Sport, and Media Institutions: Issues in Sports Journalism and Marketing," in *MediaSport*, ed. Lawrence Wenner (Routledge, 1998), 88–100.

16. Creedon, "Women, Sport, and Media."

17. Laura Grindstaff and Emily West, "Hegemonic Masculinity on the Sidelines of Sport," *Sociology Compass* 5, no. 10 (2011): 875.

18. Jennifer McClearen, *Fighting Visibility: Sports Media and Female Athletics in the UFC* (Illinois University Press, 2021).

19. McClearen, *Fighting Visibility*, 15.

20. McClearen, *Fighting Visibility*, 37, 54.

21. McClearen, *Fighting Visibility*, 52.

22. McClearen, *Fighting Visibility*, 85.

23. Kyle Kusz and Matthew R. Hodler, "'Saturdays Are for the Boys': Barstool Sports and the Cultural Politics of White Fratriarchy in Contemporary America," *Sociology of Sport Journal* 40 (2023): 98–99.

24. Sarah Banet-Weiser, *Empowered: Popular Feminism and Popular Misogyny* (Duke University Press, 2018), 5.

25. Banet-Weiser, *Empowered*, 35.

26. Kusz and Hodler, "'Saturdays Are for the Boys'," 99.

27. Derek Johnson, "From the Ruins: Neomasculinity, Media Franchising, and Struggles Over Industrial Reproduction of Culture," *Communication, Culture and Critique* 11, no. 1 (2018): 92.

28. For another example of sports ideology and politics, see Shaun E. Edmonds, *Make American Fit Again: CrossFit's Articulation with Authoritarian Populism* (Lantham, MD: Palgrave Macmillan, 2023).

29. Christopher J. Garcia and Jennifer M. Proffitt, "Recontextualizing Bar-

stool Sports and Misogyny in Online US Sports Media," *Communication & Sport* 10, no. 4 (2022): 731.

30. Kusz and Hodler, "'Saturdays Are for the Boys'," 96.

31. Kusz and Hodler, "'Saturdays Are for the Boys'," 97.

32. Garcia and Proffitt, "Recontextualizing Barstool Sports."

33. Mocarski and Billings, "Manufacturing a Messiah," 5.

34. Jason Kido Lopez, "ESPN+: Subscribing to Diversity, Marginalizing Women's Sports," in *From Networks to Netflix: A Guide to Changing Channels*, 2nd ed., ed. Derek Johnson (London: Routledge, 2023): 377–86.

35. Jonathan Abrams and Tania Ganguli, "Why Pros Like Brittney Griner Choose Cannabis for Their Pain," *New York Times*, August 1, 2022, https://www.nytimes.com/2022/08/01/sports/basketball/brittney-griner-athletes-cannabis-marijuana.html#:~:text=Griner%2C%20a%20W.N.B.A.,cannabis%20derivative%2C%20in%20her%20luggage.

36. T. J. Quinn, "Inside Brittney Griner's Russia Arrest, Detainment, and Release," *ESPN*, December 8, 2023, https://www.espn.com/wnba/story/_/id/39041673/inside-arrest-detainment-release-brittney-griner-russia-viktor-bout.

37. Neither were true, but in 2020 she did refuse to be on the floor while the national anthem was performed. Tiffanie Drayton, "The MAGA Faithful Who Refuse to Celebrate Brittney Griner's Release," *NBC News*, December 8, 2022, https://www.nbcnews.com/think/opinion/brittney-griner-paul-whelan-russia-prison-release-debate-misses-point-rcna60873.

38. "The Deal that Freed Brittney Griner," *NPR*, December 8, 2022, https://www.npr.org/2022/12/08/1141668781/the-deal-that-freed-brittney-griner. See also Drayton, "The MAGA Faithful."

39. OutKick Flash, "Why Does Brittney Griner Want to Get Back to a Nation Unworthy of her Patriotism? Tomi Lahren's Final Thoughts," *OutKick*, July 14, 2022, https://www.outkick.com/why-does-brittney-griner-want-to-get-back-to-a-nation-unworthy-of-her-patriotism-tomi-lahrens-final-thoughts/.

40. For example, Bobby Burack, "Britney [*sic*] Griner Plans to Stand for National Anthem after Months in Russian Cage," *OutKick*, May 19, 2023. https://www.outkick.com/britney-griner-plans-to-stand-for-national-anthem-after-months-in-russian-cage/.

41. David Hookstead, "'Pathetic': Former NFL QB Torches Biden for Brittney Griner/Merchant of Death Trade," *OutKick*, December 9, 2022, https://www.outkick.com/boomer-esiason-viktor-bout-merchant-of-death-trade-brittney-griner-reaction/.

42. Mark Harris, "Brittney Griner for 'Merchant of Death' Swap Makes America Less Safe: Will Cain," *OutKick*, December 9, 2022, https://www.outkick.com/brittney-griner-merchant-of-death-prisoner-swap-will-cain/.

43. David Hookstead, "'All for Show': Rachel Bush Explains to OutKick Why the Brittney Griner Trade was a Disaster," *OutKick*, December 10,

2022, https://www.outkick.com/rachel-bush-brittney-griner-viktor-bout-reaction-trade-exclusive/.

44. Mark Harris, "Steph Curry Thanks Brittney Griner for her 'Sacrifice' after her Release from Russian Prison," *OutKick*, December 9, 2022, https://www.outkick.com/steph-curry-brittney-griner-sacrifice-russian-prison-release/.

45. Mark Harris, "WNBA Player Won't Return to Russia after Brittney Griner Arrest Despite Making Entire Salary in One Month Overseas," *OutKick*, December 9, 2022, https://www.outkick.com/wnba-player-angel-mccoughtry-wont-return-to-russia-after-brittney-griner-arrest/.

46. Mark Harris, "A Grand Total of 20 People Showed Up to a Brittney Griner 'Homecoming' Celebration in Waco, ESPN Doesn't Seem Happy about It," *OutKick*, December 22, 2022, https://www.outkick.com/brittney-griner-homecoming-celebration-waco-church/.

47. Harris, "A Grand Total."

48. Harris, "A Grand Total."

49. Joe Kinsey, "British Transgender Cyclist Emily Bridges Will Now Race Cycling Legend Laura Kenny after Beating Men in February," *OutKick*, December 22, 2022, https://www.outkick.com/british-transgender-cyclist-emily-bridges-will-now-race-cycling-legend-laura-kenny-after-beating-men-in-february/.

50. Kinsey, "British Transgender Cyclist."

51. Kinsey, "British Transgender Cyclist."

52. Cyd Zeigler, "Emily Bridges Quits Cycling, A Sad Repercussion of Trans-Athlete Bans in Sports," *OutSports*, August 23, 2023, https://www.outsports.com/2023/8/23/23842400/emily-bridges-trans-cycling-great-britain-vogue-athlete-ban-olympics.

53. "Exclusive with Carl Froch," *Safe Betting Sites*, https://www.safebettingsites.com/2023/07/11/exclusive-with-carl-froch/.

54. David Hookstead, "Legendary Boxer Slams Transgender Athletes Ruining Women's Sports: 'Shouldn't Ever Happen Again,'" *OutKick*, July 11, 2023, https://www.outkick.com/carl-froch-transgender-athletes-reaction-ebanie-bridges/.

55. Kinsey, "British Transgender Cyclist"; Ian Miller, "OutKick Exclusive: Paula Scanlan Details How Penn Ignored Her Concerns over Sharing Locker Room with Lia Thomas," *OutKick*, July 29, 2023, https://www.outkick.com/outkick-exclusive-paula-scanlan-details-how-penn-ignored-her-concerns-over-sharing-locker-room-with-lia-thomas/; Ian Miller, "Transgender Athlete Case in Connecticut Will Be Heard by Appeals Court," *OutKick*, July 29, 2023, https://www.outkick.com/transgender-athlete-case-in-connecticut-will-be-heard-by-appeals-court/.

56. "Clay Travis, Tomi Lahren, and Charly Arnolt Slam Transgender Ideology in Schools in Upcoming 'OutKick on Fox' Special," *OutKick*, August 28, 2023, https://www.outkick.com/clay-travis-tomi-lahren-and-charly-arnolt-slam-transgender-ideology-in-schools-in-upcoming-outkick-on-fox-special/.

57. Dan Zaksheske, "Is It Un-American to Root Against the US Women's

National Team During the World Cup?" *OutKick*, July 19, 2023, https://www.outkick.com/rooting-for-us-womens-national-team-uswnt-world-cup/.

58. Zaksheske, "Is It Un-American."

59. Dan Zaksheske, "Majority of OutKick Fans Rooting Against US Women's National Team at Women's World Cup," *OutKick*, July 20, 2023, https://www.outkick.com/outkick-fans-rooting-against-us-womens-national-team-at-world-cup/.

60. Zaksheske, "Majority of OutKick Fans."

61. David Hookstead, "Carli Lloyd Flames USWNT's Behavior after Embarrassing World Cup Draw: 'You are Lucky,'" *OutKick*, August 1, 2023, https://www.outkick.com/uswnt-behavior-portugal-draw-carli-lloyd-reaction/.

62. Hookstead, "Carli Lloyd."

63. Grayson Wier, "Netherlands Forward Takes Victory Lap after 'Big Mouth' USWNT's Early World Cup Exit," *OutKick*, August 10, 2023, https://www.outkick.com/uswnt-united-states-women-soccer-world-cup-2023-lineth-beerensteyn-big-mouth/.

64. Grayson Weir, "Megan Rapinoe Discusses 'Dark Comedy' of Missed PK that Low-Lighted Frustrating USWNT Loss, Her Final World Cup Match," *OutKick*, https://www.outkick.com/soccer/megan-rapinoe-discusses-dark-comedy-of-missed-pk-that-low-lighted-frustrating-uswnt-loss-her-final-world-cup-match.

65. Mark Harris, "Bill Simmons Torches Alex Morgan, Gives Spot-On Comparison for Megan Rapinoe after USWNT's World Cup Exit," *OutKick*, August 8, 2023, https://www.outkick.com/bill-simmons-alex-morgan-megan-rapinoe-uswnt-world-cup-exit/.

66. Mark Harris, "ESPN Praises Megan Rapinoe for her 'Patriotism,' Says She 'Loved America' in Absurd SportsCenter Tribute Following USWNT's World Cup Exit," *OutKick*, August 7, 2023, https://www.outkick.com/megan-rapinoe-sportscenter-tribute-video-patriot-loved-america/.

67. Harris, "ESPN Praises Megan Rapinoe."

68. Kusz and Hodler, "'Saturdays are for the Boys,'" 96.

69. NCAA, "A Year for Women: Pioneers, Record Breakers and Champions," NCAA.org, April 19, 2024, https://www.ncaa.org/news/2024/4/19/features-a-year-for-women-pioneers-record-breakers-and-champions.aspx.

70. WNBA, "WNBA Draft '24," WNBA.com, https://www.wnba.com/draft/2024/board.

71. Bobby Burack, "WNBA Mean Girls Won't Accept Caitlin Clark Until She Apologies for Being White and Straight," *OutKick*, June 10, 2024, https://www.outkick.com/sports/wnba-mean-girl-wont-accept-caitlin-clark-until-she-apologies-being-white-straight-bobby-burack.

72. Alejandro Avila, "Shaq: WNBA Players 'Professionally Jealous' of Caitlin Clark," *OutKick*, June 13, 2024. https://www.outkick.com/sports/shaq-wnba-players-professionally-jealous-caitlin-clark.

73. David Hookstead, "Bill Maher Crushes Caitlin Clark's Critics, Calls Out

Her Teammates," *OutKick*, June 8, 2024. https://www.outkick.com/sports/bill-maher-caitlin-clark-teammates-critics-video.

74. Bobby Burack, "ESPN Needs to Diversify Its Coverage of Caitlin Clark and WNBA," *OutKick*, June 17, 2024. https://www.outkick.com/sports/espn-needs-diversify-its-coverage-caitlin-clark.

75. James Pollard, "GOP Candidates Elevate Anti-Transgender Messaging as a Rallying Call to Christian Conservatives," *AP News*, February 18, 2024, https://apnews.com/article/lgbtq-transgender-republicans-trump-christian-conservatives-election-83becc009d8123d96a75c2e4940ab339.

76. Matt Sienkiewicz and Nick Marx, *That's Not Funny: How the Right Makes Comedy Work for Them* (Oakland: University of California Press, 2022), 5.

77. See, for example, Dan Zaksheske, "Aaron Rodgers Repeatedly Torches ESPN While Pat McAfee Covers His Face, Launches into Coughing Fit," *OutKick*, January 10, 2024, https://www.outkick.com/aaron-rodgers-repeatedly-torches-espn-while-pat-mcafee-covers-his-face-launches-into-coughing-fit/, and Alejandro Avila, "Social Media Reactions Pour in on Stephen A. Smith Rant vs. Jason Whitlock," *OutKick*, January 11, 2024, https://www.outkick.com/social-media-reactions-pour-in-on-stephen-a-smith-rant-vs-jason-whitlock/.

11

The WNBA and Georgia's 2020 US Senate Race

A Multimethod Case Study of the Cultural Power of Sport

DOUGLAS HARTMANN and ALI BOUTERSE

One of the most important lines of research in social movements scholarship in the new millennium has involved questions about the impact of protest, activism, and social movements in service of social change.[1] Do social movements help to bring about social change? Do activism and protest make a difference? And if so, what do they do? Such questions speak to our ability to move beyond the romance of resistance to understand the larger significance and consequence of protest, activism, and social movements.

Questions about the significance and impact of activism and resistance are particularly important—and challenging—in sport.[2] The last decade has witnessed unprecedented amounts of athletic activism in the United States and all over the world, much of which is intended to contribute to large-scale movements, progress, and social change in society.[3] This activism presents an opportunity to better analyze and understand how social movements in and around sport contribute to political reforms and cultural transformations. However, even though this activism (especially the gestures, statements, and demonstrations of celebrity athletes and their allies) receives a great deal of public attention, its significance is often ignored, minimized, or dismissed in both mainstream culture and the academy. Scholars of sport have only begun to move past the performance of athletic protest to delve into the complex mechanisms by which social movements in and around sport exert their effects.[4] Many of these concerns, of course, speak to the project that unifies the papers in this volume—namely, trying to better analyze and understand the nature, power, and impact of sport as a social force in the contemporary world.

This paper takes up the challenge of documenting, analyzing, and assessing the impact of sport-based protest with a multifaceted, mixed-method case study of the activism of the Women's National Basketball Association (WNBA) and its players in Georgia's 2020 US Senate race, which elected a little-known preacher named Raphael Warnock and gave the Democratic Party a slim majority in the immediate post-Trump era.

This case is important because the political engagement of the WNBA stands out among the multitude of race-based, Black Lives Matter demonstrations undertaken by athletes, teams, and entire leagues in the aftermath of George Floyd's killing for its intentionality, focus, and impact.[5] The mobilization of the WNBA has been seen by sport scholars and socially conscious sport journalists as one of the most important instances of athletic activism contributing to concrete social change in the past decade. As the *Washington Post* put it, "The women of the WNBA . . . ultimately helped tip the balance of the U.S. Senate." The *New York Times* concurred: "The attention WNBA players brought to Mr. Warnock's campaign is widely considered to have played a role in his victory."[6] Sport scholars have since supported the contention that the WNBA's activism had decisive impact. As A. Lamont Williams put it, "The efforts of some Atlanta Dream athletes were monumental in the election of Democrat Reverend Raphael Warnock over former Senator Kelly Loeffler for Georgia Senate. Loeffler . . . was defeated in the Senate race as a direct result of efforts by Dream players campaigning against her."[7] Even Warnock himself gave credit to the WNBA for increasing his donations.[8] References to the significance and consequence of the WNBA in the Georgia senate campaign as an episode exemplifying the force of sport in making social changes are rivaled only by those to Colin Kaepernick's pregame kneeling, or the 2015 University of Missouri football boycott.[9]

We assess these claims by combining existing data and analyses of the 2020 campaign—which include public opinion polling, media framing, social media tracking, and sentiment analysis—with a close, critical reading of these analyses and our own reconstruction of events leading up to the election. Our reconstruction suggests that the activism of the WNBA did impact the Senate election, but not in the literal, unidirectional, and decisive fashion typically claimed. WNBA advocacy advanced Warnock's campaign by helping to cement his status as a leading Democratic candidate. However, these effects were short-term and his Republican opponent Kelly Loeffler experienced benefits as well, including how she used the protest to distance her candidacy from that of her chief Republican rival. Rather than determining the outcome directly, we argue that athletic activism helped to narrow the field and increase fiscal and emotional investments in the election's outcome. Broadening the scope of the analysis further reveals that Loeffler's political identity and campaign strategies were shaped in consequential ways by her status as a WNBA owner from the time she was appointed to the Senate in 2019. Based on these results, we argue that WNBA activism shaped the race by drawing public attention and resources to it, narrowing the field of candidates, and magnifying its national symbolic importance.

More generally, we suggest the WNBA and the activism of its players worked in concert with other countervailing actors and forces, and that these forces functioned mostly at symbolic and communicative levels. We situate this argument, along with these findings and analyses, within a more critical, cultural understanding of the symbolic role and communicative function of sport in society. This understanding (1) prioritizes the symbolic significance of sport over more concrete, institutional changes and reforms; (2) emphasizes the public display of contestation and social struggle (not just the performance of protest); and (3) demonstrates the communicative uses of sport for conservative as well as progressive movements and political actors. Ultimately, these symbolic and communicative functions need to be understood in relation to more concrete, institutional, social, and political forces such as grassroots organizing and political mobilization. It is a framework for thinking about the political power and utility of sport that, perhaps ironically, has been embraced and mobilized more by conservative politicians in the United States since 2020 than by liberals, as evidenced by the success the former have had in pursuing state policies that restrict transgender youth from participating in interscholastic sports.

How and Why the WNBA Got Involved

Conventional wisdom usually marks the beginning of this episode in late June 2020. This is when the WNBA and its players, in the middle of the pandemic and the bubble in which teams were competing, grew disgusted with Atlanta Dream owner Kelly Loeffler's criticisms of the protests that emerged in response to George Floyd's murder by police in Minneapolis and decided to challenge her Senate candidacy. They were specifically reacting to a public statement Loeffler made on June 24 about the protests that emerged in Georgia after the police killing of Rayshard Brooks, which bore parallels to what happened in Minnesota. Loeffler circulated a public statement criticizing the Black Lives Matter movement for being a "very divisive organization" promoting "violence and destruction across the country."[10]

The WNBA's decision was not rash. The league and its players had a long history of combating police violence against Black Americans and advocating for racial justice more generally.[11] Indeed, the WNBA had built its reputation—its entire brand—on being one of the most progressive leagues in American professional sports.[12] WNBA players had been talking about how to express their outrage and show their support for racial reckoning in the post–George Floyd moment. Even before the BLM uprisings, the players had been working with Democratic political operative Stacy Abrams and UCLA law professor Kimberlé Crenshaw to craft a "Say Her Name" campaign in recognition of Breonna Taylor, a Black woman who had been shot and killed by Louisville police in a botched no-knock raid on her home.

The WNBA was not alone in its support of the BLM movement in the aftermath of George Floyd's murder. The day after the video of Floyd's death was posted, numerous athletes, including LeBron James, Rebekkah Brunson of the Minnesota Lynx, and Josh Okogie of the Minnesota Timberwolves, released statements expressing angst and outrage. Just two days later, both the Timberwolves and the Lynx released public condemnations of Floyd's killing. In the days and weeks after, these actions spread to athletes beyond Minnesota and even outside of the United States. It was not a rarity for athletes, organizations, and entire leagues to speak out against police brutality and racial injustice. What was less common was the type of organized political action seen by the WNBA in its collaboration with grassroots political activists to promote a candidate for office.

Abrams herself had a long history with the WNBA and its Atlanta franchise. In 2007 Lisa Borders, the fourth president of the WNBA and then Atlanta City Council president, collaborated with Abrams to bring the franchise that would be called the Dream to Atlanta.[13] In 2019 Abrams joined the board of the WNBA Players' Union, and in 2020 WNBA players reached out to Abrams and Borders for advice on their plans to back one of Kelly Loeffler's electoral opponents. Abrams and Borders connected WNBA players to Senator Rev. Warnock.[14]

Loeffler, for her part, was in the middle of an exceptionally complicated Senate race because of a quirk in Georgia state law that required special elections to replace elected political officials who leave their posts in the middle of their terms. Loeffler had been temporarily appointed by the Republican Governor Brian Kemp to fill the seat vacated by the ailing Johnny Isakson. The November 2020 election would be determined by direct popular vote, which sends the top two candidates to a runoff if no candidate receives a majority of votes in the general election. This so-called "blanket" primary system resulted in no fewer than twenty-one Democratic and Republican candidates running for the seat. Loeffler, even as the incumbent who had been nominated as a centrist who would appeal across party lines, was having a difficult time distinguishing herself in the field. She was consistently outpolled by Trump supporter Doug Collins on the populist Right (see Figure 11.2). Loeffler derided Black Lives Matter to shore up her conservative bona fides.

Not long after the WNBA's criticisms against Loeffler were levied, the sitting senator's camp sent a formal letter to WNBA Commissioner Cathy Engelbert expressing her opposition to the league's plans for players to wear warm-up jerseys with "Black Lives Matter" on the front and "Say Her Name" on the back, arguing that "politics should be kept out of sports." She suggested they should instead wear the American flag on their jerseys. The statement also emphasized that Loeffler had not been actively involved with the team for months and had resigned from the WNBA's Board of Governors in fall 2019.[15]

As designed, Loeffler's letter provoked response from the players and league leadership. In their response, the WNBA players union tweeted "ENOUGH! OUT!" WNBA stars and union leaders including Candace Parker, Breanna Stewart, and Sue Bird called for Loeffler to be expelled from the league. Not long thereafter, however, the league and its players started to realize that their opposition to Loeffler appeared to be, unintentionally, helping her to build credibility among conservatives. Consequently, they shifted course and started canvassing the field for a candidate of their own to support.

In an interview with the podcast *Burn It All Down*, Atlanta Dream player Elizabeth Williams described the process of organizing a response.[16] According to Williams, Sue Bird suggested that the league should focus on supporting one of Loeffler's opponents rather than just making statements against her. As the vice president of the WNBA players union, Bird worked with the union's executive committee and the league's social justice council to vet Loeffler's opponents through a series of meetings with various Democratic candidates. They eventually settled on Warnock, whose candidacy had been surging in the wake of the support of Abrams's grassroots organizing campaign and his own moving eulogy for national civil rights icon John Lewis in late July.

After a discussion with the Warnock campaign, the WNBA and its players announced the decision for players to wear T-shirts in support of Warnock at the Atlanta Dream v. Phoenix Mercury game on August 4, 2020. From there, the shirts spread across the league. Most of the league's

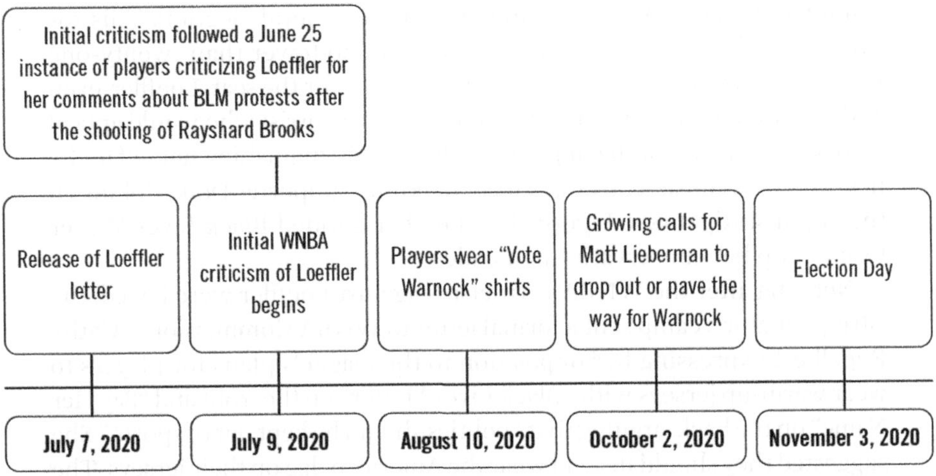

FIGURE 11.1: Timeline of 2020 election.

teams and players wore "Vote Warnock" shirts on national television and discussed their reasons for supporting him in media interviews that continued throughout the fall to election day itself.[17]

Uncertain Impacts

How—or to what extent—did WNBA support of Warnock contribute to his eventual electoral success? We can begin by looking at the polling data compiled by the website FiveThirtyEight (see Figure 11.2). The public opinion trends cannot establish any causal connections, but they do give a sense of the trajectory of the race and how it tracked with two of the key events or periods in the events detailed above. The two vertical lines in Figure 11.2 delineate those moments: Loeffler's original letter criticizing the league and its players, and the announcement of WNBA support for Warnock via the unveiling of pregame shirts in August.

Warnock's rise in the polls begins in March and runs into June. But his polling numbers do not take off until August, sometime after the league offered its public endorsement (and after a slight decline in July). They then continue to rise throughout the fall. Correlation is not causation, of course, but the fact that Warnock's rise happens in the aftermath of the league's endorsement does not seem entirely coincidental. Additionally, Warnock's polling numbers roughly paralleled those of his Democratic counterpart Matt Lieberman throughout the first half of the year, only to diverge in August. This is more significant than may first meet the eye, if

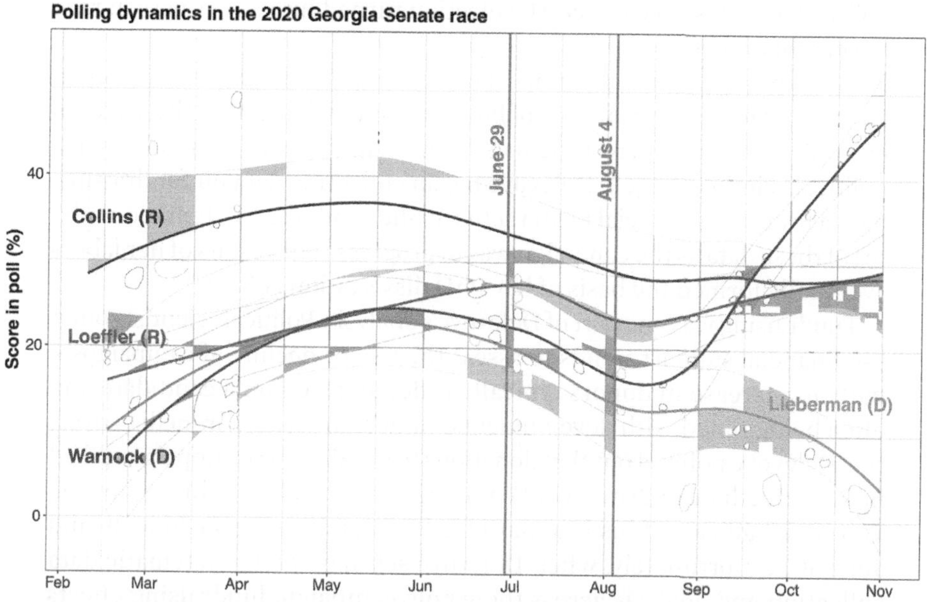

FIGURE 11.2: Polling Numbers for Warnock (D), Lieberman (D), Loeffler (R), and Collins (R). Reported in Angele Delevoye, *Leading from the Margins: The WNBA and the Emergence of a New Model of Sports Activism in the United States* (PhD diss., Yale University, 2022).

only because the special election laws that created such a crowded field for Loeffler applied to Warnock as well. In a race of this sort, candidates were not only competing against the other party, but other candidates from their own party. Any small factor could have a major consequence. It is also worth noting that at the beginning of the race, the top two Republican candidates were polling higher than any of the top Democrats. At various times in the campaign, both Republican and Democrat leaders expressed concerns that the runoff would end up with two candidates from the opposing party.

Focusing only on Warnock's numbers, however, can obscure the rise of Loeffler and the concomitant decline of her Republican counterpart Doug Collins. Collins, who was endorsed by Donald Trump and positioned to the political right of Loeffler, dominated polling in the first half of the year. It was not until June—after the Black Lives Matter uprisings and Loeffler's criticisms of them—that Loeffler began to gain momentum. While these polling numbers are, again, too blunt to establish any causal explanations, it appears that the focus on social justice within the WNBA benefited Loeffler as much as Warnock—albeit for different constituencies with opposing political agendas. In essence, the election turned into a two-person race during this period.

Conventional political science data, methods, and metrics can deepen and extend our understanding of how and/or to what extent the activism of the WNBA and its players helped Warnock to victory. To test this theory, political scientist Angele Delevoye began collecting data on fundraising, media framing, and social media activity. She conducted systematic analyses of these data as the campaign was in progress. The results of her labors eventually formed the basis of her PhD dissertation at Yale.[18]

Fundraising was one part of Delevoye's analysis. Political scientists often use financial support trends to assess the rise or decline of campaigns—with an increase in donors typically reflecting well on a candidate and often being timed with developments, campaign tactics, or media coverage. Delevoye pointed out that donations to the Warnock campaign spiked in the immediate aftermath of WNBA actions on behalf of his campaign. Warnock had two of his best days for PAC fundraising on June 29 and June 30. Unfortunately, when Delevoye set upon more systematic data collection and analysis across the whole campaign, fundraising effects proved difficult to demonstrate.

The results were not entirely negative; some trends are evident. On the one hand, these figures show steady increases in the amount of money flowing to this campaign—amounts that were clearly driven by national interest disproportionate to the size of Georgia. On the other hand, these panels (as Delevoye acknowledged) provide no way to differentiate between the effect of the WNBA protests and other factors that may have increased donations for Warnock. While donations did tick up after the July and August events, the increase aligned with donations to Democrats as a group. It is unlikely the actions by the WNBA had no effect on donations. It also seems unlikely that they had a direct or particularly outsized impact, particularly to the Warnock campaign. While Warnock and others may have given credit to the WNBA for increasing his donations, the figures show that the donations in August only slightly increased around the date of the initial announcement and did not increase dramatically until September.

These results were somewhat frustrating for Delevoye, who wanted to show that the WNBA played a decisive role in Warnock winning a Senate seat. An additional problem with using fundraising to show that WNBA activism benefited Warnock directly is what was happening on the other side of the political aisle. Such comparisons are difficult because Loeffler's campaign was largely self-funded. Having said that, the campaign finance data for the Loeffler campaign that Delevoye was able to collect suggest that even if the Republican front-runner did not need or seek donations, they began to flow in during the summer months, often with spikes just after news about developments with the WNBA. Once again, if sport-based activism benefited the Warnock campaign financially, the same seemed to hold for Loeffler.

In her quest to isolate the efficacy of WNBA activism, Delevoye turned to various forms of media and social media data. This race received inordinate attention from the national media. Using several different analytic strategies, Delevoye explored the prominence of coverage, the tone of the coverage, and the willingness of the media to lay credit for Warnock's victory at the feet of the WNBA. One of the ways she did this was by looking at the development of topics covered in the media as they were related to the election in general and how each of the major candidates were framed. These results indicate that basketball and the WNBA were defining features of this race and helped bring national attention to it. They also show that this attention cut in multiple directions.

Delevoye's comparative analysis of the coverage shows that neither Warnock nor Loeffler received significantly greater attention than the other in this context. This is interesting because Warnock, as discussed, was not directly connected to the WNBA until August. It also further demonstrates that these two candidates were centered in this coverage, to the detriment of others in the race. Delevoye's work again shows equality in the effect for both candidates, pointing to the difficulty in crediting the WNBA protests for helping only one side. It also further demonstrates how Loeffler's criticism of the WNBA and the WNBA's subsequent protests prompted media coverage to center on two contrasting candidates with starkly different racial views. Thus, the WNBA's entrance into the campaign helped to focus the contest on two candidates and subtly shift the terms of the race by making it seem more important.

Delevoye also used sentiment analysis of media coverage to examine feelings about the candidates. Sentiment analysis uses a list of negative and positive words and assesses whether media coverage or social media treatments are generally positive or negative for various candidates. In the negative sentiment analysis, Warnock's negative sentiment increases slightly and Loeffler's rises slightly. However, this effect is not sustained, or particularly large, and the candidates eventually see similar results. This is true for all of Delevoye's sentiment analyses. There are slight effects, but none that are long-term or can be isolated to one candidate. Warnock does see an uptick in positive coverage after Loeffler's letter, and Loeffler sees a very slight increase in negative coverage at that moment. However, given that the WNBA had not yet directly associated itself with Warnock's campaign when his positive coverage began to increase in July, it would be a stretch to directly attribute this increase to the WNBA.

This is especially true as positive coverage of both candidates seemed to converge after the WNBA's initial announcement of support in August, when positive coverage for Warnock dipped. Again, we see a positive impact for Loeffler's campaign as well as Warnock's. It is also difficult from the data to suggest that WNBA advocacy was the driver for increasing negative sentiment for Loeffler. The negative sentiment at the time remains mostly flat in August for Loeffler, showing that support for Warnock did not create a large negative effect for perceptions of her candidacy. Once again, such limited effects were unlikely to swing an election or even benefit a single candidate.

Delevoye's analysis of social media shows similar patterns of attention and framing. There is some evidence of an increase in mentions of Loeffler in early July and mentions of Warnock in early August, though only briefly. In terms of exposure, Loeffler seems to benefit from her criticism of the WNBA. While Warnock only begins to see increased Twitter mentions in September, Loeffler benefited from increased coverage because of the closeness of the race among the top Republican candidates. While this still may not be evidence of the WNBA directly determining the outcome of the election, it again helps to make the case that the attention brought by the WNBA helped to focus the race onto Loeffler and Warnock.

Delevoye also examined the proportion of negative and positive words in the tweets mentioning either Loeffler or Warnock, using similar methods to the sentiment analyses of traditional media coverage. These analyses show that the positive coverage for Warnock on Twitter increased after the T-shirt-wearing campaign. It also increased for Loeffler. Negative sentiment is also shown to have slightly increased for Warnock. While nothing can be directly attributed to the WNBA, and the increase in positive coverage for Warnock in July is not easily attributed to the WNBA at all, we again see the polarized responses to both candidates around the times of the WNBA protests.

Multiple, Mostly Cultural and Contextual Effects

In various post-election analyses, several left-leaning journalists and sportswriters cited early versions of Delevoye's study to claim that the WNBA helped swing the election for Warnock. Given that Delevoye ended up with mixed results regarding the WNBA's role in the election, it seems clear that journalists interpreted evidence in ways that gave more credit to the WNBA than it deserved, although this could be ascribed somewhat to the positive framing Delevoye offered in an early public presentation of her project in a then-popular political science blog.[19] In the fuller, more scholarly presentation of these results presented in her dissertation, Delevoye acknowledges the limitations of her analyses for providing definitive evidence that WNBA activism helped Warnock to his election victory.

Since these results failed to prove the direct and decisive impacts that she (and others) had hoped, they were disappointing for Delevoye. But we see the findings somewhat differently. In our view, they provide evidence that WNBA advocacy and the sporting context itself did help shape the campaigns, albeit somewhat less directly and in ways that benefited Loeffler as much as Warnock. The WNBA's endorsement of Warnock and media coverage of the controversy that led to this endorsement focused inordinate attention on these two candidates, thus reframing the contest as a two-person race. Additionally, WNBA advocacy—again in concert with the media coverage of it and pervasive political polarization—brought heightened attention to the race. Even if this attention did not change anyone's minds, it served to reinforce existing political beliefs and helped to intensify emotional (and financial) investments in the outcomes.[20]

In terms of intensity and investment, we would add three contributing factors. One concerns the emergence of right-wing sports journalism and the polarization of sports media more generally. The new conservative sports media needs to be understood, at least in part, in dialogue with the mainstream sports media's increasing willingness to cover activism and social issues in sport.[21] This dynamic alone not only reflected but ratcheted up polarization. Just as important is the emergence and proliferation of the "televised sport debate format," popularized by ESPN with shows such as *Pardon the Interruption* and *First Take*. Explicitly modeled on established political talk show formats (such as *Crossfire* or *Hannity and Colmes*), these programs are intentionally confrontational and combative, often appealing to various "race- and gender-based commitments, grievances, and tensions in the culture."[22] Which brings us to the second point: the deeply racialized nature of the WNBA and basketball itself in American culture. Race is a huge if sometimes unspoken or coded aspect of politics in the United States, and the 2020 Senate race was no exception.[23] While a full treatment is beyond the scope of this analysis, it seems clear that the prominence of Black players in the WNBA, in combination with the anti-Blackness centered in the police killing that provoked the uprisings across the summer of 2020, heightened the racial divisions, dimensions, and stakes of the election.

While WNBA advocacy may not have directly led to Warnock's rise or even victory, it is important to consider how its various communicative, cultural, and political functions worked in concert with other, non-sports forces and factors to shape the race and its eventual outcome. Conventional political science analysts would suggest that concrete institutional, social, and political forces such as grassroots organizing and political mobilization, with which Abrams and her Democratic coalition were involved during this campaign, likely played key roles in determining what led to a Warnock victory.[24] We don't disagree. However, we are also inclined to think about how standard grassroots organizing and campaigning operated in concert with the symbolic and communicative functions of sport.

Given that this campaign took place during the height of the COVID-19 pandemic, measuring the effects of mobilization and outreach efforts is complicated. While established political science studies have found that face-to-face mobilization efforts are among the most effective strategies for influencing election outcomes, this method was not an option for most of the 2020 election cycle because of the pandemic. This was truer for Democrats, as public health measures such as social distancing and masking became markers of political affiliations. In that context, the ways in which athletes and leagues engaged social and political issues provided a framework for politics.

In sports, one typically picks a team and roots for them to win. The dynamics are similar to a two-party political system like that in the United States. But in elections, the "fans" can do something to help their team win. Political parties provide a similar framework and work in concert with athletic engagement. In a twenty-one-person race, many rely on the party system to guide their voting decisions. Organizing for this race began months before the WNBA season even started. The Democratic Senatorial Campaign Committee and many nationally prominent Democrats endorsed Warnock the day after he declared his candidacy. To suggest that the WNBA won the race for Warnock would be to suggest that he still would have won without campaigning before August 4. We find that idea unlikely. Instead, it is our view that the activism of the WNBA and its players complemented, supported, and perhaps even extended the grassroots organizing and political mobilization that Stacy Abrams and her Democratic team had on the ground throughout the state. In other words, the communicative and symbolic forces that came with WNBA activism (and responses to it) combined with the ongoing, on-the-ground organizing and institutional dynamics to construct the terms of the election and its broader symbolic importance.

As we developed these analyses, we also became convinced that the impact of basketball and the WNBA on the campaign did not just start in June and was not limited to effects driven by left-leaning athletic activism and mobilization. The WNBA was implicated in the electoral process almost from the beginning with the somewhat unlikely appointment of Loeffler, one of its owners, to the Senate and her subsequent evolution into a politician and Republican candidate for reelection.

We emphasize this part of the story because Loeffler's WNBA ownership was core to her public image and political identity from the moment of her appointment to the Senate. A large part of Loeffler's appeal was that, as the owner of a sports team in a popular and progressive league, many Republicans believed she would garner support from more moderate Republicans and even swing voters, including white suburban women who not only shared her demographic but supported women's sports (an angle that would soon become even more prominent and complicated with the attack on transgender participation in scholastic sports). Loeffler's affiliation with women's basketball, in short, was supposed to make her appealing to moderates and across party lines.

If Loeffler's identity as a WNBA owner was one of the reasons Governor Kemp appointed her to fill out Isakson's term, her affiliation with the league was also one of the key reasons extreme right-wing Republicans saw her as too moderate. In a revealing Breitbart article, Debbie Dooley, a founder of the Tea Party movement, calls Loeffler a "country club Republican" with "concerning ties" to Planned Parenthood, Stacey Abrams, and Republicans who were critical of Trump.[25] Dooley makes clear that her concerns about Loeffler's "connections" to Planned Parenthood and Stacey Abrams were derived from her WNBA team ownership. Loeffler was increasingly pushed to the Right to satisfy and solidify the Republican base throughout the spring—a process that was intensified by the onset of the COVID-19 pandemic and the polarization it occasioned. This brings us to a third point and where we started: Loeffler's pivot and public break with the WNBA was an attempt to establish her conservative credibility and credentials.

Loeffler and her team were playing directly out of the playbook Trump had scripted just a few years earlier: (1) attack activist athletes; (2) accuse them of playing politics with sport; and then (3) ride the wave of publicity and media coverage that comes with the conflict.[26] These tactics were not just a matter of Loeffler solidifying her conservative bona fides among voters in Georgia and overtaking Collins as the leading Republican candidate in Georgia; they were aimed at gaining national attention and support. We might even suggest that it was Loeffler's initial appointment and eventual campaign strategies that drew the WNBA into the political/electoral fray, not the other way around.

Loeffler's eventual defeat can overshadow the success of sports-oriented politics, but her attacks on the WNBA were part of, and helped set the stage for, other conservative and Republican mobilizations of sport for political purposes. Tommy Tuberville, former Auburn University head football coach, was elected to the Senate, just next door to Georgia in Alabama in 2020, with a campaign centered on his athletic past. Warnock's next opponent, when running for a full term in 2022, was Herschel Walker, a former football player. Attacks on transgender athletes exploded post 2020, in fact, and the idea of "supporting women's sports" was entirely reframed by Republicans and used as justification for bans of trans athletes, particularly transgender women.[27] While athletes may have helped to elect a Democrat in Georgia in 2020, it is frequently Republicans who have used sports in their politics since then.

The Cultural Power of Sport

In the summer of 2020—amid the COVID pandemic, the aftermath of the police killing of George Floyd, and the lead-up to the presidential election—players, teams, and organizations across the American athletic landscape rushed to assert their opposition to anti-Black police violence and their support for the broader Black Lives Matter movement. The WNBA was a leader in this push and embarked upon a political mobilization that was more intentional, sustained, and impactful than the actions or interventions of any other league, athletic entity, or corporation.

In this chapter, we have tried to demonstrate that the WNBA's engagement with the 2020 US Senate race in Georgia exerted vital, if not entirely direct, impacts on the campaign and eventual electoral outcome. We have argued that WNBA advocacy, in concert with the public reception of it and conservative reactions to it, helped to narrow the field of contestants, amplified the symbolic importance of the race by bringing national public attention to it, and heightened emotional and financial investments in the outcome. We have also insisted that these impacts benefited both the top Democratic and Republican candidates. Indeed, broadening the scope of the analysis revealed that Loeffler's political identity and campaign strategies were shaped in consequential ways by her status as a WNBA owner, from her initial appointment and throughout the entire campaign. These actions exerted their impacts through symbolic and communicative means; they were not directly determinative.

If these impacts are not as direct, definitive, and progressive as some sport scholars and left-leaning journalists might have hoped or hypothesized, they were also far more consequential than realized by analysts or pundits who would otherwise discount or dismiss the sociopolitical significance of sport in contemporary social life. This in-between, culturally oriented analysis, in fact, captures in microcosm a larger theoretical argument about the social power and cultural significance of sport: sport and sports activism do not so much make social change as they amplify and focus the dynamics of struggle and change for broader public audiences. More generally, sport contributes to social movements and political outcomes by doing much of the cultural work that is often behind the scenes or taken for granted.

Generalizing from this case, we offer three general cultural roles or functions that social engagement and political advocacy in and through sport can have. One has to do with bringing public attention and awareness to issues, events, and policy deliberations that might otherwise be ignored or minimized. This is about establishing their priority or significance in political discourse and the public sphere, what political scientists call "agenda seeding."[28] A second cultural impact of sport extends from the role that sport-based engagements played in focusing the Georgia campaign, and involves the communicative role that advocacy in and through sport can play in defining issues and helping audiences and observers better understand the choices in front of them. In general terms, this is what sociologists often refer to as "framing." Third, and finally, is the role that sport can play in heightening emotional intensity and investment in social issues by virtue of its dramatic nature as well as by the deep passions and commitments that often accompany sports spectatorship and fandom.

These impacts and functions are best captured and gauged through what we would call a critical, cultural orientation to the study of sport. Built on the foundations of dramaturgical social theories as embodied in the work of anthropologists, feminist theorists, and sociologists, this approach emphasizes sport's primary role and social significance as a dramaturgical platform, a theater wherein audiences and observers are exposed to and learn about social issues and problems. It is, in other words, less about the internal politics of sport than the symbolic, communicative operations and functions of sport in society.

Some sport scholars have recently begun to sketch the outlines of such a critical-dramaturgical orientation.[29] Here, by way of conclusion, we will briefly note several key elements of this approach. The first involves its "critical" components. Informed by critical-cultural racial theories in the tradition of Stuart Hall and C. L. R. James (and in contrast to standard treatments of the cultural politics of sport), we believe that sport does not just provide a platform for the reproduction of the established regime or even the performance of resistance. Rather, sport is better understood as a site of contestation and struggle that, because of its cultural prominence, informs public audiences about social dynamics and power struggles outside of sport.[30] This suggests the need to situate the social messages and dynamics of struggle in sport within the context of the broader societal issues, struggles, transformations, and changes that they reflect and to which they relate.

Developing a more critical, cultural understanding of the symbolic role and communicative function of sport in social change has implications for the study of activism, protest, and social change in and through all manner of popular cultural spaces. With respect to popular cultural activism and protest in general, we suggest that attending to the symbolic and ideological dimensions of movements, mobilization, and resistance can help better understand the attention that movements receive (or do not receive), how movements can contribute to the framing of social problems, and the emotional attachment that can be cultivated in and through activism in popular, mass-mediated spaces. We believe these factors are best understood as necessary, if not entirely sufficient, aspects of political organizing and making social change.

Several features of sport make it such a distinctive cultural site (or platform) for the dramatization and display of social issues and struggles. One part of the specificity and unique power of sport has to do with its visibility, attention, and traction. In comparison with other political forms, the inordinate public visibility and influence of sport (and athletes in particular) ensures that the meaning and significance of socio-political issues and agendas played out in sport have impacts and implications well beyond the boundaries of the athletic arena itself. This is where and why media and social media play such an indispensable role bringing broader public attention and investment. And it is not just the prominence of sport in media and culture that matters, but also the deep passions and emotional investments that sports followers typically bring to their engagements. As alluded to previously, this energy and passion is—or at least can be—transferred and vicariously applied to other, non-sport issues and topics that appear via the athletic arena. Furthermore, the deep social structure and broader social significance of sport is often not fully realized or appreciated by the very folks who enact it. This is what we might call, following Clifford Geertz, "deep play"—a paradoxical engagement with culture that can heighten and intensify the social meanings in sport precisely because they are not fully recognized or embraced as significant.

All these cultural, symbolic, and communicative properties need to be understood and set in the context of and in relationship to other, non-sport social forces and factors. In the sociology of social movements, there has been a new call for setting social movements in the context of other movement actors and countervailing social forces to better specify and calibrate their impacts—what might be called a "field-based" approach.[31] So, too, with sport and the role of protest, political mobilization, and social movements in sport. The emphasis on social context and relationships within a field of struggle, and the cultural functions of sport with respect to these sociopolitical dynamics, is not intended to be an alternative to more concrete, institutional processes, forces, and factors. To the contrary, we suggest that these cultural factors are best set in relationship to more traditional notions of social power and institutional structure. An example of this is the grassroots organizing and mobilization efforts of political operatives like Stacy Abrams in Georgia. If activism, organizing, and advocacy changed the tenor and outcome of the special election in Georgia in 2020, it was this mobilization, of which the involvement of the WNBA and its players was only a part, that did the heavy lifting. Hopefully, we have made a convincing case that to make sense of the activism of the WNBA and the Atlanta Dream, we need to situate it as part of a larger relational dynamic of political actors, cultural meanings, and movement and counter-movement forces.

Notes

1. Bosi, Lorenzo, Marco Giugni, and Katrin Uba, eds., *The Consequences of Social Movements* (Cambridge: Cambridge University Press, 2016); Edwin Amenta et al., "The Political Consequences of Social Movements," *Annual Review of Sociology* 36 (2010): 287–307. See also Jennifer Earl, "The Cultural Consequences of Social Movements," in *The Blackwell Companion to Social Movements*, ed. David A Snow et al. (Malden, MA: Wiley-Blackwell, 2004): 508–30; Marco Guini et al., eds., *How Social Movements Matter* (Minneapolis: University of Minnesota Press, 1999).

2. Laurel R. Davis-Delano and Todd Crosset, "Using Social Movement Theory to Study Outcomes in Sport-Related Social Movements," *International Review for the Sociology of Sport* 43, no. 2 (2008): 115–34; Peter Kaufman and Eli A. Wolff, "Playing and Protesting: Sport as a Vehicle for Social Change," *Journal of Sport and Social Issues* 34, no. 2 (2010): 154–75; Douglas Hartmann, "Sport, Social movements, and Athlete Activism," in *The Oxford Handbook of Sport and Society*, ed. Lawrence A. Wenner (Oxford: University of Oxford Press, 2022): 571–94.

3. Joseph N. Cooper, *A Legacy of African American Resistance and Activism Through Sport* (New York: Peter Lang, 2021); Francis O'Neill et al., "Elite Athlete Activism, Advocacy, and Protest: A Scoping Review," *European Sport Management Quarterly* 25, no. 1 (2025): 143–73; Howard Bryant, *The Heritage: Black Athletes, a Divided America, and the Politics of Patriotism* (Boston: Beacon Press, 2019); Cathal Kilcline, "Sport and Protest: Global Perspectives," *The International Journal of the History of Sport* 34, no. 3–4 (2017): 157–61; Lucia

Trimbur, "Taking a Knee, Making a Stand: Social justice, Trump America, and the Politics of Sport" *Quest* 71, no. 2 (2019): 252–65.

4. These include studies of public opinions about athletic demonstrations and protest, such as Chris B. Knoester et al., "Should Athletes Be Allowed to Protest During the National Anthem? An Analysis of Public Opinions Among US Adults," *Sociology of Sport Journal* 39, no. 1 (2021): 23–34; Lisa Mueller, "Do Americans Really Support Black Athletes Who Kneel During the National Anthem? Estimating the True Prevalence and Strength of Sensitive Racial Attitudes in the Context of Sport," *Communication & Sport* 10, no. 6 (2022): 1070–1091; Jonathan Intravia et al., "The Racial Divide Surrounding United States of America National Anthem Protests in the National Football League," *Deviant Behavior* 39, no. 8 (2018): 1058–1068; Brent Smith and Stephanie A. Tryce, "Understanding Emerging Adults' National Attachments and their Reactions to Athlete Activism," *Journal of Sport and Social Issues* 43, no. 3 (2019): 167–94. On the economic impacts of athletic demonstrations and protests, see Nicholas Watanabe et al., "Market Disruption as a Regime for Athlete Activism: An Economic Analysis of College Football Player Protests," *Sport Management Review* 22, no. 5 (2019): 600–612; Judah Brown and Brandon J. Sheridan, "The Impact of National Anthem Protests on National Football League Television Ratings," *Journal of Sports Economics* 21, no. 8 (2020): 829–47. On the media perceptions and framing of athletic demonstrations and protests, see Erik Peterson and Manuela Muñoz, "'Stick to Sports': Evidence from Sports Media on the Origins and Consequences of Newly Politicized Attitudes," *Political Communication* 39, no. 4 (2022): 454–74; Adam Rugg, "Incorporating the Protests: The NFL, Social Justice, and the Constrained Activism of the "Inspire Change" Campaign," *Communication & Sport* 8, no. 4/5 (2020): 611–28.

5. See "Sportsperson of the Year: The Activist Athlete," *Sports Illustrated*, December 15, 2020, 46–87.

6. Candace Buckner, "How WNBA Players Helped Push Atlanta Dream Owner Kelly Loeffler Out of the Senate," *Washington Post*, January 7, 2021, https://www.washingtonpost.com/sports/2021/01/07/wnba-loeffler-warnock-senate-atlanta-dream/; Sopan Deb, "A W.N.B.A. Team Co-Owned by Loeffler Helped Warnock Defeat Her. What Happens Now?" *New York Times*, January 6, 2021, https://www.nytimes.com/live/2021/01/06/us/georgia-election-results#a-wnba-team-co-owned-by-loeffler-helped-warnock-defeat-her-what-happens-now.

7. A. L. Williams, "The Heritage Strikes Back: Athlete Activism, Black Lives Matter, and the Iconic Fifth Wave of Activism in the (W) NBA Bubble," *Cultural Studies ↔ Critical Methodologies* 22, no. 2 (2022): 266–75, 271.

8. Kurt Streeter, "The One Name the W.N.B.A. Won't Say," *New York Times*, October 5, 2020, https://www.nytimes.com/2020/10/05/sports/basketball/wnba-loeffler-warnock-blm.html; Jamal Collier, "Raphael Warnock Called Support from WNBA Players a 'Turning Point' in His Senate Campaign in

Georgia. And It Isn't Stopping for the January Runoff," *Chicago Tribune*, February 1, 2021, https://www.chicagotribune.com/2020/11/09/raphael-warnock-called-support-from-wnba-players-a-turning-point-in-his-senate-campaign-in-georgia-and-it-isnt-stopping-for-the-january-runoff/.

9. On Colin Kaepernick's pregame kneeling, see Dave Zirin, *The Kaepernick Effect: Taking a Knee, Changing the World* (New York: The New Press, 2021). On the 2015 University of Missouri football boycott, see Emmett Gill et al., "Freedom for First Downs: Interest Convergence and the Missouri Black Student Boycott," *Journal of Negro Education* 89, no. 3 (2020): 342–59; Bert Useem and Jack A. Goldstone, "The Paradox of Victory: Social Movement Fields, Adverse Outcomes, and Social Movement Success," *Theory and Society* 51, no. 1 (2022): 31–60.

10. Greg Bluestein and Bria Felician, "Loeffler Opposes WNBA's Plan to Spread 'Black Lives Matter' Message," *Atlanta Journal Constitution*, July 20, 2020, https://www.ajc.com/blog/politics/loeffler-opposes-wnba-plan-spread-black-lives-matter-message/ybTbHIpzZx7dbRlz3sfLiM/.

11. Jennifer McClearen and Mia Fischer, "Maya Moore, Black Lives Matter, and the Visibility of Athlete Activism," *Velvet Light Trap* 87, no. 1 (2021): 64–68; M. Blair Thomas and James E. Wright, "We Can't Just Shut Up and Play: How the NBA and WNBA are Helping Dismantle Systemic Racism," *Administrative Theory & Praxis* 44, no. 2 (2022): 143–57; Katherine Lavelle, "Change Starts With Us': Intersectionality and Citizenship in the 2016 WNBA," in *Sport, Rhetoric, and Political Struggle*, ed. Daniel A. Grano and Michael L. Butterworth (New York: Peter Lang, 2019), 39–54.

12. Dunja Antunovic et al., "'To Build a More Just Society': Women's National Basketball Association Teams' Uses of Social Media for Advocacy," *Women in Sport and Physical Activity Journal* 31, no. 2 (2023): 119–28; Mary G. McDonald, "Rethinking Resistance: The Queer Play of the Women's National Basketball Association, Visibility Politics and Late Capitalism," *Leisure Studies* 27, no. 1 (2008): 77–93.

13. TJ Macias, "Twitter Praises WNBA for Assist in Warnock's Georgia Win," *Macon Telegraph*, January 6, 2021, https://www.macon.com/news/politics-government/election/article248307575.html.

14. Interview with Elizabeth Williams, *Burn it All Down*, podcast audio, January 14, 2021; Bria Felicien, "Former Dream Star Angel McCoughtry Speaks on Loeffler, WNBA Season," *Atlanta Journal Constitution*, July 8, 2020, https://www.ajc.com/sports/basketball/former-dream-star-angel-mccoughtry-speaks-about-loeffler-wnba-season/GXScUNjoYkms6uAQXXUveK/.

15. Bria Felicien and Greg Bluestein, "Loeffler Opposes WNBA's Plan to Spread 'Black Lives Matter' Message," *Atlanta Journal Constitution*, July 7, 2020, https://www.ajc.com/blog/politics/loeffler-opposes-wnba-plan-spread-black-lives-matter-message/ybTbHIpzZx7dbRlz3sfLiM/.

16. Interview with Elizabeth Williams, *Burn it All Down*.

17. Bria Felicien and Greg Bluestein, "WNBA Players Wear 'Vote Warnock'

Shirts Opposing Dream Co-Owner Loeffler," *Atlanta Journal Constitution*, August 4, 2020, https://www.ajc.com/politics/politics-blog/atlanta-dream-players-wear-vote-warnock-shirts-opposing-team-co-owner-loeffler/L4GVFVM5AJGU5NBOE6U3F6NKSM/; Elizabeth Williams, "How the WNBA Helped Flip Georgia Blue," *Vox*, January 11, 2021, https://www.vox.com/first-person/22221250/georgia-election-results-senate-warnock-ossoff-wnba-elizabeth-williams; Kurt Streeter, "The One Name the W.N.B.A. Won't Say," *New York Times*, October 5, 2020, https://www.nytimes.com/2020/10/05/sports/basketball/wnba-loeffler-warnock-blm.html.

18. Angele Delevoye, "Leading from the Margins: The WNBA and the Emergence of a New Model of Sports Activism in the United States" (PhD diss., Yale University, 2022).

19. Angele Delevoye, "The WNBA Helped Warnock in the Georgia Senate Race, New Research Finds," *Washington Post*, November 30, 2020, https://www.washingtonpost.com/politics/2020/11/30/wnba-influenced-georgia-senate-race-new-research-finds/.

20. Sopan Deb, "W.N.B.A. Players Escalate Protest of Anti-B.L.M. Team Owner," *New York Times*, August 4, 2020, https://www.nytimes.com/2020/08/04/sports/basketball/wnba-dream-loeffler-warnock.html.

21. On emergence of right-wing sport media, see Mark Falcous et al.,"Hyperpartisan Sport Media in Trump's America: The Metapolitics of Breitbart Sports," *Communication & Sport* 7, no. 5: 588–610; Galen Clavio and Ryan Vooris, "ESPN and the Hostile Media Effect," *Communication & Sport* 6, no. 6 (2018): 728–44. On the liberalization of sport reporting on activism and protest, see Ryan Broussard, "'Stick to Sports' is Gone: A Field Theory Analysis of Sports Journalists' Coverage of Socio-political Issues," *Journalism Studies* 21, no. 12 (2020): 1627–1643; Hans C. Schmidt, "Sport Reporting in an Era of Activism: Examining the Intersection of Sport Media and Social Activism," *International Journal of Sport Communication* 11, no. 1 (2018): 2–17.

22. Taylor M. Henry and Thomas P. Oates, "Sport Is Argument': Polarization, Racial Tension, and the Televised Sport Debate Format," *Journal of Sport and Social Issues* 44, no. 2 (2020): 154–74. See also Taylor M. Henry, "From the *Tribune* to the Tube: The Development of Sports Punditry on Cable Television," *Velvet Light Trap* 87 (2021): 50–63.

23. Adam B. Evans et al., "'Black Lives Matter:' Sport, Race, and Ethnicity in Challenging Times," *European Journal for Sport and Society* 17, no. 4 (2020): 289–300; Michael Serazio and Emily Thorson, "Weaponized Patriotism and Racial Subtext in Kaepernick's Aftermath: The Anti-Politics of American Sports Fandom," *Television & New Media* 21, no. 2 (2020): 151–68; Christopher Towler et al., "Shut Up and Play: Black Athletes, Protest Politics, and Black Political Action," *Perspectives on Politics* 18, no. 1 (2020): 111–27.

24. Gary C. Jacobson, "How Do Campaigns Matter?" *Annual Review of Political Science* 18 (2015): 31–47; Alan S. Gerber and Donald P. Green, "The

Effects of Canvassing, Telephone Calls, and Direct Mail on Voter Turnout: A Field Experiment," *The American Political Science Review* 94, no. 3 (2000): 653–63.

25. Sean Moran, "Conservatives Alarmed by Kelly Loeffler's Potential Senate Appointment," *Breitbart*, November 23, 2019, https://www.breitbart.com/politics/2019/11/22/a-country-club-republican-conservatives-sound-the-alarm-over-kelly-loefflers-potential-senate-appointment-ties-to-planned-parenthood-stacey-abrams/.

26. Kyle W. Kusz, "Notes on the Uses of Sport in Trump's White Nationalist Assemblage," *Review of Nationalities* 9, no. 1 (2019): 39–59; Douglas Hartmann, "Ethnonationalist Engagements, Historic Norms, and the Politics of Sport in American Culture," *Journal of Sport History* 50, no. 2 (2023): 165–86.

27. Mia Fischer, "Protecting Women's Sports? Anti-Trans Youth Sports Bills and White Supremacy," *Communication and Critical/Cultural Studies* 20, no. 4 (2023): 397–415; Elizabeth A. Sharrow, "Sports, Transgender Rights, and the Bodily Politics of Cisgender Supremacy," *Laws* 10, no. 3 (2021): 63. See also Ajhanai Keaton et al., "Brittney Griner, Intersectionality, and 'Woke Politics': A Critical Examination of Brittney Griner's Return to the United States," *Sociology of Sport Journal* 41, no. 2 (2024): 141–51.

28. Omar Wasow, "Agenda Seeding: How 1960s Black Protests Moved Elites, Public Opinion and Voting," *American Political Science Review* 114, no. 3 (2020): 638–59.

29. Douglas Hartmann et al., "The Performance and Reception of Race-Based Athletic Activism: Toward a Critical, Dramaturgical Theory of Sport," *American Journal of Cultural Sociology* 10, no. 4 (2022): 543–69; Douglas Hartmann, "What Can We Learn from Sport if We Take Sport Seriously as a Racial Force? Lessons from C.L.R. James's *Beyond a Boundary*," *Ethnic and Racial Studies* 26, no. 3 (2003): 451–83; Trygve B. Broch and Eivind Å. Skille, "Performing Sport Political Legitimacy: A Cultural Sociology Perspective on Sport Politics," *Sociology of Sport Journal* 36, no. 2 (2019): 171–78. See also John J. MacAloon, *This Great Symbol: Pierre de Coubertin and the Origins of the Modern Olympic Games* (London: Routledge, 2013).

30. Stuart Hall, "Cultural Studies and the Centre: Some Problematics and Problems," in *Culture, Media, Language*, ed. Stuart Hall et al. (London: Routledge, 1980), 2–35; C.L.R. James, *Beyond a Boundary* (Durham, NC: Duke University Press, 2013); Brennon Wood, "Stuart Hall's Cultural Studies and the Problem of Hegemony," *British Journal of Sociology* 49, no. 3 (1998): 399–414.

31. Useem and Goldstone, "The Paradox of Victory"; Donatella Della Porta, "Building Bridges: Social Movements and Civil Society in Times of Crisis," *VOLUNTAS: International Journal of Voluntary and Nonprofit Organizations* 31, no. 5 (2020): 938–48.

Contributors

ALI BOUTERSE is a PhD student in the Department of Political Science at the University of Washington. Her primary research interests are democracy, democratic backsliding, and populism, focusing on ways in which globalization has impacted public opinion and support for political institutions and democracy. She received her BA in sociology and political science from the University of Minnesota.

ADRIAN BURGOS, JR., is professor of history at the University of Illinois. He is the author of *Playing America's Game: Baseball, Latinos, and the Color Line*, *Cuban Star: How One Negro-League Owner Changed the Face of Baseball*, and coeditor of *Beyond El Barrio: Everyday Life in Latina/o America.*

MICHAEL L. BUTTERWORTH is the Richards Chair for the University of Texas Program in Sports and Media, and professor in the Department of Communication Studies. He is the author of *Baseball and Rhetorics of Purity: The National Pastime and American Identity during the War on Terror*, coauthor of *Communication and Sport: Surveying the Field*, editor of *Sport and Militarism: Contemporary Global Perspectives*, and coeditor of *Sport, Rhetoric, and Political Struggle.*

NOAH COHAN is assistant director and lecturer in American cultural studies at Washington University, St. Louis. He is the author of *We Average Unbeautiful Watchers: Fan Narratives and the Reading of American Sports* and founding coordinator of the American Studies Association's Sport Studies Caucus.

DOUGLAS HARTMANN is professor of sociology at the University of Minnesota. He is the author of *Race, Culture, and the Revolt of the Black Athlete: The 1968 Olympic Protests and their Aftermath* and *Midnight Basketball: Race, Sports, and Neoliberal Social Policy*.

VICTORIA E. JOHNSON is professor of film and media studies and African American studies at the University of California, Irvine. She is the author of *Heartland TV: Prime Time Television and the Struggle for U.S. Identity* and *Sports TV*. Johnson also coedits the University of Illinois Press book series *Studies in Sports Media* and serves as president of the Society of Cinema and Media Studies.

ABRAHAM I. KHAN is assistant professor of communication at the Colorado State University. He is the author of *Curt Flood in the Media: Baseball, Racism, and the Demise of the Activist Athlete*.

JASON KIDO LOPEZ is assistant professor of communication arts at the University of Wisconsin. He is the author of *Redefining Sports Media*.

THOMAS P. OATES is professor in the Department of American Studies and the School of Journalism and Mass Communication at the University of Iowa. He is the author of *Football and Manliness: An Unauthorized Feminist Account of the NFL*, coauthor of *Forming the Public: A Critical History of Journalism in the United States*, and coeditor of *The NFL: Critical and Cultural Perspectives* and *Playing to Win: Sports, Video Games, and the Culture of Play*.

THERESA RUNSTEDTLER is professor of history at American University in Washington, DC. She is the author of *Jack Johnson, Rebel Sojourner: Boxing in the Shadow of the Global Color Line* and *Black Ball: Kareem Abdul-Jabbar, Spencer Haywood, and the Generation that Shaped the Soul of the NBA*.

JAIME SCHULTZ is professor of kinesiology at Penn State University. She is the author of *Qualifying Times: Points of Change in U.S. Women's Sport*, *Moments of Impact: Injury, Racialized Memory, and Reconciliation in College Football*, *Women's Sports: What Everyone Needs to Know*, and *Regulating Bodies: Elite Sport Policies and their Unintended Consequences*, and coeditor of *American National Pastimes—A History* and *Women and Sports in the United States: A Documentary Reader*. Schultz is also coeditor of the University of Illinois Press book series *Sport and Society*.

SAMANTHA N. SHEPPARD is professor of cinema and media studies in the Department of Performing and Media Arts at Cornell University. Sheppard is the author of *Sporting Blackness: Race, Embodiment, and Critical Muscle Memory on Screen* and coeditor of *Sporting Realities: Critical Readings of the Sports Documentary* and *From Madea to Media Mogul: Theorizing Tyler Perry.*

TRAVERS is professor of sociology at Simon Fraser University. They are the author of *Writing the Public in Cyberspace: Redefining Inclusion on the Net, The Trans Generation: How Trans Kids (and Their Parents) are Creating a Gender Revolution,* and coeditor of *Transgender Athletes in Competitive Sport.* Travers is also deputy editor of the journal *Gender & Society.*

TRAVIS VOGAN is professor in the School of Journalism and Mass Communication at the University of Iowa. He is the author of *Keepers of the Flame: NFL Films and the Rise of Sports Media, ESPN: The Making of a Sports Media Empire, ABC Sports: The Rise and Fall of Network Sports Television, The Boxing Film: A Cultural and Transmedia History,* and *LeRoy Neiman: The Life of America's Most Beloved and Belittled Artist.* Vogan also coedits the University of Illinois Press book series *Studies in Sports Media.*

Index